With My Love
Letha A Wiles

D1648806

So Many Mornings

Remembrances From the Life of Letha Alice Grossnickel Wiles,

including True Civil War Stories and Life in the Early 1900s

Written by Yvonne Fay Wiles Georg

Edited by Linda Blachly

Yvonne Georg

ISBN 0-9648521-0-1

Author's Note: The author has made every effort to ascertain the facts and to present events described in this book in a truthful manner. Old family Bibles and grave markers have been the source of information for the dates used in this book. The many people mentioned in this book are acquaintances, friends and family of Letha Alice Grossnickel Wiles, as she remembers them at the age of 95. It is our intent to only lovingly remember these people as they each played a role in my mother's life. My mother presents this information which is, to the best of her knowledge, and in her opinion, as accurate as she remembers it. While every attempt is made to provide accurate information, the author or her agents cannot be held responsible for errors or omissions.

Scripture quotations are from the *King James Version* of the *Holy Bible*.

Printed by McNaughton & Gunn, Inc.

To obtain copies of this book, please write:
DYG Incorporated
12428 LaPlata Street
Silver Spring, MD   20904

DEDICATION

In Memory of Russell Peter Wiles Sr., loving father of the author, Yvonne Fay Wiles Georg; and husband of my dear mother, Letha Alice Grossnickel Wiles, whose loving stories are the substance of this book. Also, with loving thoughts of Letha and Russell's two deceased infant daughters. All thanks and sweet praises to the Lord God Almighty for His hand of protection on our lives.

Dear Mom,

Thanks for the million and one unselfish things you and Dad have done for each of us! No one could have done a better job as parents.

Always with our love,
Your Children

Russell Wiles and Letha Grossnickel. Photo taken at the Paul Hayes property in 1915 before they were married.

CONTENTS

PREFACE

I was "inspired" to write this book on a Sunday evening in September 1993, after hearing and enjoying Mom laugh and tell a few stories about her past.

I often told stories from home to my co-worker and friend, Anne Marie Gillen. Anne's eyes would twinkle as I rambled out an incident. She would always comment, "Bonnie, you must write a book. Don't let these neat stories be forgotten and lost." Another wonderful friend, Joan Topalian, has listened with keen interest as well. At times, a tear glistened in her eye as I talked. She has truly been given an "earful" over the years I have worked for her.

With Anne's statement ringing in the back of my mind, I decided right there at Mom's table that September evening, and having her permission, these stories would be captured with some detail. If not, they would surely be lost forever. Never in a million years did I believe I could launch out and begin writing a book to publish. With God's help and encouragement along the way, I have taken a journey back through time with my mother and family. I have enjoyed every minute of writing this book!

My 92-year-old grandmother, Clara Rebecca Grossnickel, died when I was about 15 years old. As a child, I remember hearing Grandma tell the Civil War stories she lived through. I paid little attention because she talked about the happenings often. Now at the age of 57, I realize that I was privileged to hear these stories "first-hand" over and over again.

This book is not just about Mom and Dad, but of their love for the great Middletown Valley, in Maryland, and its people. I am a high school graduate; I do not have a college education. I went back to school at night to learn to type. I never held a public job until I was 28 years old, ten years after graduating from high school. I stayed at home those years helping Mom and Dad on the farm.

When Dad and Mom retired, I began working as a secretary, and in a couple of years I became employed at the National Institutes of Health (NIH) in Bethesda, Maryland. I married Darius Georg in 1968. I worked at NIH until our son was born in 1974. I stayed home with him for fifteen years and did substitute teaching in private and public schools. In 1989, I returned to work at NIH, where I am presently employed.

On Sunday afternoons after attending church, my husband, son, and I regularly come back home to Middletown from Silver Spring, Maryland. Often on these visits, Mom, my sister Marie and I gather around the old oak table in Mom's kitchen, sitting on the same Columbus Stottlemyer chairs she started housekeeping with 79 years ago. It was there Mom poured out her life to me as I took notes. Sometimes the three of us laughed until we cried; other times Mom's words were so sad that we wept. The time together raced by as the book grew.

In writing about my family, I realize that I love them even more than I ever knew. My family is worth great wealth to me. I found I have something money can never buy. Family love is just irreplaceable.

It took many hours to compose and rewrite my notes. Often I fell asleep at night with pen in hand or beside my bed. Due to the late hours I kept, I awakened with eyes that seemed as heavy as when I dozed off. During the course of the day, I often hastily jotted down thoughts from home on pieces of scrap paper and stuffed them into my pocket. Later, I would merge the information into the text of the book.

I continued to work my forty-hour a week job so,

without using your imagination, you know something had to go! My husband and son ate a few more leftover meals than usual. Frequently, the day's menu had the two choices you have no doubt read on signs: "Take it" or "Leave it." And quite a few more dust balls floated around in our house. My family will agree that my time was well spent as I tried to capture these treasured thoughts and memories of my parents, family and friends, and the beautiful Middletown Valley that our family loves.

The lessons taught to us from Mom and Dad's life are rich in respect, independence, endurance, truthfulness and love—the greatest of these being love.

This book was completed in August 1995, and I trust it will be a family legacy as it was written with sweet enthusiasm about my dear mom, Letha Alice Grossnickel Wiles.

YVONNE

Yvonne Fay Wiles Georg

ACKNOWLEDGEMENTS

Thanks go to my Lord for giving me such a wonderful family and Christian heritage. What a blessing to be given!

Thanks to each member of my family for giving me an abundance of love. I guess over the past two years we all refreshed a memory that has been hidden for years.

P.S.   I bet we all have some little secret Mom still doesn't know! We just couldn't tell it all.

Also, my heartfelt thanks go to my dear friend and editor, Linda Blachly. Linda received her Journalism degree from the University of Maryland, College Park Campus, in 1979. She brings over ten years of writing and editing experience to this project. She has been an inspiration to me and has given me guidance while working on this book. I could never have accomplished this project without her help.

Thanks also go to her husband, Frank Blachly, for all his wonderful help!

INTRODUCTION

Meet Our Mom:
Letha Alice Grossnickel Wiles

Our dear Mom is a tiny, delicate, vivacious woman of 95 years of age. She is a great-great grandmother who was born on September 17, 1899. Not everyone has earned the right to be called "Mom" by nine children who dearly love her. You can easily feel the warmth that radiates from her presence. Her dark brown eyes are still bright with happiness. They dance and sparkle in her small-framed face as she listens carefully or shares in conversation. She is under five feet tall and weighs just over 100 pounds. A lightweight, one could say. Throughout her life, she has shared laughter with her husband, family and friends.

God gave Mom an important and delicate assignment in this life—nine children to rear and love! There were so many times when pressing work took her away from us children but we knew eventually Mom would listen to us. Not always did she agree with the requests or demands we made of her. She never "beat around the bush" with her comments. We knew if she said she was going to do something, we could depend on it happening, Lord willing.

We children are thankful that we all grew up during an era when parents put so much value on the family and home. We never had to worry if Dad or Mom was going the leave each other, or us. They had high standards and expected us to follow their example. They taught us to have the desire to earn a respected name for ourselves.

We have never heard Mom call our father "Russell." She always referred to him as "the Mister" to strangers and "Dad" when speaking to her children.

We have never heard Mom use a swear word. She was afraid that God might hear her; therefore, she still believes He hears when she prays. Her life was always lived as a righteous example before her children. Many of Mom's evenings have been spent reading her Bible. She has been most often seen resting with that book opened on her lap. God's Word is her source of vitality. It has helped her to conquer whatever life brought her way. It put order in her life, and she knew life demands constant faith.

Mom saw the importance of simplicity in her past years and has never hid behind a sham. She has no bitterness for the wrongs done to her. She is rightly proud of her and Dad's accomplishments. Mom and Dad knew "the Man with the blueprint" for their life on this earth.

Mom has never owned the latest fashions but has always been neat and tidy. She never had a change of hair style, permanent wave, or a "dye job." She has worn her hair pulled back in a bun her entire life. Now the strands of silver hair cover her head as if to honor and crown the beautiful smiling face of a lady who has lived a full, rich life.

Mom was not exempt from the temptations of life, but she knew the consequences of giving into enticements. She always considered the cost to her husband and family. In her darkest moments, she took a lesson away from the experience. She was convinced that "character determines destiny."

God has blessed her with good health and a wonderful mind. Today, in August 1995 and at the age of 95, she is not on medication and still enjoys her own beautiful teeth!

Mom worked late into the evening hours, when her tired body surely cried out for rest. We do not know how she accomplished so much. She was the one who sat by our bedside when we were not feeling well or afraid of the storms and the dark. After being up most of the night nursing a sick child, come morning she found the strength to continue working without complaining. Her attitude has had so much influence on our lives. There were times when we thought she knew everything—the good and bad concerning us. Mom was the one who made each of us children kiss and make up before going to bed. Many times she thought we had forgiven and forgotten, only to be disappointed when she discovered we were not sincere. She did not like to hear us make unkind statements to each other. She did not tolerate that conduct! That point could be underlined. She was adamant.

Mom always cooked and baked for us. She never ate the last piece of cake or cookie if she thought someone might like to have it. Mom would always say she was "too full." She never put herself first or in front of her family. Think of the privations she has endured.

Today, Mom still keeps house. She has always spent money wisely and continues to manage her banking needs. Mom never forgets to return the first tenth of her income to the Lord, who has abundantly supplied her every need. She has never obtained or used a credit card. They never bought anything but the farm until she and Dad had the money to pay for it.

Why, just last year in the summer of 1994, right before she turned 95, a man called her on the phone one day and offered her a job. And everyone talks about "no jobs available" for the unemployed! Mom gets up early in the morning when she has work to do because she does not want to be interrupted or miss a visit with anyone because the chores are not done. She will admit she likes to rock and just look out the window over the farm more than ever. She says she finds peace and wonderful memories there.

Mom is always at the door to greet us children when we come home. A kiss and a big smile awaits us. Again, another kiss when we depart, and a wave of the hand. Many times a few tears will moisten her eyes as she watches from the kitchen door or window as we drive away. Having nearly reached the century mark, she must have kissed us children thousands of times.

Mom comments from time to time that she is "not what she used to be." And her hands are not as strong as they once were, but she never complains. There is always a spirit of "thankfulness" in her words. Those hands have handled many tough assignments. And her body may seem frail, but the determination in her heart makes her strong.

Frequently, we think of the word "old" as antique. This may be true in some cases. But Mom is no "antique." She is a "treasure of great worth" to us children.

After Dad's death in 1977, Mom has never moved his coat, overalls, work shoes and hats that hang in the closet at home. Maybe they are left there as a reflection of the past. Or does it fill the void? Maybe it reminds us to stop, look back and be thankful for all the good years we had with our parents. With Dad gone, we always knew Mom would remain a widow. She never once entertained the thought of remarrying.

We are grateful for Mom and Dad's strong character and the heritage they have given to each of us children. Just as God loves his children, so Mom and Dad dearly loved us.

Mom, even though Dad is gone, if he were to stand in our presence today and read this book, he would say, Every word is true and you have earned the tribute!

Mom, we children will never forget you and Dad!

FAMILY HISTORY

This is a short history of Letha and Russell's nine living children and their spouses:

Austin and Ruth Grossnickle Wiles owned and operated a dairy farm. They sold their farm and retired from dairy farming. They presently raise young dairy cattle.

Ralph (deceased) and **Doris** Wiles Grossnickle operated a dairy farm. They retired before Ralph's death, and Doris still owns the farm.

Carroll and **Pauline** Wiles Grossnickle owned and operated a dairy farm. They sold their farm and are retired.

Russell Jr. and Betty Harshman Wiles farmed and sold out. Russell Jr. worked at the National Institutes of Health. Betty worked at the Frederick Optical. They are now retired.

Harold and **Marie** Wiles Harshman are retired. Harold worked as a motor tank salesman for Exxon. Marie worked in food service with the Frederick County School Board.

William Kenneth Sr. (deceased) and **Janice** Wiles Hawkins. Kenneth worked as a tank truck driver for Matlock. Janice works at Vinda Bona Nursing Home in food service.

Thomas Richard and **Regean** Wiles Fogle own and operate a dairy farm.

Darius and **Yvonne** Wiles Georg work at the National Institutes of Health. Darius is a computer systems analyst and

Yvonne is a secretary.

Thomas and Myralee Garst Wiles. Thomas is president of Middletown Valley Bank. Myralee is a schoolteacher at Wolfsville Elementary School.

CHAPTER 1

LIFE BEGINS

I was born before women had the right to vote and when men still tipped their hats to the ladies. Born at a time when Social Security numbers were unheard of. Born before the popular use of modern inventions such as cars and airplanes. Born before the many mechanical and scientific wonders that reshaped the lives of the people living on the face of this earth. I made my entry into this world on September 17, 1899. I am 95 years old.

Little did I know my quiet life would eventually touch and influence so many people. My love to others has been unconditional. I have helped those in need, ministered to the hurting, listened to everyone who wanted to share their thoughts and concerns, and fed the hungry. I never thought I would witness so many friends and family falter and fall, and then regain the strength to overcome. I did not realize wisdom came with such a high price. Never did I dream of seeing so many mornings!

My life was not without pain or joy. Much of my joy has come from my family of nine living children: Austin Charles Jacob, Doris Eileen, Pauline Alverta, Russell Peter Jr., Marie Flora, Janice Mae, Regean Phyllis, Yvonne Fay, and Thomas Mitchell. The death of my two infant children, Kathleen Isabelle and a stillborn daughter, brought much grief to my life. My husband, Russell Peter Wiles Sr., died on June

1

13, 1977, leaving a void in my life.

An Adventure Begins

Back on that September day, I, Letha Alice Grossnickel, began my adventure through life in a little white weatherboard house on Myersville Church Hill Road, near Myersville, Maryland. Today the home is owned by Harold Lewis. I was delivered at home to Charles Webster and Clara Rebecca Leatherman Grossnickel. Mother was the daughter of Elder George and Rebecca Leatherman from Harmony, Maryland. I was the fourth child following three brothers. Roy Wade was the oldest child, born in 1887. Three years later, in 1890, Herbert Alfred was born; seven years later, in 1897, George Martin was born; and two years later, in 1899, I arrived. My family is of German descent.

Peter and Hannah Grossnickel were my great-great grandparents. Peter's ancestors were immigrants from Germany. The names are unknown to me.

My family spelled their name "Grossnickel." My husband's family spelled their name "Grossnickle."

CHAPTER 2

TYPHOID FEVER

Dad Has the Fever

I am very blessed to have been born to Charles Webster Grossnickel. Eleven years before I was born, he nearly lost his life to typhoid fever. There was an epidemic raging on the east coast around the year 1888. Many people became infected with the disease. My dad contracted the dreaded fever, was confined to bed, and became deathly ill. Typhoid is an acute infection caused by bacteria which enters the body through the mouth. After ten days, the victim develops severe headaches, gets a rose-red rash, has stomach distress, and is sometimes delirious. The body temperature can reach 105 degrees and remain high for two weeks before subsiding.

In the late 1800s, there were no modern antibiotics to help fight the infection. If the patient survived, it was usually due to good home nursing care, a nutritious diet that the patient may have been able to consume after some of the stomach distress subsided, and surely by the goodness of God!

Grandpap George Leatherman Helps

During Dad's illness, my oldest brother Wade was just

a baby and the only child. Since he was so young, Wade was in great danger of contracting the germ and becoming ill. Everyone understood the disease was very contagious. So many people were dying.

Mother and her father, Elder George Leatherman, cared for Dad as best they knew how. She and Grandpap lived through the Civil War and perhaps found comfort knowing that since God protected them during those earlier years of life, he would surely protect them while caring for this critically ill husband and son-in-law. Dad's fever raged for days and no food stayed in his infected body. He was rapidly losing weight and strength. The nightmare was at its worst.

Mother and Grandpap Leatherman made Dad as comfortable as possible by keeping his bed fresh. Continuously, they bathed his hot body to help reduce the high temperature. They encouraged him to drink fluids to keep him from dehydrating. One of them constantly stood by his bedside. Indeed, their presence was comforting to him. As weak and sick as Dad was, he went along with whatever they suggested. Without doubt, he was concerned for his wife and baby since he knew death could be immediate. Perhaps he wished he could die to end the discomfort and misery the disease was causing. I am convinced his wife and the baby were Dad's only encouragement to live! A great deal depended on Dad's determination to survive.

Dad May Not Live

My dad remained grievously ill and every day Mother and Grandpap Leatherman wondered what was going to happen to him. They hated to see the sun disappear over the treetops each evening, as Dad's condition got worse as the

4

minutes ticked away. Would Dad live through the night or, would the one keeping vigil soon be relieved to lie down to rest and then arise a few hours later to find Dad had passed into eternity?

Rest—they had not had a night of unbroken rest for weeks. They were so weary. Day and night they lived in suspense. What would Mother do without her husband should he die? The strain and concern was on all of my family, but Mother had a baby to care for and the possibility of becoming a young widow was great. In fact, that possibility seemed to be more real with each passing minute.

Struggling to Live

Dad clung to life for about four weeks; he was confined to bed for six to eight weeks. Many relatives and friends constantly prayed for God's mercy and healing. No one except Grandpap Leatherman came inside the house to help. It was just too risky. Everyone was terrified of becoming contaminated! Mother was extremely careful, taking extra precaution when handling the baby.

At this point, Dad was acquainted with death. He was simply standing at death's door—waiting. My family did not understand how he was able to take one breath after another.

Now it should be remembered that God has a time to live and a time to die, and it was not Dad's time to leave this earth.

Full-grown Beard

The once healthy, hearty, 30-year-old man was now a frail, 79-pound frame with a long, full-grown beard. Since Dad was so sick, no one wanted to disturb him to shave his face. Mother and Grandpap thought it certainly was not necessary. First of all, every ounce of his energy was needed for fighting to live.

Days came and nights followed and finally improvement to his health could be seen. He gained new strength slowly—a little change came a day at a time. At last he was able to get up from his bed. Painfully thin and weak, with the aid of Mother and Grandpap, he managed to stand to his feet. As he looked into the mirror to see his face for the first time in weeks, he cried and said, "Is it possible that this is me?" He decided never to shave his face from that moment on. The three of them stood weeping. There was such a spirit of thankfulness in their hearts. Dad's life had been spared!

Dad returned to his normal lifestyle as time brought new strength. During that epidemic, in many cases, the infected person was not as blessed and went to their grave.

CHAPTER 3

MY NAME

At the time of my birth, my parents had not selected a name for me. Shortly after, Aunt Salome Alice, Dad's sister, who was married to Tilghman Grossnickle, came to pay a visit and see the new baby. Uncle Tilghman was president of the Myersville Bank from 1916 to 1926. He also worked as the local veterinarian. Aunt Salome liked the name Letha. She knew a pleasant lady named Letha Fox and insisted it would be perfect. Since my aunt's middle name was Alice, she also suggested it be given to me. Aunt Salome's "hint" was accepted by Mother and Dad. I would now be known as Letha Alice Grossnickle.

Some of the Grossnickle families spelled their name Grossnickel. It would appear that "Grossnickle" was the original spelling; many of the families have gone back to using that spelling today.

Daddy, a Farmhand

My daddy worked as a farmhand for his father, Martin Grossnickel. The buildings of the Grossnickel homestead (now owned by Steven and Joann Leatherman) are nestled on a hillside off the Harp Hill Road in Ellerton, Maryland.

Ellerton was a small village then and remains so today. Beautiful hills covered with green grass and towering

7

trees meet the sky. The Middle Creek meanders its way through the flats. Then the water rushes down the hill and gushes against the rocks, creating sounds of music to your ear. Cattle drink from its supply of fresh mountain water. No one will ever count the fresh trout fish that have been snatched by hook or dipper from that creek and prepared for the frying pan by country cooks.

Majestic may be the word to explain the beauty of those mountains and valleys. Soft sounds of the night bring almost a "holy awe" as one listens to the springtime frogs in perfect chorus; the locust and katydids sing in a choir of their own. Farm life then was as simple as the lush pasture with wild flowers—and more wonderful and splendid to me than any life a king or queen could ever wish to experience. "Peace in the Valley," I would say.

"Girly"

One of my earliest memories is of my dad coming into the kitchen and rolling a scrumptious big red apple to me. I was small and sitting on the floor playing. He said, "This is for you, Girly." Girly was his nickname for me, his special little girl.

Big Farmhouse

In 1901, when I was two years old, my family moved from that little house on Myersville Church Hill Road where I was born, to the big dwelling on Grandfather Martin Grossnickel's farm on Harp Hill Road.

Grandpap retired and moved from the farm down to Ellerton. My parents then started a farming business for themselves. My mother and daddy milked approximately ten

8

to twelve cows by hand. They planted grain and grass crops without modern machinery. Dad farmed with horses; he did not like using mules.

During the heat of the day in the summertime, when the men and horses were working in the fields, they rested along the old stone or split rail fence rows under the shade of the towering trees. The horses needed a break and a chance to cool off.

Frequently, the farmer on the joining farm would be working in his fields and he, too, would take a few minutes to catch his breath after spotting his neighbor in the shade. They chatted while each man was on his side of the fence. Often, when the men where out in the fields working, the children were asked to carry a drink of water to them.

I lived on the farm with my parents until 1916, when I married Russell Peter Wiles.

Government Carries Local Mail

In 1900, one year after my birth, the United States Government began to carry mail to the homes in Ellerton and the surrounding areas. John M. Grossnickle was the local rural carrier. He was Uncle Tilghman and Aunt Salome's son, and my first cousin. No matter how stormy the weather, six days a week John delivered the mail around our neighborhood. In the winter he drove the horse and buggy, and in the summer he hitched up a stick wagon. In 1920, he began driving an automobile on his route. Just think of all the comfort he gained and time he saved!

Before this mail service, other than going in person to relay the news, there was no reliable way of sending messages to anyone in the country. Sometimes we flagged down people riding by and we asked them to deliver a handwritten note or word-of-mouth message.

Mailman's Retirement

An old newspaper article states that John M. Grossnickle retired under the United States government retirement plan in 1933 with a benefit of $95 a month. During the years he worked, he contributed five percent of his salary per month to the federal retirement plan.

Telephones

By the time I was a young child, the use of telephones was becoming popular, but we did not have one in our home. And then, all too often, the person you wanted to receive the message did not have a phone. I liked to join my daddy when he walked to Bittle's Store in Ellerton to use their phone. It fascinated me to listen to his end of the conversation. It was difficult for me to imagine he was hearing a voice through the wire and receiver he held in his hand.

Later on, I remember my folks having a telephone installed in our home. Now we could make calls and not have to leave the house. What a convenience! We had a "party line" with the neighbors. That meant we shared the phone line with a few families. When we picked up the receiver, and if they were using the phone at the same time, we could hear their conversation or vice versa. The bell rang one long and three short rings for us. The next neighbor's call had a different code of rings.

CHAPTER 4

GROWING UP

Dad's Gentle Touch

Farm life back in the early 1900s meant long days and hard manual labor. When the work was finished in the evening, and Dad had retired for the day, he would say to me, "Come Girly, I will hold you on my lap." This time was sweet bliss for both of us.

Rocking

With the darkness upon us, together, we walked hand in hand into the living room with only the flickering light from a dim oil lamp to show the way. Dad sat down on his wooden rocking chair and gently lifted me up onto his lap. As we talked he told me he loved me. I loved hearing that. He told me tales, perhaps the same stories told to him by his parents when he was a lad.

Since he was a farmer, he wore clothes made from heavy, coarse fabric. The long dark beard, which he began to grow during his illness, hung from his chin and rested on top of my head as he cuddled me ever so close to his chest. I remember that his beard was in the way when he kissed me. It tickled, and I squirmed. He always put his hand to the side of his face and held the beard back as he gave me kisses. I

11

had been told of his illness and I did not care how much his beard annoyed me—he was alive and well, and I loved him. His hands were rough and harsh from laborious work. But I felt only the soft, gentle touch of a loving father's hand as he stroked my soft, tender skin. He loved me with true love.

If we rocked long enough, the warmth from his body and the comfort of being in his arms put me to sleep. Carrying me upstairs to my bed, he gently pulled the covers up and tucked me in for the night. Whispering a prayer over me and placing one last gentle kiss on my cheek, he would leave my room knowing we had shared the same sweet love.

Making Knots

Since Dad was a farmer, he was usually around home. As a youngster, I remember helping him make the "ties" used for tying the bundles of fodder when husking field corn. This was a job Dad and I did while sitting near the kitchen stove on winter evenings. Here he taught me how to make the knot. Then he would make the loop in the other end. I liked to spend the evening helping my dad. I often commented on how much I hated the odor of the tar in the twine. In reply, Dad would lift his eyes from the twine in his hand, smile and say, "So, you do." I felt comfortable and safe there by the warm stove with Dad.

I think back on those days, and even though life was simple and the homes were not elegant, we did have all that mattered—each other. We were secure.

My Broken Polly Doll

The seasons came and went at a much slower pace for me back in the early 1900s.

One delightful warm summer day my mother and Nettie Harshman were busy doing the housework and cooking. Nettie, a teenager, was working for my mother as a maid. The air was warm and I was outside on the back porch playing with my doll named Polly. She had a rag and sawdust body with a china head, arms and legs. In my eyes she was the most gorgeous doll I had ever seen. As I was sitting on the porch steps quietly playing, Polly suddenly, and without warning, dropped from my arms. I did not think I was being reckless. Accidents just happen.

I watched her tumble down, hitting each step as she fell. On the ground at the edge of the last wooden step lay a small stone, right at the spot her china skull would land. I heard the shattering noise as her beautiful face and head broke. Oh, I cried at the sight of my broken dolly. My heart was torn apart, and my eyes were wet with tears. I immediately knew my favorite little friend was smashed and ruined forever.

Nettie Harshman—More Than Our Maid

Sometimes when the household chores were done, Mother let Nettie sew new dresses for my dolls. Mother always had extra pieces of fabric left from projects. Nettie could sew well and I was so excited about getting new outfits for Polly and my other doll, Becky. She knew the right size garment for each doll. It was just days before I broke my doll that she made a different dress for Polly. In fact, she was wearing it at the time of her fall.

13

Polly's Shroud

Nettie was out in the yard at the clothesline taking down the laundry that had been hung out to dry earlier in the day. She heard me crying and came running to see what had happened. Not knowing how precious this doll was to me, she laughed at the sight of my doll's broken head and said, "If I had known Polly was going to die and I was making her shroud or burying dress, I would have taken more care with the stitches and style." I was not only offended by the words she spoke, but to think she found my broken doll funny was too much. I was angry with her and very upset. I did not understand why she did not feel sad. After all, we both knew Polly could not be fixed, and it mattered to me.

Polly's fall was devastating. It was a traumatic moment and I never forgot her accident. Later in years as Nettie and I visited together, we often laughed about that day. Nettie was a wonderful friend and I will never forget how much I valued her friendship!

CHAPTER 5

LIFE AT HOME

Cherry Pie

In this time and place, most families planted fruit or nut trees in the yard to provide food. Folks tapped the sugar maple trees on their property and boiled down the sap until it formed maple syrup. Even if their acreage was small, people lived on the food they planted and grew.

Calmedia Brandenburg Grossnickel, Dessie Leatherman, Estie Green, Annie Main and Corie Jackson worked for my mother helping her with the daily housework. Although I was young, I can remember these ladies. I can still vision them working in the kitchen with Mother. They were nice to me and I liked to be with them.

Early one summer day when the cherries where hanging ripe on the tree out back, my folks asked one of the ladies to pick the cherries and make a couple of pies. She thought for only a moment and had made up her mind. She replied ever so bravely, "I don't pick cherries. If I fall out of the tree and break my leg, God won't give me another one." This excuse worked for her because Dad never requested she pick cherries again. He quickly learned she was afraid of heights.

Four Rubber Tires

The first time I saw a car coming down the road was around the year of 1904. I was very young. The new invention had everyone excited.

Charlie Harp was the talk of the town now that he owned an automobile. When Charlie's boys were out for a spin, they blew the horn to let us know they were passing by. All the children, as well as the grownups, ran to the edge of the road just to see them pass by in their new vehicle.

My brother George and I were thrilled with the sight of the car. Our little hearts were beating a mile a minute with excitement. Our minds could not believe what our eyes were seeing. We shouted for Mother to come look. It was difficult for us to even think people could ride down the road without a horse. The car left a trail of dust from the dirt road, and we wondered just how it could move so fast. Amazing, just amazing! Could you believe that at this time only about 150 miles of paved roads existed in the United States?

Fresh Sweet Cider

Many of the area's farms had apple orchards. In the fall of the year when our crop had been picked, Dad took a wagonload of apples to John Summers' Cider Mill in Ellerton. They pressed the apples into fresh cider and poured it into wooden barrels. Dad hauled it home with the horse and wagon. It was sweet and delicious when first made.

Sleigh Rides

As a child, I loved seeing the snow fall. When Mother or Dad suggested the air felt like snow, I could hardly wait for it to start coming down. Before the ground was covered, I started to ask my brothers when they intended to get the sleigh out of the barn. All the youth loved to go out on the road and ride on the fresh blanket. And it seemed everyone was out. Some folks had horse-drawn sleds. They were nothing more than a flat wooden bed and usually had a bench seat. I remember the horses felt so frisky in the white powder.

Wade and Herbert took George and me driving. Mother bundled us up and we covered our legs with the lap robe. The seat was not very wide in a sleigh so only two adults could comfortably fit. Often, my brothers each held one of us on their laps since we were little. Or only one of them went out and each of us sat by our brother's side.

Sleigh Bells

Oh, how I loved to hear the sound of the sleigh bells! The faster my brothers made the horse trot, the louder and more beautiful the bells rang. The air was cold and crisp with a freezing chill hitting my face and body as we rode along. The sight was so beautiful. The slopes were gentle, with the dips and hollows covered with snow. Along the road, there were occasional clumps of trees and pines with clinging white crystals hanging from their boughs. It was a sight to behold. It was truly a winter wonderland!

Learning to Sew

In the country, the ladies spent many winter days sewing. Early in my life, from the time I was four or five years old, I sat by my mother's chair as she sewed. There by her side she taught me the art. I attempted to make new dresses for my dolls; some turned out to be wearable for them. Other times, Mother would be piecing a quilt top together and, at the same time, she would give me fabric to cut and sew. I cut the pieces small as she instructed and then began to stitch them together by hand with a needle and thread.

I will never forget Mother's comment when I sewed a piece of fabric together wrong-side out or uneven. She said to me, "Letha, things done by half are never done right." I thought she was so unreasonable, but those words worked like a charm to put a guilt trip on me. I do not know why, other than I hated hearing the way she said them. I was so young, I did not care if my work was perfect. I just wanted to pass the time and have fun. I was not looking for perfection; she was.

When Mother made this statement, it hurt me and I cried and cried. But always after drying my tears, I persisted and pleased her as my little hands ripped those stitches out and I started over.

My Quilt

Children were taught early in life the skills they needed to make a good home life for their family. In 1905, when I was six years old, I pieced a four-diamond quilt top. It was made from the many pieces of fabric Mother saved when sewing my dresses. I used a paper pattern to cut the

18

blocks. The cotton bottom of the quilt was a bluish green background with a white cloverleaf design. I carefully cut and stitched the pieces together, and my finished project was nice. Mother quilted it and embroidered the date it was completed in the corner. I kept it down through the years. I have given this keepsake to our first son, Austin, and his wife Ruth.

Baking Bread

My mother baked bread in an outdoor bake oven. These ovens were built from brick or stone and joined with mortar. For convenience, they were usually situated close to the kitchen entrance with a woodpile nearby. At our house, the oven was just outside the back door and under the old pear tree that stood near the dinner bell. Cooling shelves were erected at its side. A roof extended out over them; it was intended for some protection from the rain and snow. We baked bread no matter what the weather, hot or cold.

Preparing the Oven

Early in the morning, Mother went out the back door with her "barn burner" matches in hand. She was going to start a wood fire in the bake oven. She pushed plenty of dry wood in to ensure an intense heat would be produced. Once the flame was blazing, back into the kitchen she came to prepare the dough. She mixed the ingredients in a big wooden dough tray. The tray was rectangular and was about eight or ten inches deep. She baked rolls as well as loaves.

After the wood burned and the coals died down, she dragged them with a rake from the oven and onto the ground. Then she brought a bucket of water, a long wooden broomstick, and a big cloth. She wrapped the cloth around the stick, dipped it into the bucket of water, and swabbed the inside of the red-hot oven where the fire had been just minutes earlier. This cooled it to the right degree for baking. After the oven was prepared, she stuck her arm inside the opening to test the temperature. Having no thermometer, if it felt right, she put the pans of risen bread dough in and waited for them to bake. There was no door on this oven so she propped a large stone over the hole.

Mother knew just how long to wait before rolling the stone away from the opening. Somehow she pulled those big pans of bread from that hot oven. Then she carefully sat the loaves on the shelves to cool. The bread smelled so good! It was no sooner out of the oven when I wanted a slice to eat. I especially liked her fresh bread when the crust was on the dark side. Oh my, how I did love it! Later in the day, she called me to come help carry it into the kitchen for storing.

Summer Kitchen and Wash House

At home, an old log building sat below the main farmhouse near a spring and the smokehouse. The lower level was the wash house. A spring of fresh water ran through a trough on the floor. An open fireplace was built in the opposite end from the entrance. The building had an upstairs porch that ran the length of the structure and from there we entered the main floor or the summer kitchen. It was nothing more than a small version of an early 1900 kitchen. We cooked here during the hot summer months in order to keep the big farmhouse and our bedrooms cool.

Singing on the Porch

I remember warm, summer evenings when the work for the day was finished. When supper was over, and the sunset was brilliant over the farmland in the west, we would walk across the yard, and through the grass, to the big farmhouse. Here on the porch, Mother and Dad sat on the bench, while George and I sat on the steps. We played quietly around and I can still see us there—surely it was just yesterday!

Dad and Mother talked. They discussed what was happening with friends and family. Often they made plans for the next day. Shortly the conversation would stop, and with a smile on his face, Dad would tenderly look at Mother and say, "Mom, let's sing a little tonight." Mother would nod her head in agreement and softly give a note to open an old hymn. They sang with happy and grateful hearts into the dark of the night.

On occasion, the neighbors mentioned they heard the sweet strains of my folks' voices as it traveled through the night air across the valley. Dad was a "light-hearted" man. He was jolly and he liked to joke with folks. I fondly remember those happy times our family shared.

Swinging in the Apple Tree

On Father's Day, June 18, 1995, I visited my old homestead where I grew up. This was the first time I set my feet on that ground since my parents had public sale of the farm equipment and stock on March 10, 1917. They were retiring.

Steven and Joann Leatherman own the farm now and it was such a delight to see how well the buildings and land has been cared for. Signs are, they too love their home so very much.

That Sunday afternoon while standing out behind the barn under a warm and sunny sky looking across the field towards Granny's Patch, I spotted the old apple tree I played under as a child in the early 1900s. Through the years, its branches has been damaged by the wind and storms, but it still stands. It was there under the tree where my friends, my brother George and I played so many years ago. We had a swing that was made from a long board and rope tied in that tree. Two or three children could be seated and share the ride.

Granny's Patch

Granny's Patch is a low area on the farm in the field back of the barn. There was a spring near the old foundation where once a small building rested. I have very little information but it is believed that at some point in time past perhaps someone's Granny lived in a very small house at that spot. When I was a child, my folks placed a tin cup or coconut shell by the cold, clean spring of water. Even if I was not thirsty, I always stopped to get a drink of the chilled water when passing by Granny's Patch.

One memory after another raced through my mind as I stood there enjoying the old home sweet home. It seemed as if I was dreaming. I thought how short a span of time my 95 years has been. I thought of all that has occurred during the 78 years I have been away from the home where I grew up and somehow I could not hold back a few sad tears.

CHAPTER 6

NEW EXPERIENCES

Bittle's Store

As a child I often walked to Bittle's Store in Ellerton. The establishment was owned and operated by Frank Bittle (the father of Tom Bittle). It was just a little country store where Mother and Dad shopped. When Mother was baking and needed brown sugar, or if she was sewing and needed a spool of thread, I would go purchase it for her.

Sometimes Mother asked me to get samples from the bolts of the gingham and cotton prints that were stacked on the shelves. She would instruct me to say to Mr. Bittle, "Will you please cut Mother a sample of your fabrics in stock? She is going to make a dress, apron, (or whatever) and she would like to see what you have." Mr. Bittle would agree and find his scissors. He cut a little sample from each bolt he thought she might like and I would take it home. Mother looked at each sliver and then I would return to the store with her selection and a note stating the yardage she needed. I was really excited to carry the fabric home if a dress was going to be made for me!

The Bittles had a little black dog that spent most of his time in the yard. As I walked by their home that was located next door to the store, this dog barked and ran out onto the road following after me. He ran right up to the back of my heels. He would not bite, but I was afraid. I did not trust him for one second. I walked as quietly as possible as I neared the house, but the dog always heard me coming. Talk about "treading softly." I did.

Other times when I went to the store I walked across what we called the "long field." By going that way, I would come down behind the store. It seemed when I stayed away from the front of the house and off the road my chances of keeping out of the sight of the dog were better.

Penny Candy

Bittle's Store had an old wooden floor and was heated with a potbellied stove. The items for sale were arranged neatly on the shelves. We always purchased fresh coffee beans and brought them home to grind.

On most visits, Mother or Dad gave me a few pennies or a nickel to buy some candy. The candy was displayed in a wooden case with a big glass window. I pressed my face against the glass and looked at the goodies until my mouth watered from imagining the sweet taste. After enjoying the sight of the sweets, Mr. Bittle asked, "Are you going to get a little candy today?" Most often, I could answer, "Yes." Since I always shared with George, sometimes I chose something I thought he would enjoy.

The candy seemed to make the walk back home shorter. Maybe that is why the little black dog chased after me; he caught the sweet scent.

Molasses

We used lots of dark molasses at my home for baking. We also used the lighter variety as a spread on bread and in

24

place of jelly. I remember Dad strewing it on top of apple pie, adding some of Mother's homemade smear-case (homemade cottage cheese), and smiling as he enjoyed every bite. I carried a gallon tin bucket with a tight lid to the store and Mr. Bittle filled it with molasses from a wooden barrel. The bucket had a wire bail for a handle. When the pail was full, it was heavy and the handle hurt my fingers. I kept switching it from one hand to the other. Sometimes I tucked the hem of my long dress tail under the wire. Think how many honeybees I must have fed on my way home!

Kerosene Lamps

I walked to Bittles to get kerosene for the oil lamps every couple of weeks. Sometimes Dad joined me. Again, I took a gallon tin can and Mr. Bittle filled it with oil from his barrel. I could make the purchase from either the Bittle's or Summers' Store. I preferred to stop at Bittle's when I went alone. I hated carrying the smelly container and this store was closer to our house.

Summers' Store—Sweet Tooth

Summers' Store was just across the bridge going away from Bittle's Store and my home. Now and then I liked to go there when I had only a few items to purchase. On each visit I spent time checking out his penny candy case. Mr. Summers always waited for me to finish staring at the varieties. Then, with a gentle smile on his face, he reached into the case, removing a few pieces. Carefully, he dropped them into a small brown paper bag. Gently, he folded down the top. I watched him closely as he stretched his arm across the counter. He passed the bag to me and he was still smiling.

He gave me the kind I liked, so as he watched, he must have been figuring out which pieces he would put in my bag. I liked Mr. John Summers and his candy!

It is a wonder I still have good teeth today as I think of all the candy I ate during my early childhood. I must have gotten my "fill" when young, since I do not have the appetite for sweets in my adult years.

Fine Dishes

If time permitted, while in Summers' Store, I ventured upstairs to look at the pretty dishes displayed there. I never touched anything. I just looked with a wide-eyed gaze. I had a fear of breaking one and getting myself into a heap of trouble. I was sure Mr. Summers would tell Mother and Dad if that ever happened. It seemed to me there were thousands of dishes arranged so beautifully—all kinds.

When Russell and I married, I finally got to buy dishes from Mr. Summers to start housekeeping. I bought the Blue Willow pattern and I still have them today. They were so pretty and special to me that I rarely used them.

George Eldridge

George Eldridge owned a farm at the end of the hill on Church Hill Road just beyond the Myersville United Brethren Church. He owned several durrey and stick wagons, and he had plenty of horses to pull them. Salesmen came to Myersville on the trolley car to promote their product, and Mr. Eldridge's business supplied the men the means of transportation that enabled them to travel their sales route. Some salesmen were peddling seeds and planting supplies; others were selling stoves and household items. Still others came selling magazines and books. At least once a year, you could expect a salesman who always offered a big black Bible in his display.

These men traveled over the countryside. When finished their sales campaign in that particular area, they returned the horses and wagon to Mr. Eldridge. At Myersville, they boarded the trolley car and rode to the next town to sell their product.

The trolley station was located at the Farmers' Exchange in Myersville. I would say the Exchange was the "early day shopping center!" There was an ice cream parlor, a farm supply store, and various businesses located in the complex.

On the second floor of the building, Calvin and Lola Gladhill operated a furniture store. The Gladhills are the founders of the Gladhill Furniture Store that is located in Middletown, Maryland, today. My husband and I bought our furniture from them when we married. I still use the two bedroom suites and round oak table we purchased in 1916. We also purchased a kitchen stove, chest of drawers, and some carpet at the same time.

I remember the box car delivering barrels of sugar, molasses, sacks of flour, and other staples to the Farmers' Exchange. From this point, the store owners came and hauled the merchandise back to their establishment to sell to their customers—the country folks.

I recall that fabric came on bolts and was packed in a large, tight wooden box. When my first children were little, I used one of these wooden boxes for a playpen.

CHAPTER 7

GRANDPARENTS

Grandfather and Grandmother Leatherman

My mother had a brother named Frank Leatherman. He was handicapped. There were no social programs to provide aid to help ease his burden. Folks depended on families and friends.

Grandma Leatherman smoked a pipe and Grandpap never mentioned he did not approve. He was an elder in the church and believed it was sinful to smoke. But on the other hand, he pitied his wife and thought, if she found some pleasure in this, she should not be denied the privilege. After all, she had few pleasures and was a good wife. She most often remained at home to care for Frank while Grandpap and the other children went out. Frank died when he was in his early thirties.

Visiting My Grandparents

I was about seven years old when Grandpap George Leatherman's health began to fail rapidly. Even though he was getting old, he lived down in Harmony on his farm. This was the same location where he, Grandma and his family lived during the Civil War. Mother visited often to check on him. She was very concerned about her daddy's health.

Grandpap Grossnickel and Old John

My other grandpap, Martin Grossnickel (Dad's father), lived in Ellerton in a little home near the bridge. This was just down the road from the farm. He frequently walked up to our place just to visit and pass some time away. He enjoyed tinkering around in Dad's shop and the barn. It was home to Grandpap; he had lived there while farming as well.

Grandpap owned a fine driving horse named old John. He lived on the farm with our workhorses. Mother liked to drive him but always asked permission from Grandpap first. She did not think it was proper to just hitch John up and go. She thought Grandpap deserved respect.

When Mother decided she would like to go to Harmony, she asked me to go out to the barn and find Grandpap Grossnickel. I was instructed to inquire if she could drive old John down to see Grandpap Leatherman. I remember finding him so many times sitting on the horse mounting block near the overchute. If he was not there, he was often resting in the barn. Other times I found him at some spot where he could watch what Dad was doing.

I was the one running around to find him and ask if Mother could drive old John, and I thought, "Here stands the horse so close to us, why not take him and go? Grandpap does not care." I had no problem with that and I knew my Grandpap would not have been upset with us.

Obeying Mother

Despite these thoughts, I obeyed Mother and ran to search for my grandfather. I ran around and was out of breath by the time I found him. It was amazing how quickly my little legs could carry me around when I knew we were going somewhere.

Grandpap always smiled when he saw me coming and he hugged me once I was by his side. He was happy to see me even if we had been together only minutes earlier, and even if I was only staying long enough for a quick question. I did not mess around for very long, but while standing close I would politely ask, "May Mother drive old John today? She and I would like to go visit my other Grandpap." Grandpap Grossnickel was so pleasant and kind spoken. He reached out to pull me even closer. Wrapping his arm around me and holding me ever so close, he always answered, "Sure, you may use old John." Again, he would kiss me good-bye and away I ran. He watched me for as long as he could see my little dress tail flying. I would slow down and wave when I thought I was about out of his sight. I loved my grandfathers.

Arriving back in the house and panting for my breath, I stood in front of Mother and told her that Grandpap said it would be okay to use old John. I am sure she knew this would be his answer before I ever returned to her side. Together, we then went to the barn. Dad or my brothers helped us get John hitched to the buggy and we were on our way.

I could not stop thinking about why I always had to run and ask Grandpap that question. As Mother and I drove down to Harmony, I pondered about the idea.

Grandpap Leatherman Takes Ill

I remember riding down the road to Grandpap Leatherman's and walking into the big farmhouse with Mother. I held Mother's hand. Grandpap was ill and confined to bed. We often sat up close beside his bed. Grandpap liked us to be near. I can still see his white beard

31

as he laid there with the covers pulled up around his chin. His face was so pale. In fact, it was ghostly white. Mother and Grandpap held a conversation as I sat nearby. I watched Grandpap closely and he returned a smile often.

Sometimes, while still looking my way, he would rearrange the covers on top of his chest and then neatly fold his hands on top. I think he was watching me just as closely as I was watching him. I pitied him and hated to see him feeling so badly. I know Mother's heart was touched as she watched his health fail.

Admiring the Quilt

This day before we left our home to go visit Grandpap and Grandma Leatherman, Mother told me she was going to take my quilt top squares along to show my grandparents. Mother was very pleased with my work. I, too, was proud of it. Grandpap inspected the patchwork and told me what a precise job I had done. He said I was a good girl. I can still hear his sweet voice. I can remember how Mother laid the pieces on the bed for him to admire. Again, he looked closely at my stitches and then, with his face just beaming, he looked straight into my eyes. He gave me that loving smile that only a grandfather can give his granddaughter.

Crackers

Oftentimes, when Mother and I drove down to see Grandma and Grandpap Leatherman in the horse and buggy, Mother stopped at the Summers' Store just to buy me some crackers. Crackers were a special treat. She knew how much I enjoyed them.

Grandpap Leatherman Dies

My grandfather, George Leatherman, died in February ·1907, at his home in Harmony. He was suffering from an attack of "grip" at the time. He was nearly 80 years old. I was sad.

Grandpap was a deacon and elder at the Grossnickle Church of the Brethren. His obituary stated he was a kind and gentle man who made friends with all. During his ministry, 412 people joined the church and 43 couples were married by Grandpap. His friend, the Reverend John Bussard, preached his funeral sermon from the book of Luke. *"But Jesus turning unto them said, Daughters of Jerusalem, weep not for me, but weep for yourselves, and for your children." (Luke 23:28)*

The funeral cortege consisted of fifty vehicles (buggies, surreys, and wagons). His family and friends packed the church for the service. Grandpap had lived a successful life and his estate was valued at $12,000. In 1907, this was considered "well off."

Grandmother Leatherman

I remember my grandmother, Rebecca Johnson Leatherman. She died a few years after Grandpap's death. She suffered from a stroke and paralysis. She lived only a couple of days following the onset of her illness. Grandma was a large woman and was frequently seen sitting in her big wooden rocking chair. She always kept the pipe she smoked in her hand. Grandma never smoked while we were visiting at her house. She was aware that Grandpap disapproved and thought he would not like Mother and me to see her "puffing away." Grandma was always nice to me.

When Grandma Rebecca Leatherman died, the article

33

printed in the newspaper stated she was a lady of most excellent Christian character and was held in high esteem by a large circle of friends and acquaintances.

CHAPTER 8

FEARS AND WORRIES

Trolley Rides

I never enjoyed riding on the trolley car. The ride made me dizzy, nauseated, and gave me a terrible headache. I complained to Mother, and she told me not to look out the window while riding along and then I would be fine. But it did not work for me. The whole problem was, I simply just had to look out and see what was whizzing by!

The Horse Waits

We rode on the trolley to Frederick. Mother or Dad drove from our home to the Myersville station in the horse and buggy. If it was just Mother and me going to Frederick to shop, we aimed to be ready to leave our house by nine o'clock in the morning; we were home by mid-afternoon.

Upon arriving in Myersville in the morning, we drove to Uncle Tilghman Grossnickle or Uncle Joshua Summers' home. There we tied the horse to wait until we returned. We were frequently gone for five or more hours, but the horse was used to being tied to a hitching post or fence and did not seem to mind. When Mother stopped at Uncle Tilgh's house, he usually unhitched our horse from the buggy and put him in the stable with his horse. He gave him hay to eat while waiting for us.

The Conductor

The trolley conductor, Henry Magaha, lived in Myersville off the Brethren Church Road. Henry Haupt was the engineer.

We had to climb a high step to get into the trolley. Mr. Magaha lifted me up and always assisted Mother. When all the passengers were aboard, the conductor gave the signal to the engineer to start. The signal was Mr. Magaha ringing a bell. After that, it was only a few minutes until we were on our way down the tracks.

We always caught the trolley at Myersville. It made a stop at Middletown and then traveled into Frederick. Teenagers who were fortunate enough to attend high school came from Myersville to Middletown for their classes. These students rode the trolley every day, back and forth to school. In the country where I lived, we had only elementary schools.

Overnight Trip

When I was a child, the only times I stayed away from home overnight was when we visited Uncle Scott and Aunt Sarah Derr. Aunt Melissa Harshman, Aunt Sarah, and Mother were sisters. When Mother told me she had talked with my Aunt Melissa and we were going to go visit with Aunt Sarah, I was so excited. Our family never took a vacation and this was a very special occasion for us.

Aunt Melissa and Mother made the plans and decided which day we would go. We wore our "Sunday best." We left home early in the morning. Dad drove us down to the trolley station. I always gave Dad a good-bye kiss and a promise to hurry back home.

The trolley stopped at Mount Tabor, Maryland. My great-aunt Julie Leatherman lived here. We always visited with her and she served us lunch. I loved to eat at her house. In the afternoon, Mother and Aunt Melissa would say we had "to be going." Of course, Aunt Julie was never ready for us to leave.

Again, we boarded the trolley at Mount Tabor and rode to Feagaville, Maryland, where Uncle Scott and Aunt Sarah lived on a farm. We walked to Aunt Sarah's house from the station. It was just across the field.

Stomach Distress

One time we were visiting with Uncle Scott and Aunt Sarah and, as we walked by the tenant house that was located between the trolley station and their dwelling, we decided to get a drink of water from the outdoor pump. Everyone had a tin cup or coconut shell hanging nearby to catch a quick drink. Aunt Melissa and Mother took turns pumping to flush and clean the pipes. I was thirsty and the water was refreshing. I did drink a big cupful! Mother and Aunt Melissa had a few swallows as well.

We finally arrived at Aunt Sarah's doorstep, and what a happy time began. Everyone tried to catch up on the news and I was the center of attention.

Later, I became ill with stomach distress. Aunt Melissa and Mother had not pumped long enough to clean the pipes of the outdoor pump. They had no ill effect but I was very sick! Of course, everyone was concerned and pitied me. They wanted me to be comfortable. Aunt Sarah and Mother took me upstairs and put me to bed. I was so frightened! I thought I must be going to die. I remember walking into the bedroom and looking at a high-post bed. It was covered with a white bedspread. All the covers on our beds at home were dark colors. I had never seen a bedspread. When I saw the brightness of this one, it got my attention as it appeared so pure—maybe like Heaven. I thought surely I must be by death's door.

I was laying there waiting to "die" and, who walked through the bedroom door but Uncle Scott and Aunt Sarah's son, John Derr. John was a teenager. He hesitated as he stood in the doorway. He looked at me with a big smile on his face and said, "Hey there, Honeybunch, what are you doing in that bed? I thought we'd be going out to play ball." John was so jolly and I loved him.

Mother phoned my dad and told him how poorly I was feeling. The next day he drove to Feagaville to take me and Mother home. He came with old Logan and the buggy. I recall he brought a three-legged milk stool along. Dad put it on the buggy floor, I sat on it, and rested my head in Mother's lap.

Aunt Melissa continued her visit. She spent a few days and then came back home on the trolley.

Uncle Scott Derr died in October 1928 and Aunt Sarah died in October 1946.

Mother's Illness

I remember Mother taking sick when I was just a youngster. No one ever talked to me about her illness; I just knew she was often confined to her bed for short periods of time. Dr. Davis, from Boonsboro, Maryland, came to the farm to make house calls and care for her. I do not recall much about what was happening, but I do remember watching the doctor drive in the farm lane in a buggy pulled by two

38

beautiful horses. A buggy, which is light in weight, was normally pulled by only one horse.

The Doctor's Companion

A black man accompanied Dr. Davis. He drove and cared for the horses. At our house, Dad invited the driver to unhitch the horses from the buggy. They watered them at the barnyard watering trough and then led them to the barn and gave them a couple of ears of corn and some hay to eat. The driver also kept the doctor company. There were no people of the black race living in our community, so I was intrigued when I saw him coming.

It alarmed me that the doctor had been called. I wondered what was going to happen! I was quiet and feared asking anyone questions. I was so uncomfortable about the situation. I thought maybe Mother was going to die. Years ago people did not share anything personal with their children. Children were told babies came in the doctor's black bag. Because of the unknown, I worried unnecessarily—Mother lived to be 92 years old!

I recall the doctor arriving around the noon mealtime. Dad invited him and the driver to eat with us since Mother had a maid to help care for her and cook during these times of illness. When the meal was ready to be served, Dad asked Dr. Davis to be seated by his side, and the driver sat next to the doctor.

Choking

I will never forget the day the driver choked on the food during the meal. He quickly got up from his seat, left the table, and cleared his throat. When he returned, he stood

39

by Dr. Davis' chair, laid his hand on his shoulder and said, "Excuse me Doc? Will you excuse me Doc?" The doctor never acknowledged he heard him. Repeatedly, the driver asked to be excused but the doctor would not answer.

My father, witnessing the man begging to be pardoned, and seeing that the doctor was ignoring him, stopped eating. He looked directly at the driver. With authority in his voice, Dad said, "Sit down and eat." I will never forget the somber face of the doctor. But the driver had a look of sudden relief after Dad spoke. All the while, I was at the table and I was still wondering if Mother will get better. I hated to see her suffer.

Meeting the Doctor Halfway

When folks who lived in the country became ill, many of them contacted Dr. Davis, who lived in Boonsboro. When he was out making house calls, he would arrange a mutual point to meet the patient if they were able to travel. This saved time for everyone.

One day, I remember young Russell Wiles and his mother, Flora M. Wiles, came driving their horse and buggy in our farm lane. Upon their arrival, I saw Dad greet them and show them to the house. Dr. Davis was at our home because Mother was ill.

I was down in the wash house that morning churning butter. At that time, I was too young to have an interest in Russell, but I was wondering what was going on and went to investigate. In silence I watched. I can still remember Russell seated on a chair near the back door in the kitchen. He was suffering with blood poisoning in his hand. The doctor treated the wound and applied a fresh bandage. Dr. Davis also talked with Mrs. Wiles and gave her medication.

40

The Wiles family and my family were acquainted by attending the same church.

Playing With George

One hot mid-summer day, my brother George and I were in the garden either working or playing. We were old enough to pull weeds and hoe around the plants. We each had a bottle of water to drink, and they got warm from sitting in the sun. George poured his out on a plant and informed me he was going to the spring to get some fresh water. The spring water ran through the wash house, out and down to the trough in the barnyard where the cows and horses drank. He asked if I would like him to bring me some cool water and I told him, "No, and don't you dump my bottle." He immediately picked my bottle up and emptied the water out on the dusty soil.

I guess I was hot and not in the best of moods after his defiance of my request to his question. Instantly, I knew what I was going to do to him for revenge. Without hesitation, I held my hoe high and brought it down over his head showing no mercy whatsoever. Dead? It was a direct hit! Oh, I thought, dear Lord have mercy, I have killed him! Immediately, I was ever so sorry. At the sight of the open wound and the blood running down through his hair and over his face, I thought surely he would die. Instantly, he dropped the empty bottles and ran screaming at the top of his lungs to the house to show Mother what I had done.

I started to cry, too. I left my weapon (the hoe) and ran after him, although I knew for certain I would be punished upon arrival. Mother washed George's wounded head and scolded me simultaneously. I just stood there. At that point, I had nothing to say. Nor did I want to even think of anything

41

to say. I did not care what Mother said or how she punished me; I just wanted George to live. Suddenly, I was no longer angry.

Well, George lived, I did get punished, and I was sorry I had hurt him. Kids will always be kids.

The Wagon!

George loved to play with his little red wagon. He continually pestered me to go outside with him. From my viewpoint, it was nothing special. It was just a red metal wagon bed with four wheels and a tongue. It was that simple. He was constantly telling me he needed my help to fix it. I never knew what was broken! The wagon did not look in need of repair to me. Even so, I reluctantly went to help him. I thought, what in the world is wrong with this fellow? He does not do anything but turn it upside down and look. His plan was simple, but I did get so disgusted with him and the wagon. He could never get me to stick around long at that game.

It was our responsibility to keep the woodbox filled. When it came time to bring the wood into the house, George insisted we use his wagon. So to the woodpile we would go pulling that ridiculous wagon behind us. We stacked the wood on it as neatly and securely as possible. In my mind, I knew what was going to happen before it ever occurred. And sure enough, as he pulled the wagon on the rough and stony ground, it upset every time and spilled the wood off. I told him it was easier and quicker to carry it in our arms, but he would not listen. George, who was older than me, thought I was just a silly girl.

CHAPTER 9

NEW SHOES

The Cobbler

Aaron Shepley was the local cobbler. In August, my daddy would tell me it was time to visit Mr. Shepley and have my new fall high-top shoes made. I needed new ones to wear to school. I was expected to walk to Mr. Shepley's alone. It certainly was a safe and reasonable thing to do. Off I would go down to Ellerton, a short distance beyond Bittle's Store, to the Shepley's home.

The walk was not bad. I did not mind going over the big Ellerton bridge down at the road, but to cross the Middle Creek at Mr. Shepley's home meant I must use his little creaking, swinging, wooden bridge. It shook when I walked on it no matter how softly and carefully I moved. I do believe it shook at the stillest moment. What a fright! To me, the water under that bridge seemed like an ocean at high tide during a storm. It appeared angry and vicious as it slashed and whipped against those rocks.

While walking on the swinging bridge, I dared not look down into the racing water through the cracks between the boards. And oh, how I hated to see my shadow reflect back to me in the shallow spots. I held my breath. I looked both ways before ever putting my foot upon the bridge. I did not want anyone walking on it with me who might try to play a trick. I concentrated on my destination—the Shepley's white house. I made each wide step count as I hurriedly tiptoed across to the other side. God surely must have taken my little trembling hand as I made each step.

Long Black Stockings

Before I left home, Mother made certain I had in my hand a pair of long black stockings she made for me. I needed to take them so Mr. Shepley could accurately measure for the new shoes. He allowed plenty of room for the stocking and my foot as well. Mother began knitting me those long black stockings early in the summer. She used a special yarn.

Measuring My Foot

I went barefoot all summer long; now Mr. Shepley waited patiently and smiled as I tried with all my might to manage getting that new, clinging stocking onto my tiny, sweaty foot. Maybe he pitied me, or wanted to help me. I do not know what he was thinking, but I do know what was on my mind. I hated everything about getting new shoes.

Mr. Shepley was always kind to me. He tinkered around at his workbench until I had the stockings on. Now we were ready for the fitting. He made small talk as he measured my foot that was still trembling from the walk across the bridge.

"Little Miss Want"

At this point, I was just happy to be in Mr. Shepley's house. I must say my mind was not on what we were doing because I was secretly wishing I could have the manufactured shoes from Bittle's establishment. I passed by the store on my way to Mr. Shepley's place and I desperately wanted to stop in and buy them. I knew which ones I liked—the shiny pair with pretty buttons instead of strings. I just knew he had my size.

But since nothing came of my plans, my biggest purchase at Bittle's Store was penny candy. I knew only the very rich bought Mr. Bittle's shoes. You see, it did not cost anything to dream. Those shoes appeared to me as being so soft and neat compared to the "heavy-duty" ones I was having Mr. Shepley make. But then, I would remember Mother calling me "Little Miss Want" when I asked for special things she thought were frivolous. The thought of store-bought shoes was overridden as I recalled her statement.

Heading Home

By now, the remembrance of what I—tiny, frightened Letha—was going to have to face entered my mind. Alone, and in a matter of minutes, I would be heading home and nearing the fierce, raging Middle Creek and swinging bridge. In all honesty, it was not as big a creek as it seemed. The real problem was the "unstable" tiny bridge. I thought if only my daddy could have come with me. I was convinced if I held his strong hand I would not have been afraid. I always managed to get home.

When my new shoes were completed and ready for pickup, I walked back down to Mr. Shepley's house with a heavy heart. Somehow I carried the crude leather high-tops home. I thought someone, somewhere, must surely care that I have to wear these horrible shoes!

45

CHAPTER 10

DENTAL PROBLEMS

Big Toothache

Annual dental checkups were not a common practice for the people living in the rural communities in the early 1900s. We made plans to visit a dentist only after the pain began.

When I was about ten years old, I had a decayed tooth and developed a terrible toothache. It caused such misery and discomfort that I cried both day and night. There was no nearby drugstore to offer soothing drops or modern pain killers. My dad, being very compassionate and loving, decided I needed to see a dentist. He was searching for some relief for me.

Dr. Lakin

The next day, Dad and I drove by horse and buggy to Boonsboro to visit Dr. Lakin. From Ellerton to Boonsboro was a long drive and, since I had a toothache, it seemed to take forever to get there.

We finally arrived that morning, and upon entering the office, I found my nerves jumping from the unfamiliar sight. By now my whole head was filled with severe pain. With my scrutinizing eye, I stared at the chair. It seemed so big and cold, the instruments looked evil, and the doctor did not seem like my best friend. After the dentist spoke with my father, and saying very little to me, the examination began. The doctor's decision was to pull the tooth.

The Extraction

As Dad held me in the chair, the doctor began to work. During the attempt to extract the tooth, it broke off at the gum. Now I had a new dental problem. Again they talked and I sensed I was in trouble. Dr. Lakin suggested my dad take me to Frederick, Maryland, to visit Dr. Aider for surgical removal of the roots.

Helpless

Dad took his weeping daughter by the hand and led me from Dr. Lakin's office. He tried to comfort me. Together, we walked down the street to the hitching post. The horse had waited so patiently for us. Dad gently lifted me into the buggy seat, and off we drove from Boonsboro back home to the farm. I sat very close to him. I was hurting, nervous, teary-eyed, and still trembling with fear. All the way home my dad tried to console me. Without doubt, he too, was feeling helpless. Nevertheless, I was the one who had the problem.

Another Dentist

Bedtime came at last, and ever so long was that night of pain. Since I could not sleep, all I thought about was the terrible situation I had been through. I was extremely worried about what was going to happen the next day.

Come morning, Dad and Mother got up before dawn to milk the cows and do the necessary barn work before we started off to see Dr. Aider in Frederick. I was apprehensive and afraid because I did not know what to expect.

I hated to leave home and Mother that morning. Dad hitched the horse to the buggy and off he and I drove to the Farmers' Exchange in Myersville. We boarded the trolley car that carried us into Frederick City. Upon arriving, we got off at the Town Square (Market and Patrick Streets) and walked to Dr. Aider's office on North Market Street. It was a long walk that day!

The Gas Mask

As we entered the office, I cried profusely. I held onto my daddy with all my might and strength. I was ready to stand my ground to keep anyone from so much as looking into my sore mouth. Why should I trust the doctor? I knew what happened the day before. Again, he and Dad talked, but I was too busy crying and shaking with fear to listen.

My dad and the doctor managed to hold me in the dental chair. I wanted to run away. I saw the dentist's hand coming toward me holding a contraption I had never seen before. It was a nose mask. The doctor placed it on my hurting, swollen face and gas was administered for my comfort. All these things were happening so fast. I continued to cry only to make things worse for all of us. Finally, the surgical procedure was accomplished and we left the office.

Long Ride Home

Dad and I faced the long ride home together. He helped me onto the trolley. He sat with his arm around me.

I was so sick and vomiting from the ill effect of the gas. Dad told me how sorry he felt, but again I heard nothing he said. I was so upset. Once the trolley arrived at Myersville, Dad put me in the buggy and soon we were home. Finally, the long day was over and Mother tucked me into bed.

CHAPTER 11

MY FIRST SAVINGS ACCOUNT

Middletown's Bank

Time passes by quickly both now and back then. As a young girl, my dad said, "Letha, this morning let's take a trip to Middletown to the bank. I need to take care of some banking business and today we can open a savings account just for you." Since we lived on the farm in the country, this trip took a big part of the day. Horse and buggy was our main means of transportation.

My dad, Charles Webster Grossnickel, would later be nominated and elected to serve as one of the directors from 1920 to 1934. He was a stockholder in the bank. I did not understand what being a director entailed, but I thought it sounded important and I was proud of him. My dad considered it quite an honor to serve in this capacity. He resigned in 1934, due to his bad health.

Today, the current president of the Middletown Valley Bank is my youngest son, Thomas M. Wiles. Tom took this position in 1984, at 39 years of age.

Past presidents have been George W. Gaver, Peter E. Bussard, John L. Routzahn, Robert H. Routzahn, and Charles H. Gouker.

I often think back on that childhood day. As my father and I walked into the bank in those early 1900s, I am sure he never dreamed that someday his little "Girly" would have a son, and that his grandson would become the bank's president. And by no means did the thought of ever having a son enter my mind! In fact, that day my only thoughts were on leaving my money with the bankers. I had no experience with banking procedures so it was an adventure for me to make a transaction, and I was a bit leery.

Five-Dollar Account

That day I had a five-dollar bill to deposit into my new savings account. I was curious about how this procedure worked and why they paid me for the use of my money. Dad tried to explain but his explanation did not sound reasonable to me. I did not understand what I was doing. However, if my daddy told me this was something I should do, I was willing to go along with it. Perhaps what I did not understand did not really matter. I loved him and trusted his judgment with all my heart.

Can you imagine seeing this bearded man driving a horse and wagon carrying his little daughter, and the two of us talking about the sights as we drove along? I spent so much time with my dad.

CHAPTER 12

SCHOOL DAYS

Ellerton School

George and I attended the Ellerton School at the same time. Our brothers, Wade and Herbert, were older and were out working elsewhere. George missed class frequently because Dad often kept him home to help on the farm.

Horseback to School

My brother, Herbert, and sometimes Wade, usually took George and me to school on horseback. George rode behind our older brother and I rode in front of him.

In the morning, Mother made certain we had our lunch and then out to the barn we ran. A mounting block sat under the overchute. It was nothing more than a big chunk of wood Dad saved when he cut down a huge tree. It was large and heavy so it did not turn over when I jumped onto it. With the horse standing up close to the block, I could hop on behind George. The two of us went alone once George was old enough to ride the horse down to school.

Upon arrival at school, George waited for me to get off. Then he picked up a small stone to pitch and aim for the horse's rump. If there was snow on the ground, he made a snowball and threw it at him. That was the signal for the horse to head home to the farm. Back up the road he galloped and in our farm lane he ran. He would go right to the barnyard and stay there. At the end of the day we walked home. Other times Dad came to get us on the horse.

Duties

The students carried buckets of drinking water from a nearby spring into the classroom. The pails were placed on a wooden bench. Everyone drank from the same dipper that hung from the edge of the bucket. We used outdoor privies that stood nearby the schoolhouse. At recess we all played marbles. The boys usually had a ball game going. The girls played tag, hide and seek, or house.

David Gaver

David Gaver was my teacher for my early years of public school. Maybe twenty-five to thirty students of different grade levels attended classes taught by one teacher.

The Ellerton School was located along Route 17, right in the heart of the village. The other students and I sat at wooden desks. They were old and marked from the many years of children testing the endurance of the wood with stones and knives. Most pupils liked to carve and many had showed off their finest talent on the desk tops.

The school was heated with a black potbellied stove that sat in the center of the room on a creaking wooden floor. The teacher fueled the fire with either wood or coal. Many times they threw a big chunk of wood into the stove since that burned for a long time. If the teacher did not come early to start the fire, the room was ice cold when we arrived. Blackboards and maps hung on the walls. Each child had a small slate, a pencil, and a pad of paper.

We packed and carried our food from home in a tin bucket. When several children from the same family attended the school, they often brought their lunch in one big basket. I remember some sisters and brothers bringing a whole big pie in, and they were able to eat all of it.

Young Student

Sometimes Mr. Gaver noticed the sad expression on my little face and he knew I did not feel like being at school. I was young, so he took a few minutes away from his classroom duties and held me on his lap. I enjoyed having Mr. Gaver as my teacher. He made sure the older students did not tease me.

School Lessons

Harvey Grossnickle was another teacher who taught me at the Ellerton School. Harvey was from another Grossnickle family.

What patience Dad had each evening as he helped me to learn the multiplication facts. He always helped me with my school lessons. But no task was too hard for either of us to achieve together—love seemed to make things easy.

Reverend Charles N. Freshour

When I was older, maybe ten years old, I attended the Poplar School. It was also a public school and it neighbored the Grossnickle Church of the Brethren. It sat on the opposite side of the road from the church and along the Middle Creek. My teacher there was Reverend Charles N. Freshour.

George and I walked to Poplar School. The school was several miles away from home. We could not tie the horse and have him stand all day waiting for us. That would have been too long. Neither could we send the horse home on his own from there. If the weather was not fit for us to be walking outside, we stayed home. It was as simple as that! I went to this school for about two years and then resumed my studies at Ellerton.

Russell (my husband-to-be, although I did not know it at the time) and I attended the Poplar School as youngsters. Years later, our older children, Austin, Doris, and Pauline, attended school there as well. For many years, Reverend Charles N. Freshour taught the classes. The children remember Charlie ringing a little bell he held in his hand to call them in from recess. Everyone took a turn carrying water from across the road at Charles Hoover's place.

When Russell and I were in school, we were called to the front of the classroom to stand and read. By the time our children went to Poplar School, there was a bench for them to be seated while reading.

Our daughter, Doris, recalls that while attending the Poplar School, she and some of the other children would walk up the road to the Grossnickle Church of the Brethren Cemetery and play around the tombstones. They played games, and when the spring wildflowers bloomed they gathered bouquets and placed them on the graves. When they heard the teacher ring the bell, they hurried back down to the schoolhouse. Reverend Freshour did not find any fault with them playing in the cemetery. There was no playground equipment to play on in those days.

Punishment

I remember when I was a young student, I did something the teacher thought was wrong. I cannot recall what I did now. But the teacher asked me to sit under the desk. Then I felt the teacher's feet against my legs. Indeed, I could not escape because my every move would be noticed.

Lucy Wilhide

Lucy Wilhide was my last school teacher at the Ellerton School. She was young and just beginning her teaching career. One day I was not feeling well and so I got up, walked outside, and proceeded home without a second thought. Lucy did not appreciate the fact that I left the classroom without her permission. And it was not the right thing for me to do. The next day she and I had a talk and we were both very upset.

My "Graduation"

That night Dad and I talked. I told him how much I hated going to school. As far as I was concerned, I thought I was old and smart enough to stop. He asked me if I knew how to read, write, add, subtract, multiply, divide, and did I know the multiplication facts? So I showed him what I had achieved. With a firm "I do" from me, he and I had my graduation from public school right then and there. That ended my last day of formal schooling; I never did attend high school.

I tell you, all through my life I learned so much from the "school of hard knocks." Learning the hard way seems to always stick with me. I never forgot those valuable lessons, because I lived in fear of needing to repeat the instructions. One is never beyond learning something new. Even today, at 95 years of age, I am still learning!

Home Remedies

As a young girl, when the fall came and the weather turned cold, I was often sick with the croup and a congested chest. In the winter, our home was heated with wood and coal stoves. We slept upstairs; the stoves were downstairs. The fires burned low during the cold nights and, come morning, the house was very chilly. The floors were not carpeted and they were ice cold. All we had were a few homemade scatter rugs placed here and there. As we rode the horse to school, I breathed cold air into my lungs. That combination contributed to me getting sick.

During the night, I would start to cough and croup; soon Mother appeared at my bedside. She would leave me for a few minutes, go to the kitchen, and back she came with a saucer of warm melted fat—bacon or meat drippings she called it. She never said what she was going to do, but when I heard her in the kitchen, I knew what she was preparing and I dreaded her return. Carefully, she fed me the melted fat, a spoonful at a time, until I vomited. What a remedy that was! But it seemed after the treatment, I felt somewhat better and could breathe more easily.

The Tonic

A tonic, pronounced "Scotch-a-Multion," was administered regularly to the children in our family during the winter. This tonic was for our general well-being. It had a horrible, foul taste. Most of the time, when I saw Mother coming toward me with the spoon and bottle, I ran. When she asked me to come to her, I did, but then I pulled away to stop her and the spoon holding the syrup. That was when I made the mistake. Herbert would catch me, put me between his knees, pinch my nostrils closed with his fingers, and pour the nasty liquid down my throat. That was enough to make anyone fighting mad. Sounds as if I was feisty—well maybe so, but I hated taking the tonic. I could not see the necessity for using it since I got sick anyway.

CHAPTER 13

CHRISTMAS AND SOCIAL EVENTS

Sunday School Treats

While growing up, Mother always made a few goodies and cooked a delicious turkey dinner for the family on Christmas day. She was a good cook. My parents bought hard toy and stick candy as well as plenty of fruit for the season. The toy candy was in the shape of farm animals, sleighs, traction engines, and different types of wagons. Each piece was about two to three inches tall and had a flat base. I remember standing the candy on the window sill, on the mantel, and in the china cupboard.

We did not decorate for the holiday or have a Christmas tree, so the toy candy was something festive for the house. It was either a bright clear red, yellow, or green. It was also hard as a rock. When I was ready to eat it, Mother cracked it with a clean hammer into pieces that would comfortably fit into my mouth.

On Christmas morning, we received just a few toys—maybe a doll and a ball. The Sunday School Department at the Grossnickle Church of the Brethren gave the young and old in the service each a beautiful china dish filled with candy (some years an orange was added). We looked forward to this treat. It did not bother me that we did not have lots of gifts. Most country folks lived very modest lives. We did not put importance on having "things"—we knew what "needs" were all about. And we recognized the difference between the two!

We can ruin our life with envy and strife. Mother and Dad tried to live simple and righteous lives.

Charles Shank's Confectionery Store

I often joined Dad when he went to Myersville to take care of business. Charlie Shank ran a confectionery store in town. Any time of the year, while walking down the street, Dad asked, "Girly, would you like to have some ice cream today?" I never turned the offer down.

Upon arriving at the store front, Dad would open the door and we walked in. We each ordered a plate of vanilla ice cream. I liked mine plain. Dad liked strawberry syrup on his. I stood on my tiptoes trying to see Charlie. I wanted a big scoop. I thought if I watched as he dipped he would pile it up—and he did! Mr. Shank had small tables and chairs in the shop so patrons could be seated and enjoy the treat.

New Dresses

I was by no means ever mistreated or abused by anyone or my family, but I was a lonely little girl with big brothers. My daddy did all he could to make me feel I was his special girl. When I was about twelve or thirteen, he bought me a mink fur muff and neckpiece. I was pleased to have such a luxury and, indeed, it was a very special gift. Dad also made certain I had nice dresses for church. Often, when he went to town, he bought a piece of fabric for me. Once he purchased navy blue silk that changed color as I moved. I remember it well. He purchased dark brown fur

62

and white lace to edge the yoke and hemline.

Josephine Hays, who lived in Middlepoint in the tenant house on the C. Upton and Ella Grossnickle farm, was a seamstress. She made the cloth into a beautiful dress. I loved it and Dad was proud to see me look so pretty. About the only time I wore this dress was to go to church since social functions in the country were limited.

Long Dresses and Sleeves

As strange as it may seem, Mother insisted my dress hems touch the top of my high-top shoes. It was stylish to wear them a little shorter. And many girls were wearing their dress sleeves above the elbow. I wanted mine shorter also. Josephine knew Mother's wishes and, as she was fitting the dress on me, she commented, "Letha, I know you would like to have your sleeves above the elbow, but you know how Mother feels about that." I nodded my head because Mother made it very clear to me that I would not be seen with my elbows or legs showing. She thought people would be quick to judge her if she allowed this. What would she think if she saw today's styles?

The Lavaliere

I remember Mother going to Frederick to shop one day. I wanted a lavaliere to wear with my new silk dress. A lavaliere is a necklace. I especially liked the chain style with the pendant hanging from it. I was going to stay home with Dad that day so I mentioned to him how much I would like having one. I knew he would understand.

Before Mother left home that morning, Dad gave her extra money and asked her to buy me a lavaliere. I also knew

63

Mother would not forget it if Dad asked her to make the purchase. I watched and waited for her return.

I was excited when I saw the buggy come up the road and turn into the lane. When she handed the package to me, I was elated. Mother chose a pendant of red stone with a long tear drop pearl hanging from the ornament. The pendant was on a gold chain; it was so beautiful and I treasured it.

Sunday Afternoons

On Sunday afternoons after church, my brother Herbert and his friends (Harry Mock, Albert Palmer, and Reno Rice) gathered at our home. They all played string instruments. The singing and music rang from the old farmhouse.

Torture

I was the little sister who seemed to be in the way on these afternoons. I had no one to play "little girl" games with and I became so bored. Herbert was always teasing me. My father usually defended me and he instructed me not to put up with him. I think Dad knew I was lonely and he pitied me.

Nevertheless, these sessions of playing their medallions, guitars, Autoharps, and harmonicas just went on forever in my young mind. This music was acceptable "torture" and I had to put up with it. And Dad was defending Herbert. First, one of his friends asked for a note to tune his instrument and then another made a request. I thought the entire afternoon was being wasted on that everlasting tuning. Once they got themselves together, the music did sound nice.

Quilting Parties

When I was young and at home, Mother attended quilting parties with the other neighboring ladies. The host of the party prepared and served lunch to her guests. They quilted, talked about what was going on in their lives, and enjoyed the day together. Mother left our house early in the morning. I hated to see her drive off in the horse and buggy. I was lonely unless I was in school.

The Frames

Many of the homes had big rooms that could accommodate the large quilting frames. The two horizonal bars were about nine feet long and the two vertical bars were about three or four feet long. The frame was set so the corners were at a true angle. Ticking (a heavy fabric) was nailed to the horizonal bars and the underlayer of the quilt was sewed to this fabric to hold it in place. The filler or cotton batting was placed on next, and then the pieced top. Next, a pattern for the stitches was marked with pencil or chalk, and it was ready to be stitched or quilted.

CHAPTER 14

NEW RESPONSIBILITIES

The Hens

Mother had trying times getting her old hens to sit on the nest each year. She needed new chickens to replace the ones she slaughtered to cook, and she needed new hens to lay eggs. In the spring of the year, she prepared the boxes or coops and then carefully placed one egg on the straw. She hoped the hen would let nature take over and she would sit on it. Once the hen made the decision, more eggs where slipped under her to make the time spent on the nest worthwhile. It took three weeks to bring forth a chick.

Chicken and Geese Feathers

We made and used straw ticks for mattresses and feather beds for bedcovers. We did not have springs for our beds either. To make a straw or feather tick, heavy fabric (ticking) was sewed into a large bag the size of a bed mattress. Then it was stuffed and sewn closed.

We saved the feathers that were plucked from the chickens we killed to eat. As difficult as it was, we washed them in a bucket of water and put them into a cardboard box to air dry in the sunshine. They were used for making feather cushions for our chairs.

Rope Beds

We slept on rope beds. The frame had little knobs around the edge where a mattress would normally rest on the springs. The ropes were tied across the bed frame, back and forth, forming a netting for the straw tick to lay directly on. It sat on four legs.

After I was married, I used the feather beds as covers on the children's beds to keep them "toasty" warm in the dead of the winter. Our home, as well as many others, was not centrally heated. During the spring and fall housecleaning, we put fresh straw in the ticks. We shook the feather beds to dust and fluff them up a bit.

Plucking Geese

While I was growing up, Mother and I plucked the geese's breast feathers. The geese were alive! We did this once a year, in the spring. Since their feathers have a soft texture, we used them to fill the pillows for our beds.

We chased the geese into a stable in the barn and closed the door. Dad often helped. Mother always sat on an old wooden box and had a bucket for holding the feathers close by. When the geese flapped their wings, they created a breeze. Mother covered the top of the bucket with a damp cloth to keep the feathers from escaping.

Only the breast feathers were plucked. We had to be careful to leave a "lock" of them under the wing. If too many were removed from this area, they could not hold their wing up. If that happened, until more feathers grew back, they walked around dragging the wing on the ground. Dad instructed me not to pluck them too close.

I hated plucking the geese! Mother and I held the

goose by its legs so it was upside down. Then we stuck its head under our arm. If we happened not to hold it tight enough, the old goose would grab and pinch us. It hurt! But, what we were doing to them was hurting as well. Have you ever heard, "turn about is fair play?"

Bringing in the Cows

On the farm, one of George's and my duties was to bring the cows in from the pasture field at milking time. We each rode a horse unless the men were working them in the field. George always ran to reach the horse stable before me. You see, he wanted to use the saddle and he suggested I use a burlap sack. Well, sitting on the sack was the same as trying to ride on "greased lightning." So, I rode bareback! What did it matter? At least I had an opportunity to ride the horse! My little legs clung to the horse's sides and I held to the bridle with all my might. As my long dress bounced in the breeze, I did enjoy the ride! We pretended to race our horses up the hill, but I tend to believe we were only forcing them to gallop!

Learning to Milk a Cow

When I grew older I helped Mother milk the cows. Most often, the farm women and girls milked while the men did the field work. I remember learning to milk an old cow named Beck. She was very gentle. Beck never kicked; she was probably just too old to get her feet up.

If Dad was not doing field work, he always curried and groomed the horses, and fed the other livestock while Mother and I did the milking. My parents did not sell the milk, but churned the cream into butter for the market. They raised young calves on the skim milk.

Aunt Susan Shepley

I never forgot walking to Aunt Susan Shepley's house. Aunt Susan was Dad's sister. Her husband was deceased, and one of their grown sons lived with her. She had a diabetic condition and was in poor general health. Mother felt sorry for my aunt and knew it was difficult for her to get around in the kitchen to cook food. Every couple of weeks, Mother prepared chicken or beef, made soup from the broth, and baked either bread, rolls or a pie for them. Then it was my duty to carry the food and walk to her house to visit. I started out across the field that took me up to the Church Hill Road. I stayed on the road that went past Uncle Caleb Harshman's farm and the Church Hill Lutheran Church. Aunt Susan's house was the second one past the church.

I remember arriving and, if Aunt Susan's son was home, he answered the door. They was always happy to see me. I handed them the bucket of soup and the handkerchief holding the baked goods. I never stayed long, as it seemed I never had much to talk about with her.

The handkerchief was made from the extra fabric Mother purchased when making aprons. The country women bought an additional yard of material when they planned to sew, cut it into a big square, and then hemmed the edge. It was just the right size for carrying food when you tied the four corners in a knot. The men would hang it from the knob on the horse's hame and carry lunch with them to work.

No matter how long I may live, I will never forget how afraid I was to walk by myself over the countryside. Folks allowed their dogs to run loose and I was frightened of them. Going alone took courage beyond my years.

70

CHAPTER 15

HORSE EXPERIENCES

Spooked Horses

Al Bartgis and Will Gouker lived in Ellerton. Will married Al's daughter. Together they ran a huckster route and operated a slaughter shop.

A huckster, or peddler, travels from farm to farm and buys or sells the farmers' produce. They also hauled the meats to Myersville by horse and wagon, and from there it was shipped to the markets in Baltimore by railroad car.

On their weekly run through the countryside with the horse and wagon, they carried cantaloupes, watermelons, bananas, oranges, and fish to sell to their customers. They bought butter, eggs, lard, poultry, and cured pork from these folks. In fact, they would buy almost any kind of produce you wanted to sell.

During the early 1900s, there was no electricity for refrigeration in our area. In the winter months, when Middle Creek was frozen, the men cut big blocks of ice and put them in an ice house or the ground cave between layers of sawdust. The sawdust served as insulation and helped to preserve the ice. The Bartgis cave was at Dam Hill on Route 17, near the Church Hill Road.

The Slaughter Shop

The slaughter shop was near the road. It was nothing more than a shed with the front side wide open. We could see the men in there butchering when we traveled down the road. A big log was positioned inside this building. They hung the calves from it while they cut their throats. The chickens, ducks and turkeys were also hung from this log, and the men stuck a knife under their tongue to kill them and let the blood drain from their veins. You could see a big black iron kettle of water over a blazing fire down by the creek. The water was heated to the boiling point and was used to scald the poultry. By doing this, the feathers could be easily removed.

When we passed by in the buggy or wagon and before we neared the property, I recall how excited the horses became. They did not like to pass by the Bartgis place. The horses were spooked when they heard the poultry clucking with excitement. Without a doubt, they had a deep inner feeling that something was wrong. They pointed their ears and snorted before they ever got to the scene. We prepared ourselves for a "hard jolt" of the buggy. We really had to hold on tight to the line or the horse would run away with us.

They pranced and danced as we drove them past the property. To gain control of them, we gave a hard, quick jerk on the line, pulling their head in both directions. They clearly hated the area and so did I! I can say I understood the fear they were experiencing.

I never wasted time when passing the butcher shop. I recall being afraid to walk by there on my way to school, if I was alone. I knew Mr. Bartgis and Will, and I was not afraid of them—I just hated what they were doing and the fact that I was a witness.

Selling Eggs and Butter

Years later, when Russell and I were living at Middlepoint, Will stopped at our farm on his huckster route and bought eggs and butter from us. When Will came, if the children were around, he would never leave without giving them a penny. Anywhere he went, if there were children around, he handed them a cent. He was such a kind and gentle man.

George and the Log Wagon

Young boys helped on the farm and worked alongside of the grown men. One day in 1911, George, who was about fourteen years old, and my dad were driving the team of horses hitched to a big steel-wheeled farm wagon. They were coming home from the Gravel Hill mountain lot. The wagon was loaded with wood to burn in the stoves at home. They were driving along on Route 17 just below the Grossnickle Church, when George, who was standing on a large flat stone alongside the road, attempted to jump on the lazy board of the wagon. A lazy board is attached to the side of a large wagon. The person who is going to draw the brakes rides here so he can easily jump on and off the wagon. George missed his aim and fell under the rolling wheel!

Dad's Heart Sank

Dad was riding Logan, the saddle horse. Mae was the lead horse on the left side of the four-horse team. A four-horse team consists of a front left-lead horse and a right off-lead horse; a back left-saddle horse and a back right off-side wheel horse. The team is driven from a line to the harness of the lead horse.

When this mishap occurred, Dad happened to look back and saw George lying on the road. The wagon wheel was about to cross over him and Dad could not get the horses stopped. He drove over George's leg! If he had tried to stop at this point, he risked dragging George with the pressure and friction of the wheel. Dad's heart must have broken. It hurts to see your children suffer.

Will Gouker

I do not know who passed by, but someone saw the accident and was kind enough to go summon Will Gouker to come with his horse-drawn dating wagon to carry George to our home. A dating wagon is a type of covered wagon. Will's wagon had a smooth floor that was large enough for George to lie down flat. He was a huckster who lived in our neighborhood, and folks often called on him to help in an emergency.

Dad had to get the horses and wagonload of wood back to the farm. He could not just leave them tied to the fence alongside of the road. I remember them arriving home. Mother and I saw them coming and wondered what had happened. Even before we walked up to the men, we sensed something was wrong. Mother questioned, "Why is Will following?" Within minutes we learned why.

With tears streaming down George's face, it was obvious he was suffering excruciating pain. Oh, I felt so sorry for him and Dad. Dad's heart was filled with pity and compassion for his son. We were all concerned and excited, but I am sure George was, beyond any question, more frightened than any of us.

Now that Dad was home with the wood, he, Will, and

George quickly headed for Myersville in the dating wagon. From there Dad and George boarded the trolley car and traveled to the Frederick Memorial Hospital to have George's leg cast and set.

George had a compound fracture! Just think of all the discomfort he must have gone through as they lifted him without using a stretcher to support his leg. And imagine riding in a horse-drawn wagon on a bumpy, dirt road and having broken bones! My, oh my, what he must have gone through.

In the early part of the 1900s, few people who lived in the country ever made it to a hospital in time to get help to save their life if they were critically ill or seriously injured. It was such a long drive. Many died on their way for help.

Driving the Horse and Buggy

Between 1904 and 1910, the car era began. I was a little girl. For a long time, I can recall only the Harps owning a car in our community. We used horses and horse-drawn vehicles as our main means of transportation. There was no such thing as a license to drive a horse! Parents permitted their children to drive when they thought they were capable of handling the animal.

Youngsters were comfortable with horses, as we grew up around them. There were no police patrolling the highway. Well, there were no highways, just dirt roads.

Too young to be an experienced horse and buggy driver, my dad often accused me of driving dangerously fast. I knew the horse, and I had ridden bareback for a few years, so why did he constantly lecture me; why did he have such fear for my safety? He often remarked that I never knew I was in a hurry until I got behind the horse. I thought he was overly concerned, to say the least.

Deck, My Horse

Deck was the little horse Dad gave me to drive. He was gray and had a gentle disposition. Deck broke his leg when he was young. As a little girl, I remember it happening, but I cannot recollect how it happened.

To aid his recovery, Dad and my brothers fastened a sling to the rafters in the horse stable and somehow put the horse in a canvas belt holding him up off the sod stable floor. I remember going to the barn and seeing Deck hanging there with his broken leg bound and dangling. It seemed he hung there for a long time before his leg mended.

When the broken leg healed, it was shorter than the other legs, thus causing him to limp. After his recovery, he could still move along at a good "clip." To me it just seemed that the horse had speeding in his blood. My judgment told me if Deck had a mind of his own, just go ahead and use it, and let that buggy go! I tried not to think of Dad's warning. He really hated to see me drive fast and I knew it.

Dad preferred I use Deck—I know he thought, with the limp, he might be a "slow trotter." He was wrong! The plain fact was I dreamed of a good, fast horse. It compared to a "hot" sports car of today. And the more quickly I got to where I was going and back, the more time I had for doing other things. And, besides, I just liked to feel the wind in my hair and on my face as I drove along.

Dad seldom let Deck out of the horse box stall in the barn, and with good reason! Sometimes he did tie him outdoors to the fence or to a tree to eat grass.

As much as I liked Deck, he could be so aggravating. If he saw me coming toward him with his collar in my hand, he would run in a circle. I hated him doing that. Deck knew I was going to hitch him to the buggy. By the time I outfoxed him or got him cornered, I was worn-out. I caught him by his mane, tail or head. Once I got my hands on him, he would stop immediately. It was as if he was playing with me, only I did not like the game! He also had a bad habit of standing and digging in the dirt with his hooves. He kicked the soil up over his coat of hair making it all dirty and dusty.

I remember George and me taking the broom and leading Deck from the stable down to the watering trough. He knew what was going to happen. There was plenty of run-off water and we nearly always gave the old boy a bath before we started out for church on Sunday mornings. I am sure Deck felt our compassion was at a low as we scrubbed him with the broom.

Organ Lessons from Miss Eleanor Stine

Once a week, I drove down to the little town of Harmony, by the way of Summers' Hill, for private organ lessons. Being the only girl in my family of boys, my folks decided I should be given that privilege.

When I arrived in Harmony, I tied Deck to the fence, and then walked to the kitchen door of the Stine home. Miss Eleanor Stine, my music teacher, greeted and escorted me to the front room. Together we sat down at the pump organ and began the music lesson. We usually played hymns. Here I pumped and played until I was hot and exhausted. Miss Stine was about 25 years old and was a kind lady. When the lesson was over, I paid her 25 cents, and she showed me to the door. From there I dashed to the fence, untied the horse's leather strap from the post, hopped into the buggy, and with the line in hand, I raced up the road. When I gave Deck a "kind" slap on his rump with the buggy whip, I was home in minutes.

My Reputation

As I drove in the farm lane, I surveyed the fields and around the buildings, searching for the sight of my dad. I needed to know if I should slow down. You know my reputation. Often I could not see Dad outdoors or anywhere in sight. I then had high hopes of escaping him. But on second thought, I was sure he would meet me and inspect the horse. I did not want him to see how sweaty Deck was. Dad did not like the horses to be forced to the point of sweating when they were pulling the buggy.

It seemed never to fail—Dad was waiting in the barn. Eagerly, he helped me remove the gear from the horse. And then, yes, it was then he saw the sweat under the gear. Trust me, he knew without doubt that I was racing Deck. No matter what I said or how much I explained to him my need to hurry home, the reasons were never accepted. He knew exactly what to say to make that expression of guilt come to my young face. I never had to confess for the truth to be known. Dad knew how much I loved to drive a fast horse. The "pity" was I had no willpower to change my desire.

Loving Lecture

Next came the loving lecture that needed to be repeated time after time. He told me how dangerous speed on those hills could be, and how a horse could get spooked, and that I needed to listen to him when he talked to me. I did listen, but I seemed to forget so soon! He never forgot to remind me of the time the horse jerked the line out of my hands. As a matter of fact, I could not forget that either and

I hated to be reminded of it. I was frightened out of my wits on that occasion.

"Whoa, Deck!"

One day I was driving the horse and buggy home from a music lesson at Miss Stine's. I was breezing along and happy—Deck was moving ahead at a steady pace. Going down the hill at Summers' Store at the bridge in Ellerton, ever so quickly, the horse briskly switched his tail and jerked the line out of my hands. I do not know how he did this since I was holding it so tightly. It happened in a split second. My heart was leaping with fright. I had a "runaway horse" hitched to my buggy! I thought everything was out of my control. Then with God's help, I hollered "whoa" loud and with such a command of authority that I got the horse's attention.

Deck obeyed my young, strong voice and stopped. I swished my long dress tail out of that buggy and quickly picked up the line. Holding onto it for "dear life," I hopped back into the buggy, my tiny feet dragging my clumsy high-topped shoes with me. I now had a "death's grip" on that piece of leather. I seemed to want to drive a bit slower the rest of the way home. I needed time to think. I wondered what I should say to Dad. Or should I even tell him? I surely did not want to discuss the incident!

I was so thankful to be alive that day that I confessed to Dad what had happened. Of course, he scolded me, but I somehow knew how much he cared. He was justified in what he said, even though I had heard him repeat those same words for what seemed like a million times. He really was concerned for my safety. He did not want anything to happen to his "Girly." After it was all over, I decided my guardian angel was on duty and about his business of keeping me safe that day.

The Talent Mastered

Well, I *did* accomplish and master the art of playing the pump organ, only to lose the talent in the years that followed. I answered the pressing needs of my family and thus neglected to spend time in playing. But I tell you, I do not to this day remember ever developing a sincere desire to drive a slow horse!

Harmonica

In later years, when my older children were grown, the younger ones would often gather around me while I played the harmonica. I was hardly a professional at this, but they thought I was the greatest. My son, Tom, always laughed and said when I played I looked like a horse chewing on an ear of corn. Guess it was a funny sight now that I think back on it.

Logan, the Black Beauty

I remember asking Dad, well maybe it was more like begging him, to let me drive Logan. Old Logan was a big black horse, and he was beautiful. He was also much faster than the other horses. We all liked him and my brothers thought he was Dad's favorite. They thought he took "special care" of him.

If Dad had not been working Logan in the field, he would let me drive him, especially if one of my brothers was going with me. I shall always remember looking into Dad's eyes and pleading, "Please Dad, may I drive Logan today?"

I will never forget the smile that came across his face when he answered yes—and how disappointed I was when he said no and explained that Logan needed to rest because he would be working in the field the next day.

Mother's Driving

Mother was a good driver. She never encouraged the horse to trot beyond a reasonable pace. She drove slow and easy. Maybe, just maybe, my dad had given her "the lecture," and maybe she chose to listen.

Dad's Horse Purchase

No matter what age we live in, husbands and wives have differences of opinion. John Gaver (my school teacher's father) was having a public farm sale. He was going to auction off a beautiful workhorse named Mae. She was black, short and stalky. For some reason Dad had to have her. Dad attended the sale and purchased the horse for $300. I remember Mother got so annoyed with Dad because she thought he paid too much money for old Mae. Dad thought he needed her, had the money to make the purchase, and did so without a second thought of what Mother might think. One does not need to read between the lines—he learned what was on Mother's mind. Dad listened, but knew what he had done was of sound judgment. With time, Mae had three beautiful mare colts that he raised and sold. He regained his investment and made himself a nice profit.

It seems this is the only incident I can recall where a difference of opinion was voiced by my parents in a manner that I would remember. My dad and mother truly loved each other.

CHAPTER 16

CIVIL WAR STORIES

Mother Lived During the War

My mother, Clara Rebecca Leatherman Grossnickel, was the daughter of Elder George and Rebecca Johnson Leatherman and was one of twelve children.

Mother's brother, my Uncle John C. Leatherman, was about nine years old when the Civil War began in 1861. He was born in 1852. Mother was born in 1861, but since the war did not end until 1865, she did recall and was adamant about some happenings that impressed her young mind. However, Mother did not recall as much detail about the events as her brother, John C.

Family members rehearsed these war stories to Mother throughout her life. Down through the years, she repeated them again and again to me and my family. Periods of the war were fought in Frederick and Washington Counties. The Civil War was between the North (the Union) and the South (the Confederacy)—the cause was political.

Working for One Hundred Dollars a Year

My uncle, John C. Leatherman, married in 1873, just eight years after the Civil War had ended. He worked on a farm and earned one hundred dollars a year. Not much money, it seems, but think of eggs selling for 6 cents a dozen and butter for 8 cents a pound!

Guns and Cannons Blasting

The Civil War was raging. Many folks thought of the conflict as a madness or as an insanity. My mother's parents were farming in Harmony on the homeplace presently owned by Carroll F. Leatherman Jr. This location and adjoining areas were controversial regions over which Confederate and Federal troops swarmed during these days of war. The Middletown and South Mountain areas held bloody battle scenes. It is said the Union soldiers covered the six-mile area as they camped the night before the Battle of South Mountain.

During the dark of the night, the men moved out, but the home folks could hear the noise of the guns; they were certain lives were being wasted away with each blast. At times, the fighting was hand-to-hand and nearly silent. But still the residents were sure the fighting was ever so near. What frightening, devastating days for everyone.

My Grandma Sold Bread

The year was somewhere between 1861 and 1865. Remember now, my mother and her family were a part of these Civil War stories. They lived through them! And I, her daughter, am repeating these stories to you, the reader, at 95 years of age.

It was in warm September and Grandmother Rebecca Leatherman had just baked bread. She placed the hot loaves on a bench that sat on the porch outside the kitchen door.

A young, thin, black lad came riding in the gravel farm lane on a horse. He rode up to my grandparent's house.

My grandmother was approached by the boy at the door. Without wasting words, he asked her to sell him bread.

He looked like a child to Grandma and she felt sorry for him. He was but a lad! Her heart was simply broken as she looked into his sweet face. She knew somewhere he had a mother who was no doubt worrying about him. Grandma's heart was touched. Guess she thought some warm bread would taste good to him. So she agreed to his request.

Grandma just happened to look out the lane, and who else was riding up but a military private. She paused. He too came to the house asking to buy bread. Grandma Leatherman was honest and, with a gesture toward the little fellow, told the private she had just sold the bread to the boy. The private backed off.

Supper's Ready

The boy thought he had "supper in the bag," so to speak. He felt good! Then he thought: What could be better for his master, a Yankee officer, than some milk to drink and butter to spread on the fresh baked bread he had purchased? Bravely, the lad inquired about getting some. Again, Grandmother agreed to oblige him. The lad just knew the officers at the camp were going to be pleased with his success when he returned that evening. I am sure his mouth was yearning for a piece of Grandma's delicious butter bread.

Stolen Bread

The private was still hanging around, as if resting his horse under a tree, as Grandma quickly made her way across the yard to bring the butter and a jar of milk from the springhouse. She thought, "What is this man contemplating?"

But she continued on. Food was kept cool by storing it in a tight container or jar and placing it in the trough of running spring water that traveled through the springhouse.

Still mounted, but now having sharpened the end of the stick he held in his hand, the private closely watched for his chance to spear the bread from the bench. As the boy's attention was focused elsewhere, he "made the kill." With the fresh bread bouncing on the stick, off he rode in a gallop across the fields. Guess he thought bread without butter and milk was better than no food at all. The young lad, who had so carefully planned supper, was now without one bite to eat. The smile on his face faded away as his young heart sank.

Worried

I cannot begin to imagine how worried my grandparents must have been for their children's safety during these days of war. These folks did not know for certain when or which direction the battle would move. I am sure my mother, her brothers and sisters stayed close to their parents, especially when they heard the noise of the battle in the distance.

Overnight "Guests"

Another happening told to me by Mother is about three military officers spending the night in my grandparents' home.

It was late in the evening as the officers rode on their horses up to the farmhouse. Grandfather Leatherman heard the sound of the horses' hooves and saw them coming. There was a cloud of dust following them. He came out of the house to meet them. As they approached my grandfather, they politely asked if he would allow them to come into his house and sleep in beds for the night. They explained to Grandpap their weariness and need for a night of safe rest. They assured him they would not bring any harm to the household.

My grandfather knew they were tired, and they appeared to be trustworthy gentlemen, so he consented. It was a small thing to do, he thought. They followed Grandpap into the farmhouse and he showed them to the bedrooms. They seemed so pleased with Grandpap's generous hospitality.

Get Up!

Uncle John C. often told the story of how, during the night—actually, it was about two o'clock in the morning—while he was tucked into bed, he was suddenly awakened by the sound of the guns and shells. The noise was sharp and blood curdling. He quickly jumped up from his warm bed and ran to his bedroom window. He looked down on the lawn and saw his father and still another soldier talking with great concern and excitement in his voice. My grandfather was listening intently while holding a candle that flickered in the dark of the wee morning hours. The soldier was demanding the sleeping officers return to camp immediately.

Grandfather Leatherman clearly understood the message, turned, and came back into the house. Slowly, he climbed the stairs to awaken the soldiers. As one of his feet hit each step, his heart seemed to pick up speed. The very thought of war made his heart race with grief and compassion for those involved. He hated what he had to do. Grandpap despised fighting and war! He could not find a reason to approve of it, no matter how hard he searched.

Once Grandfather appeared at the bedroom door and the soldiers heard the message, the three men scrambled to get into their clothes and boots. Down the steps and out the house they went. They rode off toward the sound of battle. Grandpap was very concerned for the soldiers' safety that night. I know he must have prayed. He was so unyielding about his belief that there was just no place for war in the world. He often repeated how strongly he felt against active hostility. He wanted it known to all that he was against it! Grandpap was very "sick at heart" that night.

Turkey Hill

Come mid-morning, neighbors united on Turkey Hill in Harmony to talk about the happenings of the night. There were also moments when they stood in silence. From time to time, they looked stunned as they listened to the distant sound of the guns. Tears came in their eyes. They had hoped the hills and valley would be silent, but it was not!

That morning, Grandpap told everyone about his experience with the tired soldiers. They all wondered if the officers had made their way out into the night from Grandpap and Grandma Leatherman's house only to end their life in battle. There was something uncanny about the morning after the men left. The possibility of not living through the day was so real for all the soldiers. Just think of the horror these battles brought.

Pain and Grief

When you think of having no pain killers other than whiskey and booze, maybe death was welcomed more often than not by the wounded soldiers. There were no sterile operating rooms in the makeshift hospitals. Most often, open-air tables held the wounded during surgery. Infections and gangrene ran wild among the injured. Amputees, their bodies racked with pain, crowded the recovery areas. Using sticks for crutches, they struggled to move about.

The moans of the ever-so-brave could be heard from the areas that lay thick with fallen soldiers. The crippled bodies were trying to drag themselves for help or to locate a safe area to rest. Or maybe they were struggling, searching for a place to die with a little dignity. The air itself must have reeked with the stench of blood and gunpowder.

Devastation and horror could be seen everywhere. War causes the most horrible sights and mutilation to mankind.

Burying the Dead

One of Uncle John C.'s friends, Jim Bussard, Jim's father, and Grandpap Leatherman went to the battle site the next day to help bury the dead men. There were so many graves to dig. Uncle John C. was younger than his friend Jim. Grandpap would not allow Uncle John C. to go along. He could not understand the problem. Grandpap only told him that he was too young to walk so far.

It was many years later before John C. perceived that Grandpap was just trying to spare him from the sight of the battlefield—the bloody wounded, the still dying, and the dead men. Seeing horses that had been massacred, the young boys and men in the prime years of their lives lying dead on the ground was a sight that remained vivid in the minds of all who were a witness. It was an "alive" nightmare.

The Tragedy is Buried

The Leathermans were Unionists and the Bussards were Confederate sympathizers. These men forgot their differences and worked together to dig the graves with pick and shovel. It took strong men to overcome the emotions involved and get the job done. They buried as many as ten casualties from both sides in the same grave. Over and over, hour after agonizing hour, the thought of burying these men and boys returned to their minds. These men, no doubt, carried these memories to their graves.

Years later, bodies that could be located were removed from those crude graves and laid to rest with honor in the Sharpsburg National Cemetery in Sharpsburg, Maryland. What tragedy, what tragedy!

Riding the Horses to Safety

Not only did the military men come to your home to spend the night in a comfortable bed, or to buy or steal food, but they also came to take your horses. When the farmers got the news, by neighbor telling neighbor, that the soldiers were coming on a "horse-stealing raid," the men and the boys who were old enough to ride, gathered and journeyed together into parts of Pennsylvania. Here they scouted for a safe location to temporarily hold the horses. Finding areas where the fighting was not in progress, they waited, hoping and praying for protection. They did not return home until they received word that the soldiers had moved from their farms.

The Beautiful Colt

My grandfather had horses and two little colts. One

colt was beautiful and perfect. Grandfather felt this colt was too young to follow the horses and safely make the trip. It was a long distance to Pennsylvania, and who knew how long they might be staying. Thinking he was more protected hidden in the cellar of the farmhouse, the colt was left behind with Grandma and the young family.

The Crippled Colt

The older colt was crippled in one leg, but Grandfather thought he would chance taking him along. He decided he was strong enough to keep up with the horses.

Husbands said "Good-bye," and with a hug, gave a few last minute instructions to their wives. Mothers kissed their sons' cheeks and said, "I love you. Hurry home and, please be careful." With food, a bed roll, a Bible, and maybe a gun, off the men rode away from home, looking back and waving good-bye. The little children tugged on their mothers asking, "Where is Daddy going?"

The women and families watched them leave and cried. They did not know what might happen to the men or the horses. The husbands and fathers left with agonizing thoughts ripping through their minds. They realized their families who were left behind were in danger should the mishap of a stray bullet occur or a desperate, mean soldier appear. There seemed to be no peace of mind for anyone at that time. Long, lonely days and nights followed for everyone.

He Nickered

A few hours after Grandpap Leatherman and the men where gone, some soldiers on horseback came upon the farm.

91

The little colt, uneasy in the cellar, heard the sound of the horses' hooves. Perhaps thinking it was his mother coming back home, he nickered. The soldiers heard him! They stopped, listened, and made certain they truly heard the colt. They suspected someone was hiding him. They looked toward the barn, but the cry of the colt seemed for sure to be coming from the house. These soldiers were about to prove how bold they could be at helping themselves to whatever they wanted.

Grandma saw some of the soldiers get off their horses. She watched. Her heart grew faint. They came toward the house talking to one another as they entered the cellar without Grandma's permission. They stayed in the basement only minutes and brought the little colt out with them. They found him!

Grandmother was afraid, but she had to do everything she could to rescue him. With her long apron flapping as she briskly walked along, she followed the soldiers out of the house. The children all scampered to tag along behind. They hustled to keep pace with their mother.

Grandma Begged and Cried

Looking straight into the eyes of the men and, with her most sincere plea, Grandma Leatherman begged the soldiers not to take the colt from the farm. They did not give her the time of day. Paying no attention whatsoever to her words, they mounted their horses, held the colt by the bridle and strap, and headed off. The family was heartbroken. They were all scared and crying. My mother, who was very young—probably about four years old—her sisters, brothers, and Grandma Leatherman followed the soldiers on their horses out the lane, still pleading all the more with them not to take their colt. Grandma thought surely it would die in battle.

Heartless

Finally, recognizing their plea was not going to be honored, slowly the sad, weeping family turned and headed back to the house. Grandma was brave and did all she could do to stop them. The children walked ever so closely to their mother. They all wanted to hold her hand or, at least, cling to her dress tail. Their hearts were heavy and fearful.

Grandma did not know when Grandpap and the men would return home. She was anxious for their return, but she dreaded to even think of telling them that the colt was gone. No one, especially young men and young horses, deserved to be drawn into such a terrible battle. They did not have a chance to live yet!

These women, left behind while the men were away from home with the horses, were forced to be brave. They could have given up and hid in fear, but most of them stood in strong faith when danger lurched at every corner. They knew the men were depending on them.

George Blessing: Hero of Highland

The year was 1864. I had often heard the account of George Blessing who, at 70 years of age, had a clash with the Rebels. He was a farmer at Highland, Maryland. On Saturday morning, July 9, George, his son, and another man stood off Confederate raiders who intended to steal George's horses. George was also protecting his property since the soldiers often "stole the homestead blind."

There was an abundance of "worm or rail" fences on

the farms. Just as surely as not, the soldiers tore down the fences and used the rails for firewood. It was handy, cured, and ready to burn. They needed a fire to keep warm in the cool weather and to cook their food if they were setting up a campsite for the night.

In some areas where the fighting was heavy, the residents had to abandon their homes in fear of losing their lives. Crops were ruined by the troops marching through the fields. Living in and around the Middletown/Myersville areas where our families owned homes was "risky business" during these Civil War years.

Stealing the Horses

The Rebels had planned and scheduled the raid on the Blessing property for the early morning. Five men were instructed by Major Harmon and Captain Walker to go to the farm and steal the horses. They were backed by a company of Cavalry men. So, clutching their orders, the men came storming onto the Blessing farm.

The story is told that George Blessing took his stand against the Rebels in "the name of the Lord God of Hosts." George and his family gathered to read the Bible and pray before he went out to battle. George gave his son two guns. Another friend was willing to help so he received a gun as well.

The three brave men took cover behind the trees in a wooded area on the farm. They carefully loaded their guns and were ready to fight. As the thieves rode onto the Blessing property, George and his men quickly opened fire. They hit one soldier and wounded him.

Wounded Enemy

Another badly injured enemy rode under the overchute of the bank barn, but the fire did not stop from either side. George killed a man as they were retreating. He captured still another and held him prisoner. The rest of the men made it back to the company of forty to sixty men. It was learned the Rebels took a wounded man back to Middletown for medical attention, where he died. Other wounded men probably lost their lives as well.

That peaceful homestead was now the scene of bloody conflict. It certainly was a battle of faith and courage for George.

George's Men

George gathered more ammunition and, before he could load his guns, nineteen Rebels returned with four of George's neighbors marching before them. They were being held hostage by the Rebels. These hometown folks were pretending to be guides. George's son and the helper decided they had seen enough and left him to fight alone. George knew God was still on his side!

The enemy was coming head-on for George. He scampered to a cluster of cherry trees carrying all four of his guns. One of the guides ran when George hollered, "Halt!" George took a shot at him but missed. As soon as this man reached the Rebels, they returned rapid fire on George, who was now standing alone.

Lead Balls

The Rebels' shots were knocking splinters and limbs

off the trees scratching and beating George's body as they fell. When the lead balls hit the fence, parts of the wood shattered and hit him in the face. These balls fell around his feet. He still had three guns for "sure work," as George put it. After a few more "cracks" at George, the Rebels hastily rode off. Dead and wounded men were laying over the ground in bloody pools, but George was still standing "in the name of the Lord of Hosts."

The Enemy's Return

Later that day, the military sent word to George that they were going to return and shell him. George sent back word that he had wounded men from their company in his barn. George's message was, "Burn the barn and your soldiers in it, if you like."

Before dark that same day, Cole's Calvary, with Lieutenant Colonel Vernon in command, appeared on the Blessing property. George had not let down his "lone" guard. He thought it was the Rebel battery returning, so he took the dead Rebel's carbine, which is a rifle with a short barrel, and hid himself in a bramble of bushes out near the farm lane. A bramble is a cluster of berry bushes or prickly shrubs of roses.

George was certain the shells would start flying any minute. He waited breathlessly, but was happily mistaken. This time the Rebels meant no harm. George crawled out from under the bushes. The men and soldiers started to cheer as they rode toward the house.

Burying the Dead

The Rebels helped George bury the dead. They spent the night with him in his home.

Just think of this—a true "war story" of that day and time. It is hard to imagine. One minute—fighting, with the intent to kill, and the next minute—friends. Whether friend or foe, one could never deny the fact that George Blessing clearly earned the title of "Hero of Highland."

I remember hearing my mother tell this story and I recall her relaying the thought of George Blessing being so brave. He loved his homestead, had worked hard to earn a living, and believed his God would not let him down in his hour of great need. *"A thousand shall fall at thy side, and ten thousand at thy right hand; but it shall not come nigh thee."* (Psalms 91:7)

Horses Stolen from Elias Grossnickle's Farm

Elias Grossnickle was a farmer and a Union Sympathizer. He lived between Ellerton and Wolfsville. The farmers looked out for each other during these days of the Civil War. Elias was aware his horses were about to be stolen by the military. He decided that he and some of the neighboring men were going to ride back over the hill to the creek. He took all of his horses but three.

There they stood in the water making it difficult to be tracked down by the enemy. Elias was trying to "outsmart" the soldiers.

Elias reasoned, what farmer does not have a horse? He felt the soldiers would use the same rationale. Elias knew that if he hid all the horses, the military would return, since they would suspect he was hiding them. Elias felt that losing three horses was better than losing all of them.

C. Upton's Hat

On another occasion, a little boy was with the soldiers while they were on Elias' farm. During the encounter with the men, Elias' son, C. Upton Grossnickle, was standing by his father's side. Elias' heart was touched and he felt so sorry for the little fellow tagging along with the men. The lad's clothing was scanty and he was thin. What danger surrounded this child? And why was he allowed to follow the men to war? In pity, Elias reached down and took the hat off his little son's head and put it on the young boy who was with the military men. I am sure Elias wondered many times if the child survived the war.

CHAPTER 17

GROSSNICKLE CHURCH OF THE BRETHREN

Strong Family Heritage

The Grossnickle Church of the Brethren is located at Middlepoint, just north of my home place. This red-brick church with the slate roof lies at the foot of a mountain area filled with chestnut, evergreen, maple, and hickory trees. Fertile farmland is patchworked in the midst of rocks and mountains. Just across the road from the church runs the Middle Creek. Early on, the church did not have a baptistery. The preacher baptized converts in the creek.

The Grossnickle Church of the Brethren rests at the bottom of a hill upon which tombstones of the deceased stand. Folks from as early as the 1700s are buried in that cemetery. Many tears have been shed by the strongest of men while standing there as they mourned the loss of family and friends. The cemetery is on such a slope that the grave markers have shifted down the hill over the years. They were realigned and cemented in place some years ago. Even today, a large slate rock remains standing at the top of the hill as if to remind us that Christ is still the solid rock.

Back in 1847, the Grossnickle Church was a wooden structure built on the present site. It was known as the Meeting House. Today's brick church was built in 1899, on the same location.

Services Held in Houses and Barns

Prior to either of these structures, the congregation met and worshipped in homes and barns. When you, as a member, hosted the meeting, it was customary to invite the entire membership to the preaching services and to stay for lunch at your house. Later, permanent arrangements were made to regularly meet at the same farm. These early church members did not have a name for their congregation, but by common usage it became known as the Middletown Valley Congregation.

The usual places of worship were the Peter Grossnickle farm (now owned by Robert T. Grossnickle), the Upton Grossnickle farm (that Paul and Jennie Grossnickle owned for so many years), and the Elroy Leatherman farm (owned by Gladys Naille; the barn was destroyed by fire a few years ago).

German Family Roots

Between 1738 and 1747, three Grossnickle brothers, John, Peter and Daniel, came at different times by ship from Germany to Philadelphia, Pennsylvania, to settle in the new country. "Old" John Grossnickle was the first to arrive, while Peter and Daniel came in the following years. "Old" John married Catherine; her last name is unknown to me. He cleared the wilderness and built a barn and a stone house, which still stands today. Upon his death, the homestead was passed down to his son. The farm has remained in the family and is now owned by Robert T. Grossnickle, who is a descendant of "Old" John. This is the farm that Russell's grandfather, Peter of J. Grossnickle, owned and where Russell

100

was groomed by his grandfather to be a farmer.

Permanent Meeting Place

The Grossnickle farm, where Russell grew up, was the first permanent meeting place selected by the congregation. The next permanent place of worship was the Elroy Leatherman farm. Many Love Feasts were held at these homesteads in the spring and fall of the year. The Love Feast is the sharing of a meal, feet washing, and serving Holy Communion. Members of the congregation, who lived too far away to drive home at night, stayed in a friend's home. These folks' horses were stabled and fed as well. Various types of wagons, surreys, and buggies could be seen parked around the farm hosting the meeting.

Boys Will Be Boys

Years later, C. Basil Grossnickle was told that when the families were holding services, the teenage boys sometimes took the horses for a bareback ride. Because so many folks drove horses to attend the Love Feast or communion service at the Elroy Leatherman farm, they were also stabled down in the Peter Grossnickle barn located nearby.

Church Privies

Two white wooden privies stood near the Grossnickle Church of the Brethren. Years later, bathrooms were installed. The ladies used the outhouse in front by the main road. The shed that housed the coal for the stove which heated the church was adjacent to this one. The men used the privy out back in the woods near Charlie Hoover's place. Russell always parked our buggy and tied the horse to the fence in back of the coal shed.

Both young and old attended the services at the Grossnickle Church. Many a date has been arranged on the grounds of this church. The cost for the date, if you could say it "cost" at all, was a free-will offering when the old metal collection plates were passed down the rows of pews.

Lennie Grossnickle and Grandpap's Horses

Leonard Grossnickle and my grandpap, Martin Grossnickel, always tied their horses to the same tree in the Grossnickle churchyard. Lennie's horse was a reddish-brown bay who pulled a stick wagon with an umbrella that covered the driver. Grandpap drove old John, a "long-legged" sorrel with a blazed face, and his horse pulled a stick wagon without a top. I liked old John—he was nice and gentle. I can envision those horses standing there just as clearly as if I were looking at them right now. Metal rings were fastened to opposite sides of the tree. The horses wore a soft leather strap attached to their bridle. The strap was used to tie them to the rings. They stood facing each other as they waited for the service to close and the return of their masters. When the weather was cold and stormy, the men put blankets on them to keep warm. Many of the horses fought, kicked, and picked on the one standing beside them—but not Lennie or Grandpap's. They were content with each other's company.

Mother's Great-Grandfathers Were Ministers

My grandfather, Elder George Leatherman (Mother's father), was a deacon and elder at the Grossnickle Church.

Mother's great-grandfathers were both ministers in the German Baptist faith. Grandpap Martin Grossnickel was the son of Peter Grossnickel Jr. He was a member of the German Baptist Church, which later became the Grossnickle Church of the Brethren. Both Russell and I have strong family ties to the heritage of the Grossnickle Church of the Brethren.

Newspaper Article Explains Ancestry

In 1965, an article was printed in *The Frederick Post* giving information on Reverend C. Basil Grossnickle and his ancestry. Basil's grandfather, Charles C. Grossnickle, and Russell's mother, Flora Grossnickle Wiles, were sister and brother. The article states:

> Basil was inspired by his ancestry to dedicate his life to the service of Christ.

> Two Grossnickle brothers sought to escape religious persecution 225 years ago by crossing the vast, newly-explored Atlantic. They came to the New World from Germany and eventually settled in the Middletown Valley. John Grossnickle set sail from Germany in 1738. He was a member of the new German Baptist or Dunkard faith. His migration was part of the vast Pietistic Movement, which saw the beginning of many new Christian sects deviating from the established Lutheran Church of Germany.

> After arriving in Philadelphia, John Grossnickle and his family moved to

103

Lancaster County where he was joined eight years later by his brother, Peter. There was a difference in the spelling of their names.

The two families merged and later drifted down into Maryland. They were lured by the shining target offer of free land. They founded a community. A tract of land near Ellerton, over the mountain from Wolfsville, Maryland, became known as "Two Sons," after John and Peter. The families cleared the land and laboriously created two farms.

As devoutly religious folks, they worshipped together in private homes, practicing their ancient faith, whose members were later to be called the Church of the Brethren.

Both farms had among the buildings a large stone house which still stand today, one of which became the place of worship for the German Baptists.

There are other Grossnickle families living in Lancaster County today and it may be explained by a reference made to a third brother, Daniel, who also made the Atlantic crossing. Daniel may have stayed in Pennsylvania when his brothers came to Maryland. And Daniel may have been a small boy at the time. It is believed that the names of passengers aboard ships from Europe under 16 years of age were unlisted.

CHAPTER 18

MY SOCIAL LIFE

Social Events

For most teenagers in the early 1920s, the popular social events happened in the church. Russell Peter Wiles (known as Pete to all his friends) and I attended the Grossnickle Church of the Brethren. I did not become a member of the church until 1918.

My Friends, Nellie and Elmer Leatherman

As a young girl, I remember my friends and I walking up the road and across the fields to the Grossnickle Church. As we strolled across the farmland, the boys and girls who lived in the homes along the way joined in; by the time we reached the church, maybe as many as eight or ten of us would be in the group.

I also enjoyed attending special services held at the Harmony Church of the Brethren. When I went there, my parents preferred that I rode with the neighboring youth, Nellie and Elmer Leatherman. They did not like the idea of me driving the horse and buggy alone at night. And I did enjoy Nellie and Elmer's company. Off we would go to meet with our friends for the service. Elmer drove a horse named old Lark hitched to the buggy.

Ministerial meetings, or what we call evangelistic meetings today, were held in the spring and fall of each year. As the preacher closed the sermon, and the last hymn was "lined" and sung, the young people gathered outside. (Lining a song means that the song leader reads a line of the words at a time, and then waits for the congregation to sing.) We greeted one another, chatted a bit, and then went to the tree or fence post where our horse was waiting. We hopped into the buggy and Elmer drove us home.

Church Music

Many years ago, musical instruments were not used in Brethren churches. They had a song leader. The leader used a pitch pipe and led the congregation in singing the hymn. Charles C. Grossnickle, Charles Delauter, and Effie Delauter led the singing for many years at the Grossnickle Church.

As much as we enjoy hearing the piano played in church services today, it was a big adjustment when it was first introduced. Many of the Brethren folk thought the very idea of playing a piano in church was "sinful."

Lil Stottlemyer's Millinery

Lil Stottlemyer operated a millinery shop in Wolfsville. She sold beautiful hats. It was fashionable for the young girls and women to wear them when they went out. Each season, Mother and I drove up to Lil's shop in the horse and buggy to purchase a new hat for me. It was a fun trip. I loved trying on the hats, and sometimes I had trouble deciding which one to buy. There was always a good selection in stock and I liked most of them.

This season, around 1914, I selected a wheat-colored

straw hat with the brim's edge trimmed in navy blue velvet ribbon. It had a wide navy band around the crown with a big bow attached. It was a pretty hat and I was thoroughly delighted to have it.

Mary Moser

I noticed a friend of mine, Mary Moser, suddenly always sat beside me at church. I suspected my brother George was sweet on Mary, so one day I questioned him. "George," I said, "I don't know why Mary never sits with anyone other than me. Could there be some interest brewing between the two of you?" George answered, "Yes, I have been talking with her."

My Hat!

Well, soon on a Sunday afternoon, George, Mary, and I went out for a ride in the horse and buggy. You realize the opportunity for something to do was not the greatest!

I wore my hat since I was wearing my "Sunday" clothing. For some reason I took off my brand-new hat and laid it behind the seat in the back of the buggy. With it off my head and out of sight, it was out of my mind as well. When George and I returned home, neither of us thought about the hat. We parked the buggy in the shed, put the horse in the barn, and that was it.

Days later, I thought of my hat! I ran to the barn to get it from behind the buggy seat. Well, I found my hat right where I left it, but I also found a disaster!

Not in My Hat!

The hens were free to roam around the farm and one had entered the buggy shed. Being a good hen, she jumped in behind the buggy seat and looked for a spot to make a nest. Finding my straw hat, and thinking she found a ready-made nest, she plopped herself into it. That may not have been so damaging; even if she had laid an egg, everything may have been all right. But the old hen decided to answer "a call from Mother Nature" right into my hat! It was soiled and ruined. I was so sorry, but what could I do?

"Getting Even"

I ran back into the house to tell Mother what had happened. She did not say much to me about it. What was done, was done. It was not intentional on my part. I do remember George chewing me out good for being so forgetful. I listened as I was thinking that Mother did not scold me. I thought, what is it to him? I continued to give him what appeared to be my full attention, and then I reminded him it was my turn to talk.

I said with authority, and maybe a little bit of pleasure, "Remember George, Mary's parents will not let her go out with you unless I go along." There was no need to say more. He got the message loud and clear in one sentence. I knew he acknowledged what I had said without an outward gesture. I am afraid I had that "get even" attitude that day. I tell you, after I reminded brother George of the consequences, that got him off my back. He now had something to think about other than my hat. He loved Mary and certainly did not want anything to get in the way.

CHAPTER 19

THE LOVE OF MY LIFE

Russell Peter Wiles

It was in the early fall of 1914 when Russell Peter Wiles asked me for a date. I knew he was a good man. He was born May 10, 1892, to Jacob E. and Flora Maria (Grossnickle) Wiles. I was 15 and he was 22 years old.

May I Take You Home?

This Sunday evening was different from any other that I had experienced in my life. While talking and laughing with my friends outside in the churchyard at the Harmony Church of the Brethren, perhaps standing under the tall maple trees, Russell Wiles came over to me. He asked me how I was doing. Then he asked the big question, "May I take you home tomorrow evening after the service if I drive my horse and buggy?" He rode horseback when he came to church alone. I replied to Russell's question, "I came with Elmer and Nellie and I feel I should return home with them." Now what he wanted to hear was not what I had just remarked. Actually, it was not the answer I wanted to give to him either. Russell just smiled and said nothing more. Turning away, he walked over to old Phil and off he rode alone from the church.

I can still remember the many times I had seen Russell

ride horseback up to the church lot, tie Phil to a tree, and walk into the sanctuary. He rode tall and straight. I was interested in his company.

As Elmer drove old Lark home and, while we were going in our farm lane that night, I contemplated if I had made a mistake by making my comment to Russell. I wondered if he would disregard what I said. Would he come driving his horse and buggy to church the next evening? At this point, my plans were "without doubt" already made up in my mind. I would be at church the following evening! I did not tell Russell the truth. I did want him to take me home.

The Longest Church Service

The next evening came and I was back at the church with my friends Nellie and Elmer. As the service started, I noticed Russell come in and take a seat. I was trying to determine in my mind if he had driven the buggy. I thought, if only I could take a peek outside the church door. The service seemed to go on forever that evening. It was as if extra verses were suddenly added to the hymns. I am sure the Reverend preached longer than usual on purpose! I could not concentrate as I tried to listen to his sermon.

Nellie's Advice

Again, when the benediction was finally over, out my friends and I went to the churchyard under the dark sky filled with thousands of stars and a bright moon. I was watching out of the corner of my eye for Russell. Again, he came to me and asked if he could take me home. Once more I said, "I feel I should go home with Nellie and Elmer." Why did I keep saying that? For some reason I just could not bring myself to being honest and say I would love to be with him. Nellie, looking at me, said, "You don't have to go along with him!"

Russell did not want to listen to more nonsense from any of us, so he took the situation in his own hands. Gently, but firmly, he took my hand in his strong hand and whispered, "You are going home with me tonight." We walked together to his buggy. He helped me in, covered me with the lap robe, and off we drove toward home. I was so excited and happy!

Our New Relationship

Russell was a handsome young man. He was tall and his stature was as straight as a tin soldier. He was muscular from the hours of hard farm work he had done from the time he was a young lad. His hair was shiny black and curly, his black eyes twinkled, and his dark olive skin was tanned to perfection. A gold tooth sparkled as he smiled. He came to church wearing a white shirt trimmed with a black pin stripe fabric, and a gold tie pin stuck in his dark tie. To me, it was as if a picture frame surrounded the face of this wonderful young man.

To think of Russell as a young man seems like only yesterday to me. I enjoy the clear and vivid memories I have of him. How quickly the years have rolled by.

The "Country Cadillac"

Russell's horse, Phil, was fast and beautiful. He was a heavy horse and he carried his head high. Phil was black with a tiny white mark on his forehead. His feet trotted with a rhythm of a rolling drum. He had that keen step of a good driving horse. Maybe the horse's speed could be attributed to the encouragement of the buggy whip that Russell smarted on his rump every once in awhile. The buggy he pulled was perhaps the top of the line—it had rubber wheels that were nearly silent as they turned. The black leather seat was tufted with covered buttons and the top was covered with a smooth black leather. This buggy was the "Country Cadillac" of the day! Russell wore black leather driving gloves and, of course, he covered his new sweetheart with a black crushed velvet lap robe printed with yellow, red, and brown flowers.

When I grew up, the teenage boys were fortunate to have a horse to ride. And if you had a buggy, you really had it made.

The Drive Home

For some reason, as we drove home from church, the ride seemed so exciting. I knew I was falling in love. The night air was cool and crisp, and I was driving with a splendid man. I may have even dreamed of a life with him. No doubt he had been dreaming of me. The drive home seemed so short that night. Once we made our way into the winding, gravel farm lane, he showed me to the kitchen door and bid me good night. He briskly walked off the porch and through the damp grass to untie Phil; then he drove away.

I stood at the window, straining my eyes to watch him leave in the dark. I could hear the sound of the horses' hooves as he left in the stillness of the night. Deep inside I was so thankful Russell had taken my hand and led me to his buggy.

Russell's Life

Russell was accustomed to life's "hard knocks." He was only four years old when his father, Jacob E. Wiles (born

December 23, 1863), died of typhoid fever at 33 years of age. Russell had an older sister, Mary, and a younger sister, Flora. These children were young, and Russell did not remember his father.

An article in a local newspaper reported that Jacob E. Wiles died on a Friday morning after being ill for about three weeks from the disease. The funeral took place on a Sunday morning at the Grossnickle Church and the article stated it was a "sad occasion with a large attendance of relatives and sympathizing friends."

Grandfather Peter Grossnickle (Russell's mother's father), who was living on the farm near Middlepoint presently owned by Robert T. Grossnickle, arranged to have Russell, his sisters, and mother move into the corner house on the property. His grandfather gave his widowed daughter, Flora, the opportunity to work for him. When the children grew older, they worked as well. He paid them so they could be somewhat independent.

Russell's Great-Grandfather, Pete Wiles

Russell's great-grandfather, on the Wiles side of his family, was a veteran of the War of 1812. His name was Pete Wiles. Very little is known about him. He was born in 1795 and died on October 22, 1869. He lived to be 74 years old.

Sixth Grade Education

Russell completed first through sixth grades of public school. Back then, young boys often had to fill the shoes of a man, especially if the father was deceased. The family's need to survive when death came was urgent, so Russell quit school so he could do the work that needed to be done on the

113

farm.

Aunt Amanda Dies

When Russell reached the age of 14, his great aunt, Amanda Stottlemyer (his grandfather, Pete Grossnickle's sister) died, and her farm at Middlepoint was for sale. His grandfather, Pete Grossnickle, purchased his sister's farm.

Russell, his sisters, his Aunt Alverta (Flora's sister), and his mother moved to the Stottlemyer property. It was then that Russell became the "man of the household" at 14 years of age.

Now, Russell's Grandfather Grossnickle and his wife Mary (Russell's step-grandmother) retired from farming down at the homeplace with the stone house. They moved into the corner tenant house so they were still living nearby. Charles C. Grossnickle (Pete Grossnickle's son and Russell's mother's brother), moved to that farm.

The Fourteen-Year-Old Man

Russell's grandfather, Pete Grossnickle, and his sons Harlan, Charles, Webster, Thomas, Welty, and John gave advice and instructions to this 14-year-old lad. These men were Russell's uncles and he was very fond of them.

Russell had to fill a large pair of shoes, and so he did with the respect of his family and neighbors. He was up before dawn and, instead of going off to school, he went off to the barn and field. I think many drops of sweat and tears must have come from this lad as he carried on a man's work alone in those fields from sunup to sundown. Farm work is difficult for grownups. Just think of the strain and responsibility on this young boy.

114

Years later, Russell's mother bought the Stottlemyer farm from her father, Pete Grossnickle. Mother and young son continued farming.

Our Courtship

Now a courtship commenced between Russell and me. We had many a fun time together. He came to my parents' home to see me on Saturday and Sunday evenings, and again on Wednesday nights. I looked forward to the time we shared.

George and his friend, Mary Moser (who later became his wife), were dating at the same time as Russell and I. The four of us (each couple in a buggy) went to community festivals, church events, or just out for a buggy drive through the country. By now, George and I had "matured" in our opinions of each other. We put our disagreements as children behind us and all of us truly did have good times together.

On one occasion, on a Sunday, we drove up to Black Rock. That was a special occasion for us. The hotel in Black Rock had recently burned. The wealthy folks from Baltimore, Washington, and cities in Pennsylvania came there to spend the summer or a vacation there. I remember seeing a part of the kitchen that remained after the fire. Jars of jelly, and salt and pepper shakers were in the debris.

We especially enjoyed our drives through the woods in the spring when the wildflowers and some of the bushes were in bloom.

At Christmastime, Russell took me to the Wolfsville Lutheran Church and the United Brethren Church services. This was the highlight of the holidays. Folks packed and crowded the churches for the special programs, or "entertainments" as they were addressed back then.

Horse and Buggy Picture

I have a snapshot of Russell and me taken in 1915. He and I often went alone for a buggy ride on Sunday afternoons. This day we were driving around Wolfsville when Russell stopped by Paul Hayes' house. Paul came out of his house and snapped a picture of us in the buggy. I still have that original photo, and it means so much to me today.

Dressed Up

That afternoon I was wearing a light blue dress and off white hat. The hat had a wreath of tiny pink, yellow, and blue flowers, and a black velvet ribbon was tied around the crown. The black streamers hung down from the back of the hat. Russell was wearing navy pants, and a white shirt trimmed in black and white pinstripes. The necktie matched the trim on the shirt. Even now, without the aid of the black and white photo, this is so vivid in my mind.

Gold Bracelet

About one year after we started dating, I had my sixteenth birthday. On September 17, 1915, Russell gave me a wide gold bracelet for this special occasion. I had dreamed of having one someday, and I was so happy with the gift. It was beautifully engraved with flowers and was about three-fourths of an inch wide. He made the purchase from Doll's Jewelry Store in Frederick. About 30 years ago, I gave it to my youngest daughter, Yvonne.

Mantel Clock

That same year Russell gave me a black Sessions mantel clock for Christmas. Today, 80 years later, the clock keeps accurate time and sits on the fireplace mantel in my living room. It has ticked away many hours while Russell and I were together, and now that I am a widow, alone and older, the "ticks" seem to race away even more rapidly. I do miss my husband and have thought of him so often during the past 18 years since he has passed on.

Chocolate Drops

While courting, when Russell came to see me on Saturday nights, he brought me candy. It was the custom of the day. Usually in the evening he rode horseback to Wolfsville to the barber for a haircut. Harlen Stottlemyer operated a barber shop, combined with a small clothing store. He carried men's work clothing and shoes for the family. The store was located on the corner in Wolfsville. While in the village, he also visited Charles Kline's Store where he purchased candy for me. Today that establishment is owned by Milton Harne.

Upon arriving at my door, Russell presented whatever delicacy he had chosen for me. He often brought me chocolate drops. I do not know why I could never inform Russell that they were not a favorite of mine. In fact, I just could not eat the "things." Since he liked them, he assumed everyone did, including me.

My dad liked the sweets. So, without fail, the day following our date he would say, "Well, Girly, where's the chocolate drops?" Dad could never have imagined how very welcome he was to every one of them.

117

Getting Married

It must have been very difficult for my parents when Russell and I decided to get married. I was standing on the porch one morning as my father was coming from the barn to the house for breakfast. I saw him approaching so I waited for him. As he walked up the steps, he looked at me and said, "Well Girly, your mommy tells me you and Russell are going to get married. Your mother and I wish you the best, but you know when you get married and leave home, you must stay." I answered, "Yes."

From that statement on, I was determined in my heart to love and stay with Russell, no matter what happened. Dad loved me so much but he wanted me to know how important our marriage vows would be. Our commitment was to be forever, or as long as we both lived. We would make our promise before God and it was an important decision.

Empty Chairs

Having lived to see my nine children marry, I now know "first-hand" the sadness parents feel when their children leave home. That empty chair at the table causes a heartache. It is so true that our children are not ours, but merely gifts on loan from God. The responsibility of rearing a family is vast and should not be taken lightly for one moment.

Partners for Life

Little did I know that fifteen months after the first buggy ride home from the Harmony Church of the Brethren, Russell and I would be husband and wife. Russell was about to make me his bride and partner for life. We knew our marriage and life together would not be perfect, but we were willing to devote it to one another. This magical evening I was wearing a dark wool suit, a pair of off-white gloves, and my black high-top buttoned shoes. I finally owned a pair of "store bought" shoes! At least I did not have to wear the "handmade Aaron Shepley specials" on my wedding day. My hat was off-white with large matching silk flowers circling half the band. It had a large brim. Russell wore a dark suit.

Reverend Charles Ausherman and Elizabeth

It was Saturday evening, January 1, 1916. Russell came to pick me up in the horse and buggy. We were going to get married! We were excited and happy as we drove from my parents' house that dark, misty New Year's Day evening to the home of Reverend Charles Ausherman. Reverend Ausherman was Russell's uncle. He was married to Russell's mother's sister, Caroline A. Grossnickle, who died when she was a young woman. The cold, damp air meant nothing to us as we drove to the Ausherman's farm. We were in love!

Russell parked the buggy out by the barn, tied the horse, and holding my hand we strolled to the house. The Reverend was waiting for us. Here in his living room we were to be married before one witness, the Reverend's daughter, Elizabeth Ausherman (Brandenburg). It was a simple wedding for the beginning of a long and binding relationship that withstood the test of time for sixty-one-and-a-half years. After this short ceremony, we hopped into the buggy and drove back to my parents' house.

Back then, couples seldom had a formal wedding. Usually they slipped off alone to the preacher's home and were quietly married.

Our Wedding Night

On our wedding night. Ben Gouker. friends and neighbors gathered to give us a "banding." The banding custom was an event to travel to the home of the bride and groom. Upon their arrival, they beat on pans, blew whistles, and shot guns into the air. They made any kind of noise to surprise and startle the couple.

Every farm had a dinner bell to beckon the family to meals. This was the choice noisemaker at the banding. The folks waited in the yard making the noise until the couple came to the door and stepped out onto the porch. They visited for a few minutes and everyone gave their congratulations to the newlyweds. Sometimes refreshments were served, especially if you were expecting to be banded and had made preparations.

No Honeymoon

There was no honeymoon for us. We spent our wedding night at my parents' home. Russell's mother, aunt and sister, who were living at the farm, took care of his chores that Sunday morning.

My parents planned to have some guests in our honor for Sunday dinner. They invited Reverend Ausherman, his daughter Elizabeth, my grandpap Martin Grossnickel and his second wife Eleanor Taylor Grossnickel, my brothers Herbert (and his wife Sallie), Wade (and his wife Maudie), and George (and his sweetheart Mary Moser), to come. Everyone visited, wished us well, and had a wonderful afternoon together.

Waiting to Live Together

Russell's mother, sister, and his Aunt Alverta still lived with Russell in the house on the farm his mother owned. I did not move in until they moved to Aunt Alverta Grossnickle's home in Myersville. That house is located across the street from the old Myersville Savings Bank, now owned and occupied by the C. Basil Grossnickle Insurance Agency, Inc. This bank was built in the 1800s. Aunt Alverta's brother, Webster, lived in her house while she was on the farm with Russell's family, so we were all waiting for each other's move!

Russell came on horseback to my parents' house to see me on Wednesday and Saturday nights. I was thrilled to see him come riding in the lane. He was my husband and I wanted to be with him. We also saw each other on Sundays at church. This arrangement continued from New Year's Day through March of that year.

Chaperone on Our First Night

Some things in my life I have never figured out. When I finally moved to Russell's farm, Mother asked a lady friend of ours to spend the first night with us. Mother never said why she thought we needed a chaperone. If I was old enough to get married, I was old enough to spend the night alone with Russell in our home.

CHAPTER 20

MARRIED LIFE BEGINS

Cooking my First Meal

Harry (Hank) Delauter was working for Russell on the Mandy Stottlemyer farm when we first got married. I cooked three meals a day, and the hired hand ate with us. On the day I arrived at the farm to stay, I opened the cupboard doors in that old kitchen in search of a surprise that might have been left for me. I did find the surprise—a heel of bread, a ham bone, probably left for the dog, and a jar of peaches. The lady staying with us that first night brought a yellow cake with a caramel icing. I was most grateful for it. I managed to scrape enough meat from the ham bone to make sandwiches for Hank and Russell, opened the jar of peaches, and cut the cake. With my first meager meal under our belts, I made a promise for a nicer spread in the evening. I should have checked what I had to work with before I made my promise! I did not find much and there was no nearby store to come to my rescue. The next meal consisted of slap jacks (biscuits baked on a griddle), fried potatoes, sausage and gravy.

Barn Work

From the beginning of our marriage, I started going to the barn to help with the work. I milked cows tied in a stable bedded with corn stalks. When field corn stalks (fodder) are dry, they become as hard as a stick. It took some nerve on my part to walk into that barn with a bucket and sit down amidst the mess on a three-legged stool to milk those cows. I was a stranger to them and so they turned, pranced around, and switched their tails at me. An iron stanchion built in a barn will hold a cow in a tight position and limit her movement. These cows had only a rope or chain to their halter. I tied them, but they could turn in a complete circle if that is what they had in mind. There was nothing to restrict them but me! What a sight this must have been.

Dad and Mother's Farm Sale

About one year after I married, Dad and Mother had a public farm sale on Thursday, March 1, 1917, at 10 a.m. They sold sixteen head of cattle, three bulls, nine head of shoats, and six horses (named Mae, Cola, Panny, Pet, Fanny, and Logan). I know the amount five of the six farm horses sold for that day: $167, $266, $201, $208 and $106. They also sold a little one-year-old black mare colt named Hattie, who was listed in the sale bill as "kind and gentle." Dad also sold one share of stock in the Myersville and Ellerton Horse Company. Farm machinery, such as a binder, mower, hay tedder, grain drill, corn planter, plows, spring harrows, wheat fan, hay fork, and lots of harnesses were sold as well. H. R. Lease was the auctioneer. John L. Routzhan and George W. Bittle were the clerks. M. O. Gladhill had the right to huckster, or sell, his produce on the farm that day to the folks attending the sale. Terms of the sale were: A credit of six months was given on all sums over ten dollars. Think of that!

My Parents Retire

After my parents retired from farming in 1917, they moved to the house on the corner of Church Hill Road and Route 17 at Ellerton. Dad bought the Church Hill home from my Uncle Caleb Harshman. My parents were farming on Grandpap Martin Grossnickel's farm when my uncle put the house up for sale. Dad thought he and Mother had worked hard and long enough and should retire.

Now that Dad discontinued farming and was planning to move, Grandpap Grossnickel sold his farm to Harvey Leatherman. It was sold on March 10, 1917. Grandpap was already living in Ellerton.

CHAPTER 21

OUR CHILDREN ARE BORN

Austin Charles Jacob

Our first son, Austin, was born on March 22, 1917. We were so happy to have this little boy. He was a sickly child and we had many sleepless nights after his birth. I needed full-time help, so Russell hired Edna Biser and her mother to come give me a hand. Having a maid did not mean that I could sit down and rest. It did mean that I was free to go to the barn and milk the cows while Russell headed to the mountain lot to cut timber, or to market to sell produce, or to the field early in the morning to get work done. Without modern machinery, farm work with horses was a slow process.

C. Upton and Ella Grossnickle Visit

Our good neighbors, C. Upton and Ella Grossnickle, always came to visit when we had a new baby. Upon their arrival, Upton asked Ella to hold the baby on her lap, then he pulled up a chair, sat close, and loved the little one. He enjoyed just sitting there tenderly patting the baby. He would say "hua, hua, hua," as he put his face down close to the little one. He rubbed his cheeks on the baby's face and held its hand.

Beautiful Little Kathleen

On July 29, 1918, a tiny girl, Kathleen Isabelle, was born to us. When she arrived, Dr. Lamar, informed Russell and me that this little one would not be staying long in this world. When we looked at her little spine, our hearts broke. There on her back, near her kidney, was a blister the size of an egg. She had spina bifida. What devastation we faced!

We loved her each minute of her short life with us. It was in the hot, humid, and busy summertime. No matter, we held her as much as possible. Kathleen was so beautiful. How we wished she could be healthy, but we could easily see that was not part of God's plan.

After Kathleen was born, C. Upton and Ella Grossnickle's daughter, Nellie, came during the day and helped me around the house. Austin was just sixteen months old and needed my attention. At the same time, I wanted to spend time with Kathleen. It was apparent Austin sensed our sorrow.

Each day, Russell and I wondered if this would be Kathleen's last day with us. Just one month after her birth, God, in his almighty mercy, took her home. At the time I was holding her on my lap as we rocked in the rocking chair.

A funeral was planned with Tom Bittle, who owned and operated the funeral home in Ellerton. Tom brought the baby back to our house to lay in state. The little casket was placed on the bed in the spare bedroom.

There was nothing anyone could have done for Kathleen. Medical science had nothing to offer back then. As each evening came, Russell and I went into that bedroom and wept in a helpless state of mind. Being there with her made death no less real to us.

Little White Casket

The funeral was held at the Grossnickle Church of the Brethren on a hot, sticky Saturday afternoon. The service was soon to begin. With heavy hearts, Russell and I got into the buggy and drove there. The little white casket was brought in Bittle's buggy from our house to the church. The pallbearers were Louisa Bussard Brandenburg, Nellie Blickenstaff Rice, Elizabeth Hays, and Madeline Stroup Ahalt.

Grandma Wiles came to our house to sit with Austin that day. He was young and did not realize what was happening, but he knew that once there was a baby in the house who was no longer there. Death ripped at our hearts and we had that feeling that cuts deep inside our beings.

World War I

The year of 1914 brought World War I, a global conflict. Russell was exempt from serving. Since we did not have a radio, we were never up-to-date with current events.

One day around noon we heard bells ringing—church bells, school bells, and dinner bells. A few airplanes flew over and we were outside watching, wondering what was going on. Seldom did we see a plane in the sky.

Our neighbor, Cyrus Blickenstaff, had a radio and he heard the daily news. If we were outside when Cyrus came to his mailbox, he shared whatever information was making the news. Today, by wonderful technology, we see what is happening, as it happens, around the world, from television in our homes. Then, we did not know what was going on in the next village.

This day Cyrus made it a point to come talk with us. He asked Russell if he knew the war was over. Of course we had no way of knowing, but we were thankful. If there is ever a reason for rejoicing in this world, it is when war and its battles are ended—and so it was in 1918 at the end of World War I.

Russell's Haircut

In 1918, when Austin was one year old, I decided his hair needed to be trimmed. We were trying to save money at every opportunity, so I thought I would give him a haircut. I placed the scissors and comb near my rocking chair as I sat down to rock him to sleep this afternoon. With my tools handy, and Austin sound asleep, I began. I situated his head on a pillow to free my hands to work. Cautiously I combed and snipped. When done, I thought the cut looked pretty good.

Russell came into the house and was pleased with what he saw. He suggested I give him a haircut as well. I resisted since his hair was very curly and dark. I said, "I cannot cut it for you." He insisted everything would be all right and that no "mistake" would be seen. Little did he know!

Russell took a seat and I draped a cloth around his shoulders. Again, with scissors in my hand, I nervously snipped away. I cut a little off and handed him a mirror to check it out. He said he would like it shorter and instructed me to cut again, taking "a lot more off." Once again, I told him this was against my better judgment. I was not confident in what I was doing.

Well, I did cut more off—in fact, when I stopped cutting it looked as though I laid scissors against his scalp and cut. For certain, I should not have listened to him. I made such a mess out of his hair this time that it made me sick.

What I did was simply awful! We were ashamed for him to go off the farm. Believe me, he did not go to church for awhile, and he wore his hat most of the time. We proved wrong the statement, "The only difference between a good haircut and a bad haircut is a week."

However, upon remembering our tight money situation, I attempted to barber again and, with practice, I became pretty good. I cut Russell's hair from 1918 until his death in 1977.

Doris Eileen is Born

Our third child, Doris Eileen, was born on August 29, 1919. She grew up to be the "second Mom" to all the younger children. She was my very best nursemaid when the younger children were born.

Grandpap Martin Grossnickel Dies

Martin Grossnickel (my grandfather on my father's side, and the son of Peter Grossnickel Jr. and his wife Sophia Brown) died on Tuesday, December 9, 1919. He died of congestion of the lungs at age 82. He was born on February 1, 1837. He was a farmer and a stockholder in the Middletown Savings Bank. He and Grandmother Selina Warner Grossnickel were German Baptist. Selina was born in 1837 and died in 1900. Grandpap's second marriage was to Eleanor Taylor. Eleanor died three years prior to Grandpap's death. Grandpap spent a few years of his younger life living in Bladensburg, Maryland, in Prince George's County, before settling in Frederick County.

Pauline Alverta is Born

On October 18, 1920, Pauline Alverta was born. Mary Pryor Beans and Eva Delauter Shultz helped me around the house with the babies. All these young girls who worked for us were so very good to the children. I never had to worry. I knew they would take excellent care of them.

My Helpers

In the country, most girls did not have public jobs. They grew up and married young. Susie Pryor Early worked for us when Doris and Pauline were toddlers. Susie was eager to work and please me. She, too, loved our children.

Mary Delauter Gladhill came to work in the summer months after Susie left us. When I baked bread, Mary would slice a warm loaf, get the butter, take out the bucket of syrup from the kitchen cupboard, and sit down on the floor with the little ones. They all gathered up close to her. Mary spread the bread and they had themselves a sticky feast. They had syrup over their hands, up their arms, and on their faces. And, if one decided to touch their hair, they really had a mess. No matter, I enjoyed seeing them have such a good time when we had so little to have a good time with.

Visiting Mother and Dad

I left my folks to marry at the age of 16. Like any young woman, I too, enjoyed going home for a visit. Sometimes, when the weather suddenly changed and we got caught in a shower, or if the wind was cold and strong, the buggy ride was anything but pleasant. I went, not only for my satisfaction, but to give my parents the opportunity to enjoy their grandchildren.

Before I started out on these trips, I served breakfast to the family, prepared a lunch for the men left behind, and got the little ones dressed. Russell would gear up the horse and hitch him to the buggy. I gathered the children to the barn and hopped into the driver's seat. He helped get the children settled, handed me the driver's whip and line, and off we went down the road about four miles from our farm. Again, the accusation of being a fast driver could probably have been proven to be the truth as I seemed to always be in a hurry to get to my destination, and again in a hurry to return home. For sure, I did like the horse to "move along."

Picking Berries

Berry season meant a trip to Hamburg Mountain, which is located above Highland. We picked huckleberries for pies, cobblers, and jelly. First, we got up early to do the morning milking and barn work. Russell's Aunt Alverta enjoyed going to the berry patch so she often joined us. Russell and I took the spring wagon (a long-bed wagon with one bench), a picnic lunch, and buckets for the berries. Off to the mountain we went.

I never enjoyed this event much. I always feared snakes might be hiding in the bushes or underbrush. We seldom took the children along because I worried one might wander off and get lost. All the trails headed into the thick woods. It seemed clear to me that no berry was worth what I was going through. I knew that I would have to clean the berries and bake when I got home. Besides all that, the children's little tired faces looked to me for some rocking and love. No one will ever know how many times I wished I could have stopped to hold them whenever they wanted to sit on my lap.

It was a long, hot, and tiring day for us. And the cows were waiting for the evening milking as well. Someone, or something, was always clamoring for my attention.

Austin is Lost!

Most often, Russell's mother came to the farm and kept the children for us while we went berry picking. One day, Austin was "bound and determined" he was going along. He cried and his little heart would have been broken had we drove off without him. As best I can remember, he was about five years old.

Just as surely as not, there were other families in the mountain picking berries. This morning, the Charlie Keller family had parked their wagon and we pulled in beside them. Their children were playing in their wagon and Austin decided he was going to play in ours. I proceeded to walk away for a short distance and began picking berries. I told him I would come back to check on him. I instructed him not to leave the wagon.

All was well until Austin decided he was no longer interested in playing and was going to come find me. Suddenly, I heard someone calling at the top of her voice, "Letha, Letha." It shocked me and I quickly answered. And then I heard a child crying for Mommy. Nellie Lewis, who was picking berries, called back to me. "Your son is close by but he is lost. He is heading back into the woods." Frantically, I shouted for her to catch him and wait until I could get there. I ran with my dress tail catching on the bushes, and the branches whipping my legs, but I hardly noticed as I was so distraught. I found Nellie and Austin in a flash and hugged him close to me as the big tears rolled down over his cheeks. I really could not scold him for leaving the wagon; I was so happy he was all right. I was so upset I declared I would never go berry picking again.

Tired and Cranky Little Ones

The evening barn work was always hard to get through. The older children came home from school and sometimes had homework. The little ones would be tired and cranky, and the baby needed extra attention as well. There was always a baby! I put the baby in the playpen which was nothing more than a crude wooden box with a quilt lining the cold, hard, unfinished bottom. The baby could not see out unless he/she was old enough to stand up and hold onto the side. No modern conveniences for anything or anyone during those days.

Make-Believe Horses

While I was outdoors, the children entertained themselves and kept an eye on the baby. Sometimes the baby would be fussy and fretful, and I knew their tiny arms ached when they carried him/her around.

I remember Austin turned the old Columbus Stottlemyer straight chairs upside down and tied a rope to the knob on the chair backs. Now he had himself a team of imaginary horses. Next he, Doris, and Pauline sat on the kitchen table, which turned into their imaginary wagon. Off they drove their team of horses to do whatever they were pretending that day.

Every once in awhile, they tied the door shut on me and I had to wait outside until they let me in. And then again, I was the one picking open the knots they tied. Austin loved to play with a rope and, trust me, he knew how to make tight knots.

"Mom, the Baby Is Wet!"

When I finished the chores and approached the kitchen door, I could expect to hear or see anything—someone giggling or crying, and occasionally, I would find one sound asleep. But as I opened the door, everyone came to life!

They all hustled to me, waiting for their turn to tell me something. Sometimes they did not wait for a turn, but everyone spoke at once. As one talked, another patted me to get me to look their way. To each question, an answer was expected. One of them always reported the baby needed a change of diaper. What a commotion!

Sometimes, while I was at the barn, Pauline came and stood on the gate calling for me to come to the house because the baby's diaper needed changing. Or, if she saw the other children disagreeing, she came to me with her big brown eyes wide open and filled with concern saying, "Mommy, come quick. Two's a fighting."

Often, Austin would coax Pauline to go out to the barn and tell me to come to the house. He would tell her to say they needed me, thinking I would come right away. The poor little ones looked for any reason they could think of to get me back into the house. I cannot say that I blamed them, because they spent many lonely evenings waiting for me to finish the outdoor work. In the winter months, darkness fell before I finished. The children were often afraid since they could see shadows caused by the flickering oil lamps.

We were all tired, they were hungry, and I often wished for a split second that I would either drop dead or the

Lord would come. I would take whichever could be arranged quickly. Just how much stress can I endure, I wondered.

The Prune Box

Russell bought twenty-five pound boxes of prunes and I canned them so they would be ready and handy to use. They came packaged in a wooden box. When Doris was little, she stood by my side on one of these wooden boxes and watched as I worked in the kitchen. There beside me she would say, "I can do that. Mommy, let me do that." I would let her dry the dishes and she would say, "Let me wash them for you. I can do that." She followed me like a little shadow.

Punishment

I never did spank the children often. But the same hands that spanked, held and loved them as well. They knew when I spoke to them I meant exactly what I said. When I did punish, I often sat them on a chair and did not allow them to talk or look at one another. This had a two-fold purpose. They were out from under my feet and they most often fell asleep waiting to finish their sentence. I had no intention of breaking their spirit, just their wills. After all, our kindest words belong to our family.

Pauline and the Goats

One evening, Russell came to the house and Pauline was doing her reading homework assignment. She seemed to have a problem at school reading a particular story about goats in a turnip patch, and so we practiced reading it at home every night for weeks. I can still see Russell opening the kitchen door and hear him saying to her, "Polly, aren't you ever going to get those goats out of the turnip patch?"

CHAPTER 22

GOOD OLD DAYS?

Life of the Farm Woman

Life for farm women was not easy in the 1920s. The toilet and the water pump were out back. I had to pump the water and carry every drop I used indoors. I washed our clothes in a wooden "hand-powered" washer. It was not much of an invention, but it was better than the washboard. It was my energy that turned the crank as the paddle swished the clothes in the tub of water. My hands were red and often appeared ready to blister when the laundry was done. You could surely work up a sweat doing the wash!

No Electricity

We did not have electricity for lights or heat. We used oil lamps to light the house. I washed the globes, trimmed the wicks, and filled them with oil every day or so. Lanterns were used for light in the barn. This was dangerous.

Russell was in the barn once when the lantern exploded. I do not know what caused this to happen, but I do know we were fortunate he was able to pitch it out of the barn in time to keep the building from catching on fire. So many times in my life I have been reminded of Psalms 73:23, *"Nevertheless I am continually with thee: thou hast holden me by my right hand."*

Barn Raising

I have never witnessed an old-fashioned barn raising, but I do remember my dad going to them. After I married Russell, he also attended a few.

Charles Harshman lived at Wolfsville when his barn burned down. Russell helped to construct the new building. A barn raising was an all-day event. Frequently, the men came from distant areas to help. The men did not expect to be paid for their work. It was done out of the goodness of their hearts for someone, most often, less fortunate than themselves.

We had sold Phil, Russell's driving horse, to Charles Harshman a few years after we were married. When the fire broke out in his barn, Phil was in the horse stable and burned to death. This happened during the night, killing the cattle and other horses as well.

Cutting Firewood

Before we needed it, Russell cut firewood so it could age and dry. We had a woodbox in the kitchen that had to be kept filled the year round in order to have dry wood for the cookstove. We also heated the kitchen during cold weather with the range.

In the springtime, I planted a garden and canned food for the winter. In warm weather, the kitchen became so hot while cooking that I could hardly stand being in there, not to mention working under those conditions. No fans, no refrigerator, and no ice.

140

Kitchen Range

I guess I should have been thankful for a range. That was a step above the fireplace! The kitchen range had a water tank on one end that held about five gallons. This was the only hot water heater we had. The tank opened with a wide lid so I could dip from it with a small pan. I carried water from the outdoor pump to fill the tank since the house did not have plumbing. I had hot water only when the fire was burning. It was handy if I had a baby to bathe or if I had lots of dirty, greasy dishes to wash. When I bathed the baby, I saved the water and scrubbed the kitchen floor. And, I did not pour it out yet! I scrubbed the porch so that the final drop was used. When I carried my water into the house, I thought of ways to make the most use of it. I always had a big tea kettle on the stove, but just when I needed a few cups of hot water, it was most likely boiled dry.

The Icehouse

We did not have an icehouse, but there was one on the neighboring C. Upton Grossnickle farm. An icehouse was usually a hole dug in the ground at the side of a hill with a small entrance. In the wintertime, chunks of ice were cut from the frozen creeks and preserved for emergency use. The men cut the ice with hand saws and stored it between layers of sawdust. The neighbors set a day aside for doing this chore and all the men helped. If someone became very ill, the icehouse was opened and the ice was used to help break the fever. Once in a great while, they opened the icehouse to make ice cream. This was a very special occasion.

Sleigh Bells

While living at Middlepoint, during the winter months when the ground was covered with snow, we often heard the Walter Lewis family ride by our home in the stillness of the night on their horse-drawn sled. The ringing of the sleigh bells from the horses' gears was a sweet sound to my ears. Occasionally, the horse neighed as they passed by the farm.

The Lewis family visited relatives and gathered to sing and spend the evening. I shall never forget how they harmonized as they sang those old hymns while riding along in the night air. Their voices blended so beautifully, and it gave me such a happy feeling to hear them.

Preserving

We buried some fruits and vegetables in the fall of the year in what we called a cave. It was a hole dug in the ground. Usually, it was near or in the garden. We buried apples, cabbage, and turnips. The cabbage heads were buried upside down. We covered the produce first with straw and then with a thick layer of soil. That kept the fruits and vegetables from freezing.

Dried Fruits

I dried fruits and vegetables for winter use. I used herds to hold the food while drying. Herds are heavy wire screens in a wooden frame (like a tray). I washed the produce and prepared it for drying by slicing and removing the pits. I dried shelled beans and whole green beans. I filled the herds and placed them in a low-temperature wood burning oven for a few days. We completed the process by air drying inside the house. It took a long time to dry for storing. If the moisture was not thoroughly evaporated, the food molded or rotted. By the time the entire process was finished, I had spent days preserving a little bit of food.

Canned Food

I canned jar after jar of vegetables, fruits, and meats. My hands cramped and ached from peeling. And now we say the "good old days." Well I tell you, I truly would not care to live through my life again.

Homemade Bread

Every couple of days, I baked bread for the family. The little ones liked to carry the fresh baked loaves back to the pie cupboard that stood in the hall in the old farmhouse. I remember every loaf our second son, Russell Jr., carried. He took a bite right out of the top. He was just a little boy. We did not have plastic bags to use for storing. I just sat the loaf on the shelf and covered it with a bread cloth. Of course it dried out, but we ate it anyway. For a change, I baked corn pones, slap jacks, and biscuits. I made corn cakes, buckwheat cakes, flannel cakes, and Johnny Cakes. These are varieties of pancakes that we ate for breakfast. Russell enjoyed these cakes for supper during the winter months.

Making Lye Soap

We used homemade lye soap to wash dishes and our clothing, and to bathe. I made two kinds—boiled and cold soap.

I made boiled soap by mixing and heating twenty-two

quarts of water and two cans of Banner's Lye until it boiled. Then I added ten pounds of rendered fat from pork rinds or other fat I saved when cooking meat.

The hog lard sometimes became rancid due to the hot weather. By the end of summer, the lard was about nine months old, and had been stored in a tin can without refrigeration. We used this in the soap since it was too "strong" to cook with. I also added turpentine to the soap I used for doing laundry. It helped to clean.

We boiled the soap mixture in a black butchering kettle that swung from a crane over the fireplace out in the wash house. I used a wooden broomstick for stirring. I cooked the soap until it became thick-like jelly. To test it, I lifted that stick out of the kettle so the hot, liquid soap could drip in a small spot, about the size of a quarter, onto the cold cement floor. When the liquid sat up and held its shape, I swung the kettle from the fire and let the soap cool and harden. After it dried for a few days, I cut it into cakes and laid it on a shelf or the porch to complete the process.

When making cold soap, I began by mixing the lye and water. The lye makes the water hot. Next, I added clean rendered pork fat. It mixed well while the water was warm. If I could afford a small bottle of perfume, I added it to the ingredients to give it a soft fragrance. I also poured in a bottle of mercurochrome to make it a delicate pink color. We used this soap for bathing only. I guess we considered this the "luxury" form of lye soap!

How to Make Lye

I have never made lye, but I remember my mother's procedures for doing this. She made it instead of using the cans of granulated lye like I purchased at the store.

Homemade lye is produced from wood ashes. Hickory ashes make the best lye.

Wood Ashes

An ash hopper sat out behind the smokehouse. It had a spout which allowed the liquid lye to drain down and into a large crock.

Mother cleaned and scraped the wood ashes from the kitchen range firebox. She saved them until the barrel or ash hopper was full. Then Mother poured a couple of gallons of water over them and waited for it to drip through. She packed the hole in the hopper with straw or corn husks to keep the ashes from going out as well. She repeated adding the water until she had the desired amount of lye.

The lye was a black liquid and caused the soap to become a dark gray instead of the ivory color produced with Banner's Lye.

As ancient as these skills may seem, to me it was only yesterday when I was living through that era. Remember, I was born in 1899. Just think of the water that has run under my "bridge of life" since then.

Sears, Roebuck and Company Catalog

In the mid-1920s, when the older children were small, we did not have the time to go shopping in Frederick or Hagerstown, Maryland. In fact, it was impossible to take the little ones shopping by horse and buggy or trolley. Next best thing was a shopping trip through the Sears, Roebuck and Company mail-order catalog. Everyone was excited when the new catalog arrived in the mail.

Talk about a wish book! We spent hours looking and

wishing for the latest fashions we never ordered. When the time came to make an order, the children and I sat down with the book opened on the table. Everyone was pointing, talking, and justifying why they wanted whatever. Everyone had a chance to tell me about their heart's desire. Whether we ordered it or not was another subject. But I tried to get them something they liked, whether it was shirts, coats, pants, or dresses.

I mailed the order off and everyone anxiously waited for the package to arrive. We knew approximately how long it took to be delivered. On the day I expected it to reach us, I informed the children. They either watched for the mailman from the kitchen window or played out along the fence until he arrived. If no one was outside, the mailman blew the car horn and hung the parcel on the picket fence that enclosed the yard. Our mailman was John M. Grossnickle, and he delivered the mail to my home when I was a little girl.

The children tried on the new garments. Sometimes the clothing did not fit and I had to wrap it up and return it to the mail-order house. Again, they waited out by the mailbox with the parcel. When John arrived, he told them how much postage was needed for shipping, and they paid him. He then took the package.

New School Shoes

Russell took the children to Harlen Stottlemyer's Store, in Wolfsville, to buy them new shoes every fall before they started back to school. It was difficult to buy shoes from the catalog. They needed to be fitted on their feet.

New Hats

I took Doris and Pauline up to Wolfsville to Lil Stottlemyer's shop when I needed to buy them a "Sunday" hat. All the women and girls wore them. This was the same store where Mother purchased my hats when I was growing up. I could make the trip in the horse and buggy and take all the children along.

Fried Frog—The Delicacy

One day, Hallie Delauter, Harry Delauter's son (the hired hand) was out working on the farm and caught a frog in the spring down in the meadow. He stabbed it with a pitchfork. I do not know how, but he cleaned it. I noticed the frog was still moving as he brought it to the kitchen in a crock of cold water. Hallie said it was dead! Then he asked me to prepare it for the evening meal. I could not believe what he was asking me to do. Hallie instructed me to roll the pieces of frog in flour, salt and pepper; then pan fry this "thing." He carefully placed the crock behind the kitchen door to wait for suppertime.

It is a wonder we all did not die of food poisoning before we reached sixteen, since our food was exposed to the heat for so long a time before cooking.

Hot Stove

Before I prepared supper that evening, I pushed more wood on the fire in the cooking range. I placed my skillet of lard on top to heat. I was about ready to prepare the frog. Not knowing that fat heated to a high degree would cause the frog to jump, I had quite a shock when it started to move again. I had the strangest feeling I was cooking it alive!

The men came into the house that evening and Hallie inquired if the frog was ready to eat. No doubt I was hungry, but I was not about to eat something that stayed on the move in hot fat. Hallie, Austin, and Russell tasted the delicacy. I said, "No, thank you" when passed to me. I tell you, I do not recollect any of them rushing out to catch another frog for the next meal!

Nine O'Clock Bite

We may talk about "keeping up with the Joneses" today, but in the early 1900s, the farmers' concern was not to let the neighbors catch them getting to the field after the sun came up. It was embarrassing to be late! Every farmer wanted to be out there and working before daybreak.

I served breakfast early. By the middle of the morning, that food had been worked off so the farmers ate a "nine o'clock bite." I either baked hot bread rolls, pies, or cakes for Russell and whomever was working for him. Sometimes I made sandwiches. If the men were close to the house working, they would stop, tie the horses to the fence or take them for water, and then come into the house for something to eat and drink. If they were working in a distant field, the children ran something out to them.

CHAPTER 23

MORE BABIES

Russell Peter Jr. is Born

On February 21, 1925, Russell Peter Jr. was born. Ruth Delauter Main came to help the family after his birth. In the summer months that followed, she worked alongside me as we cooked and baked in the kitchen. When Ruth wanted to go home to visit her family, Russell let her ride one of the horses. Her home was only a few miles away, but sometimes she liked to visit overnight and then return in the morning. We all enjoyed Ruth's jolly personality and good nature. Down through the years, the occasional visits I have had with these old friends have been enjoyed immensely.

Expecting Again

In March of 1927, we were expecting another child. I worked hard up until the time the babies were born and my body never had a chance to recover or get complete rest. It was not time for the baby's arrival, but I was so sick I thought I was going to die. I was sure my time was up, and my feet had made their last steps on the face of this earth. I thought I had pulled the covers over the children for the final time. Russell called the doctor to come see me. I was afraid for him to leave the room long enough to make the phone call.

149

I thought I might die before he returned. The doctor came and said I had too much strain and worry on me again. With time, I gained new strength to carry on.

Marie Flora is Born

Early in the morning on March 24, 1927, Marie Flora was born. Long before daylight, Russell awakened Austin and asked him to get out of bed and ride old Pet to Charles Delauter's house. He was to tell Ruth, Charlie's daughter, that I was about to deliver the baby. We had arranged for her to come work for us during this time since I needed some assistance when a new baby came.

Austin was only ten years old and was not only afraid of the dark, but also of the dogs that lived along the way. He was just a little boy, but he jumped up and did as he was instructed. He never mentioned he was afraid and never whined saying he did not want to go.

Austin passed by the Lewis' home and their dogs always came to the roadside and barked at the horse. This excited old Pet, and she would nicker and snort as she changed her pace. But Austin kept her in control; he was a brave little boy.

Let Me Eat My Breakfast

Austin tied Pet to the fence at the end of the road and walked down to the Delauter house. It was still dark outside and he hated walking by the bushes. It was so spooky. All of the family was not out of bed yet, but with a knock on the door, someone appeared. Austin entered the house and nervously explained the situation as best a 10-year-old boy could.

The Delauters were planning to have fried fish for breakfast that morning. Ruth said she could come but she had to have some breakfast first. After eating, Ruth jumped onto the horse with Austin, and home to the farm they rode. Austin did not waste time—he knew what was about to happen. A new baby was coming!

Stress

The winter Marie was born, we moved all the beds into one big bedroom. We had five children from ten years old to newborn. The old farmhouse was dark, cold, and spooky. We did not have electricity, so once the oil lamp was turned out, the house was pitch dark. The floors creaked with the softest step. The windows rattled and the shutters banged and beat the sides of the house with the lightest wind. We stuffed rags and paper around the windows and doors to stop the draft. When the children heard the noises, they were afraid. Since the rooms were not heated, we needed to be sure all these little ones stayed covered through the night.

Pauline was tiny and young, so I had her and baby Marie in the bed with me at the same time. I always felt sorry for the little one that had to move over when the new baby arrived. Russell slept with Russell Jr., who was next in line to the newborn, in a bed beside me and the other babies. Austin and Doris were young so they slept in their small beds in the room also. There seemed to be no way to get any sleep other than having us all together.

CHAPTER 24

LIFE IN THE FAST LANE

"Little Bird"

My daddy always said Marie was his "Little Bird." My life was more than busy by the time she was born.

I was seldom able to go home and visit—there were just too many little ones. With only the horse and buggy for transportation, it was next to impossible to give the whole day it took to make the trip. In the summertime it was a hot ride. In the winter it was too cold.

When those special visits were made, upon arrival, Dad and Mother always came out from the house to greet us. Dad kissed and hugged each child as we got out of the buggy. The children did not see him very often. Marie, the youngest, was afraid of his beard. He wanted to hold and love her, but she did not want anything to do with him. The older children were well acquainted and enjoyed being with him. Mother was anxiously waiting to see all of us as well.

"Little Doll"

Annie Stottlemyer, the Reverend's wife, seemed to enjoy Marie also. On Sundays, while we were at church, she would say, "Oh, she just looks like a little doll."

Going Home

One day, I decided it had been a long time since I had visited with my parents in Ellerton. They were growing older and I seemed to notice this fact more with each trip home. So, even though it was a long and hard day's journey, this would be the day I must go.

Pauline rode on a little wooden box placed on the buggy floor. I drove the horse while seated on the left side of the buggy seat. Doris sat between me and Austin. Austin held Russell Jr., and Doris held baby Marie.

Lathered

I must stop and tell you this. Doris recalls and laughs about how hot and sweaty she became on warm days while riding on the buggy seat in the middle of Austin and me. On these trips she always held Marie so close. She was being careful not to let her slip and fall. She recalls arriving home one day after the sun had been blazing down on her all the way home. We pulled the buggy into the barn, she got out and looked up at me. She said, "Look Mommy, I am all lathered up." I guess she heard us talk about the horses being lathered when they were sweaty, and she thought she was too.

Back to My Story

Anyway, this day we made the trip to Mother and Dad's house, visited for a few hours, and we were returning home. I had a nice visit. The thoughts of my aging parents were on my mind, along with how much work was waiting for me upon my arrival at home. I could see more gray in Dad and Mother's hair and they looked so sad as I drove away after the visit.

Steam Engines and Horses

With Kate, our horse, traveling briskly along, we had crossed the bridge coming around Slate Hill, and there traveling in front of us was the steam engine and thrash machine owned and driven by Roy Poffenberger. Roy was on his way to our farm to thrash the wheat crop. I may have been speeding again, since I overtook the engine!

Rescue

The steam engine made a chugging noise as it spouted out steam. Neither Kate nor the other horses heard the noise of an engine very often, so it caused them to become wild with excitement. They would jump and just go crazy. Once in awhile, you might find a horse who would work near an engine.

When Roy noticed us, he jumped off the machine and hurried to the side of the dirt road. He motioned and shouted for me to stop the horse, who was very nervous from the scene before her. I could tell by the look on Roy's face he was concerned. The sight of a stranger coming near, and hearing the noise of the steam engine excited Kate all the more. Roy quickly told me he was going to lead the horse past the engine and assured me that everything would be all right.

Since taking control of the situation was going to be tough, he grabbed old Kate by the bridle and instructed me to loosen up on the line. He held onto her as she jerked and bucked. At times, Kate lifted him off the ground. I was uncertain about what was going to happen and thought surely the buggy would flip over. The children and I were jostled around and frightened. We were all speechless.

Talk about angels of mercy being on the scene! Taking all this man's strength, he led Kate past the noisy engine and up the road a short distance. By now he had quieted her down, so I drove on home.

If Roy had not come to our rescue I do not know what would have happened to me and that buggy-load of children. Most likely, we would have been spilled from our seat and perhaps not lived to tell about it. Auto accidents were almost unheard of in our neighborhood, but plenty of tragedy happened with horses and their buggies. I had just got the children home safely when the engine arrived at the farm.

The next few days were busy for Russell and me. The farmers supplied the coal for fueling the engine. Roy brought a horse-drawn water cart loaded with two big barrels. The farmer hauled the water to the steam engine. It needed water to operate.

When Roy finished thrashing the grain crop, he blew the whistle on the engine to signal to the man on the next farm that he was ready to move on. The shrill sound of the whistle carried across the valley and there was no problem hearing it.

Breaking the Horse

The farmers broke their own young horses for riding and working in a team. This day, Russell was training a new young sorrel horse he bought. He had not been told by the previous owner that the horse was "false." A false horse is one who will not carry a rider on its back.

Today was the day set for triumph! We both went to the barn because I was afraid he might get hurt. Somehow,

Russell was able to get the bridle on the horse. He held on as he led him out the barn and over to the fence that enclosed the barnyard. Russell stood on the rails, managed to quickly jump on the horse's back, and kept his mount! I held my breath in amazement and fear. The horse took off running around the straw stack. He rubbed up against the rick as closely as possible trying to dislodge Russell from his back. Russell stayed on!

Open the Gate

Russell was going to ride to the mountain that day to check on some timber cutting that was being done for him. He planned to take a small sack along. Russell shouted to me to open the gate and pass the sack to him as he was going to ride by me again. It was like passing the baton in a marathon race! I will never forget the sight as he rode off the farm that morning. I wondered where that horse might take him.

Tooter

I recall a local man often came by the farm at Middlepoint to visit. He would knock on the door and I asked him to come in. When I inquired how he was doing, he would reply, "Oh, I'm tired and hungry." So without fail I would prepare him something to eat, no matter what time of day it was.

One day, Russell and the man were in the house chatting. He was a tall, lanky fellow, and a bit "laid back" in his personality. When he visited, Tooter, his little black "lap" dog, came as well.

I was busy in the kitchen and was in and out of the back door for what seemed like a hundred times that morning.

Tooter was stretched out in the warm sunshine on the back porch, right up next to the door. He appeared to be determined to come into the house as I came in or out. He insisted he was only content at that spot—right at the entrance of the kitchen. Never failing, each time I disrupted his rest, he became more intent on having his way. Tooter seemed to be sure he was eventually going to wear me down. I did not allow our dogs in the house, and this dog was not coming in either. The children were small and I had enough to do to keep the floor clean without a farm dog's dirty footprints as well.

At last, I became so desperate to get this dog out of my way, that I picked up a pan of hot water and pitched it on old Tooter. I do not know why I did such a thing. I guess you just have to understand the situation. Tooter jumped higher and more quickly than I had ever seen him move. He barked and yipped as he ran off the porch and out into the yard.

At once, his master was up from his chair. There was a sudden increase in his step and attention. He was soon out the door with a smooth, quick motion as he checked on his dog. He remarked and, with the intent of me hearing, "Tooter, I don't think that woman likes you." It was not a matter of me being fond of his dog; I just could not put up with this dog's insistence of coming into the house.

CHAPTER 25

MAKING A LIVING

Cutting and Hauling Timber

Russell sold timber. When the fall of the year came, Russell (and whomever happened to be working for him at the time), hauled timber from our mountain lot off Gravel Hill near Wolfsville Road. Usually he hired men to cut the trees. Russell dragged the logs out of the thick mountain with the horses. Then he loaded them on the log wagon.

He hauled the logs to Myersville and they were shipped away by railroad cars. Much of the wood was sent to the West for building the early cross-country railways.

In those days, there were no chain saws to make the job easier. The trees were cut down with a crosscut saw and ax. I packed a lunch in a cloth and Russell tied it to the hame of the horse's gears, or he put it in the wooden box attached to the side of the wagon. He used a four-horse team of workhorses to pull the load. With the wagon whip in his hand, off in the early morning hours they traveled, deep into the mountain.

Left At Home

In the morning when the men left home for the mountain, I stayed at the farm to do the milking. I fed and took care of all of the other animals—pigs, chickens, and whatever was running around alive on the farm. When evening came, it was back to the barn to repeat the chores. During the busy seasons, I had a maid who stayed in the house with the children.

Rocking the Children, Alone

With Russell still out in the mountain, late at night I sat at home with a sleeping baby on my lap, a child on my knee, and maybe one standing on the rocker of the rocking chair holding onto my neck. They were trying to get some attention. I rocked until I heard the sound of the steel wagon wheels and the hooves of the horses coming up the road. Once Russell made it home, it would be only a little longer until he would be coming into the house. First, he had to unhitch the horses, feed, and take care of them.

I watched for the flicker of the lantern as he walked from the barn. It was always a welcome sight to see Russell's face at the kitchen door. I had waited so long for him to come. He would lift one of the sleeping children off my lap, freeing me to get up from the chair. He, too, was tired and together we carried the little ones to their beds. With everyone tucked in for the night, we could give a sigh of relief and fall asleep for what seemed like only a few minutes of rest. Morning always came quickly.

I recall that when Russell was in the house in the evening, we sat down and rocked all the children. As I rocked the baby, I sang and Russell hummed along.

Selling Produce

From 1917 to 1929, we planted and harvested large

crops of potatoes and other vegetables for our use and to sell. Russell got up early in the morning and loaded the produce onto the spring wagon. If the load was heavy, the shaft was removed from the wagon and replaced with a tongue so two horses could pull it. He went up Highland School Road, across Hamburg Mountain, and came out at Spout Springs Road. At Spout Springs, Russell stopped along the roadside. Here at the spring-fed watering trough, he let the horse drink and rest before continuing to Frederick.

The Catholic Convent, located in Frederick, bought large quantities of his produce. Upon Russell's arrival, the Sisters peaked out the "peephole" and then opened the door. They made their purchase. If it was cold and stormy weather, they gave him something hot to drink and offered him a bun or sweet roll. It was a long, cold hike up over those mountains in the early morning hours of the winter. Russell always commented that the Sisters were some of his best customers.

Mr. Staley and Roy Leatherman's Market on Market Street, as well as Hamilton's Store, also bought his produce. After these purchases were made, anything leftover was peddled door-to-door to residents in nearby homes.

Horse Milk for an Ailing Child

Russell drove over the Hamburg Mountain to go into Frederick to market. One day, a lady, whose house sat alongside the road, came out and flagged him down. He had our horse, Mae, hitched to the wagon and she had recently given birth. She was still nursing her baby foal. Russell stopped when he noticed the lady and she asked if it would be possible for him to take some milk from the mare for her child. The youngster was very ill with the whooping cough

161

and she had heard that horse milk would help speed his recovery. Russell saw the desperation on her face and heard it in her voice. He nodded and answered, "Yes." She gave him a small pan. There by the roadside he proceeded to milk the mare. After a few minutes, he gave the warm milk to the lady. She was most grateful. Then Russell jumped back up on the wagon seat and continued on his way.

Limited Medication

Medication was very limited in the early 1900s, and folks were desperate for whatever medical help they could find. Everyone swallowed their pride and did whatever it took to get the help they needed.

Uncle Tilgh, the Veterinarian

Uncle Tilghman Grossnickle worked as a veterinarian. When we needed some medical attention for an animal, we called Uncle Tilgh and he came to check if there was anything he could do.

After working with the animal, he always came to the house to wash his hands and then he would sit and visit with me for a few minutes. Uncle Tilgh wore a pointed goatee, was small in stature, and had a squeaky voice. He carried a little black satchel. The children loved Uncle Tilgh; indeed, he was a delightful man.

Home Remedies

Most of the folks living in the country searched for home remedies as the cure instead of going to the doctor for help. It was just too inconvenient to travel to town for an office visit.

I made a "drawing" salve from equal parts of brown sugar, soap, and beef tallow. Mother taught me how to prepare the ingredients. I chipped or shaved soap into fine pieces. I rendered beef tallow and let it slightly cool. Then I mixed the three ingredients until it formed a soft salve. It was stored in small jars with tight lids and set on the pantry shelf. This salve was applied to the flesh to draw out splinters or for infections on the skin. I still keep some on hand today.

CHAPTER 26

ANTICS AND MISFORTUNES

"Ruckie Boy"

Uncle John and Aunt Bessie Grossnickle and their children, Maurice and Mildred, often visited us on Sunday afternoons. They lived on a nearby farm. Aunt Bessie had a nickname she used when addressing Russell Jr. She called him "Ruckie Boy." He was just a little boy when we lived at Middlepoint. He was under five years of age.

One Sunday afternoon, Maurice, Mildred, Austin, Doris, Pauline, and Russell Jr. were out playing in the wagon shed. They were jumping in and out of the wagons, just having a good old time.

Suddenly, someone had the brilliant idea of offering "Ruckie Boy" a horseless ride in the spring wagon. For the moment, he thought he was someone special and was delighted to be so honored. He was going to be the only child to get the ride! He quickly got into the wagon and the other five applied their energy. "Ruckie Boy" was on his way out of the wagon shed. All was fun and wonderful until the gang decided to play a trick on him. They pushed until all four of the wagon wheels were in the branch that ran down behind the barnyard. With a quick turn, they ran away from "Ruckie Boy" and the wagon, giggling and laughing with each other. There he sat, alone and screaming for help!

The children huddled in the shed, peeking out around the corner every now and then. It was the funniest thing they had ever thought of doing.

Poor "Ruckie Boy" was in a very bad situation. Everywhere he looked around the wagon there was water. It might as well have been flowing up under the wagon bed, as far as he was concerned. "Ruckie Boy" just knew for sure he was going to drown! Well, the water was only a couple of inches deep at the most, but he certainly was frightened. Finally, the five came and rescued him.

Racing

I remember that Mildred could run so fast that her little legs carried her ahead of all the other children. And do you know who was always coming along behind? Poor little "Ruckie Boy"! I remember Aunt Bessie and I watching the children as they raced across the yard. She said, "Oh, look at poor little Ruckie. He is really working hard trying to keep up." Well, the truth is, he never did catch up with them. By the time he got halfway to meet them, they were coming back.

Uncle Caleb Is Ill

My Uncle Caleb Harshman was married to Mother's sister, Melissa. He died in 1929. We were living at Middlepoint at the time. I knew he was very ill with bronchitis and the flu, but I did not realize his illness was so grave. His health had been poor for about eleven years.

I had been sick with the flu as well, and seemed to have so many things happening in my own young life.

On a Saturday afternoon, my daddy stopped at our house on his way home after attending Uncle Caleb's funeral at the Grossnickle Church. Dad was checking on how I was doing. Finding me still confined to bed, I am sure he noticed my straining circumstances. Seeing the worn, pale look on my face, he could not bring himself to tell me he had been to the funeral. I was worried about Uncle Caleb, but when I asked how he was doing, Dad answered, "Oh, he's all right." He never said a thing to make me think my uncle had passed away.

I have never been able to understand why no one would tell me Uncle Caleb had died. I guess they thought I had my hands full of my own problems. That never seemed to satisfy the fact that I did have a right to know. I was very fond of my Uncle Caleb.

Some days later, Etta (Sis) Stottlemyer came to help me catch up with some work around the house. As we were talking, and not knowing that I was not aware of Uncle Caleb's death, she told me. I was surprised, saddened, and hurt at the news.

An Interrupted Bath

Basil and Quentin Grossnickle, Elbert Grossnickle's sons, walked home from Poplar School with Austin. The homeless, or tramps, sometimes camped under the wooden bridge that crossed the Middle Creek near the Grossnickle's farm. Not having a home and needing a bath, what could better meet that need than the clear, clean water in the creek?

This sunny, warm afternoon, the boys were walking across the bridge on their way home from school, and who was bathing? None other than the tramp. The boys noticed him and decided this fellow's bath was going far too peaceable. They stopped, laughed, and whispered a suggestion. No one would admit whose idea it was. So,

167

meaning no harm and just having fun, the boys picked up stones and threw them at the tramp. This immediately confused and angered him. The old fellow jumped around, shouted, and got annoyed with the boys, to say the least.

The Race Is On

We often sent Austin to Ellerton or Myersville on our horse, Pet, to run errands for us. Now I know that perhaps he may have inherited a desire to ride a fast horse from his mother. I will not deny I liked to "move on down the road."

This day, Austin was riding near the bridge at the Charlie Grossnickle farm when the school bus caught up to him. As the bus passed Austin and old Pet, someone called from the window, "Come on!" Now Austin did not refuse the invitation for a race and so he encouraged Pet to charge ahead with full speed. When the horse's steel shoes hit the bridge, it was like thunder clapping in a storm.

Austin had a witness—Charlie Grossnickle, his great-uncle. I know how much he enjoyed the speed, but the "gig was up." Austin was truly in big trouble that day!

Extra Lunch

Austin always insisted he carry a big lunch to school. I wondered how this boy could eat so much. Nevertheless, he convinced me that his big appetite was caused by the long walk to school. Many years later, I learned that Austin wanted one of his good buddies, who was a few grades ahead of him in school, to share his food.

Pet and the Ice Storm

I will never forget one Saturday morning, probably around 1925. It was in the middle of winter. Russell hitched Pet to the spring wagon and was going to drive to the Farmers' Exchange in Myersville to purchase grain for the cattle. The children enjoyed riding with their dad in the wagon on these trips to take care of business.

Sometimes they stopped for a few minutes to visit with the children's Grandmother Wiles who lived in town. Always in the summertime, and usually on Monday mornings, Russell and some of the children took her milk and butter. The children remember going up the street by her house with the team and wagon in the early morning hours and, if they did not stop, she would be standing by the window waving to them.

Anyway, this Saturday Doris and Russell Jr. decided to go along with their daddy in spite of the cold, cloudy winter weather. They dressed warmly and crawled into the wagon. They had arrived at the feed supply store when a heavy sleet and ice storm commenced. Within minutes, the roads were covered with ice and were dangerously slick.

Sliding on the Ice

After the grain and supplies were loaded onto the wagon, and everyone was aboard, they started down the slippery hill out from Myersville toward home. There was no cover on the spring wagon. They were fully exposed to the inclement weather. Russell knew the road was treacherous and was concerned about the children's safety. Suddenly and without warning, old Pet's feet slipped out from under her like a flash and down the hill she slid on her rumps. The wagon carrying the feed, Russell, and the children, looked as if they were pushing Pet.

Russell tried to stay calm and instructed the children to "sit tight." Doris and Russell Jr. held onto the wagon until the skin on their little knuckles turned white. They were scared speechless. They all just stared at the scene before them. The right-hand side of the road dropped off in a steep hill. It would be hard to say what would have happened to them had they slipped off the road that day. Russell held to the line, trying not to show fear.

Pet did not regain her composure until she reached the flat at the bottom of the long hill. There she conquered the situation and was able to stand to her feet. Russell got off the wagon and stood still for a moment in amazement.

Everything and everyone was "upright." Lo and behold, the horse stayed hitched to the wagon and only the gears became tangled. He checked and straightened them, and continued home. We were so grateful for God's protection. Only by the control of a "Higher Being" did that horse and wagon stay on the road.

I had been worried about Russell having the two little ones with him in the storm and was happy when they returned. Every one of them was frightened, wet and cold. We thought nothing of riding in the cold weather, but riding in an ice storm was a different story. However, it was the only way we ever traveled, other than an occasional trolley ride. I hate to think of what could have happened that day!

The Milk Pitcher

I had never wondered what to do, but always wondered what to do first. The little ones looked forward to making butter since they rode on top of the churn as the older children and I turned the crank. I laid a blanket on top and the child who was riding pretended he or she was riding a horse. As the paddle turned in the barrel of cream, the butter fat separated from the milk, thus forming butter. Our churn was in the shape of a barrel and laid flat on its side in a set of crossed wooden legs.

We did not sell the milk to the dairy, but churned the cream into butter to sell to the huckster. We also sold the sweet cream.

Intruder in the Kitchen!

The milk separator sat behind the door in the kitchen at the Middlepoint farm. It was used to drain the skim milk from the butterfat. We fed our calves the skim milk after we weaned them from their mothers. I was doing some outdoor chores and was hastily scampering around trying to get back into the house to prepare the evening meal.

It was a nice evening—the children were either playing or doing their jobs around the farm when I returned to the house. As I stepped onto the porch and neared the back door, I heard an unfamiliar noise coming from behind the opened door. It sounded as if someone was stirring around in my kitchen.

Carefully, I listened for a few moments. I knew I was right, someone was in there! I turned and ran as fast as I could to see that all the children were near. Then we hurried to the back of the hog lot where I could see Russell heading towards the edge of the field. He had the team of horses and had been working in the "eighteen acre" field. He saw me and the children running and knew something must be wrong. When he finally reached me, I quickly and excitedly told him of the noise and frantically suggested that he be the one to

171

enter first and check this out.

He left the team and we all hastened back to the house. Not knowing what or who he might find inside the kitchen, Russell picked up a piece of wood as he passed by the woodpile at the edge of the yard. Cautiously, he crossed the wooden porch. He opened the screen door, and stepping carefully, entered the kitchen. Clasping tightly to the club he might need for a weapon, he looked behind the door.

There appeared before his eyes a stray cat with its head wedged in my white and blue earthenware milk pitcher. Russell chuckled, stepped back to the open door where he could see me, and said, "Come look. What a sight this is!" The cat could not so much as pick up his head from the weight of this vessel. That pitcher was wedged on tight.

The cat had been trying to get the last bit of milk that was left in the pitcher. When it put its head into the oval top, the pitcher overturned and the cat's head became trapped.

The Buggy is Full

During the last years we lived at Middlepoint, and after Russell Jr. and Marie were born, the older children, Austin, Doris, and Pauline, walked to church on Sunday mornings. They were growing up and the buggy was full by the time Russell, the younger children, and I were aboard.

Riding Home in a Model T

C. Upton Grossnickle and Uncle William Harshman owned cars by now. It was in the late 1920s. As they came upon the children walking alongside the road, they always gave them a ride. No one ever rode by without picking them up. There was no fear of any harm being done to them back in those days.

Austin remembers Archie Brandenburg, who was dating Louisa Bussard, giving him and his sisters a ride to or from church. Archie and Louisa came to Grossnickle Church together on Sunday morning. He drove a one-seated Model T Ford. When he stopped the car to pick up the children, Austin hopped onto the running board by Archie's side; Doris and Pauline were on the side by Louisa. Then Louisa put her arm out the window and around the girls to protect them from falling as they stood riding along on that running board of the Model T.

CHAPTER 27

TIME PASSES QUICKLY BY

Time passed quickly on the Mandy Stottlemyer farm—eleven years of our lives were spent there farming. Then Russell's mother died.

Again, Death Comes

When Russell's mother (Flora Maria Wiles) died on July 13, 1929, at her home in Myersville at age 66, she left two of her three children, Russell and Flora. Her daughter, Mary Wiles Gaver, died in October 1927. Mary left two daughters.

Flora's farm at Middlepoint was sold to Russell Harshman. The estate was to be divided between my husband, his sister Flora, and Mary's two daughters.

Russell and I had been farming on shares with his mother. New plans and hopes of a home of our own came into mind. By great sacrifice, we thought we could accomplish buying one. But a home for us to purchase was not found.

We moved to the George Toms farm on the south side of Myersville in the spring of 1930. There we farmed on shares with Mr. Toms for two years.

Moving to Myersville

It was April 1, 1930, moving day for the Wiles family. We moved from Middlepoint to the Toms farm at Myersville. Well, there was more work to be done that day than should be imposed on any mother of five. Days had already been spent packing boxes, remembering where I put things, preparing food, catching up on the laundry, and a little time was spent wondering how I would ever survive the ordeal. Everywhere I looked there was something to do. I cannot imagine what we would have done without the help of our relatives and friends during this time of transition.

Where is the Mother Pig?

Of all times for one of our sows to leave the farm, what could be worse than moving day? Russell knew she was going to deliver her little ones at any time. When she could not be found this morning, he and Austin began to search. They probed for hours trying to locate her with no success. Finally, the two gave up and returned home. The rest of our livestock and possessions had to be moved down the road and time was slipping away.

Charles Freshour to the Rescue

Later that day, Charlie Freshour, who lived across the field from our farm buildings, came upon the mother pig. She and her newborn pigs were down by the Middle Creek. Austin still laughs about how he and his dad struggled to get the mother into a hog crate. They loaded her and the new pigs on the wagon and headed down the road to the new home in Myersville.

A Real Cattle Drive

We owned about six horses, six hogs, and seventeen cows. Russell made plans to drive the cattle down Route 17, up Myersville Hill, through the town, and to the Toms farm. Folks did not have cattle carriers or trucks to carry animals from farm to farm. We had no choice but to drive them. (The George Toms farm was destroyed by the Interstate highway in later years.)

Lee Delauter, Callie Long, Clinton and Jack Brunner, Stanley Grossnickle, James Grossnickle, my brother Wade and his son Clyde, my dad, and Russell (and others I have forgotten) planned to move the cattle early in the morning. Austin was a young boy but he was in the crowd helping. After our helpers had milked their own cows, and as soon as these men could get to our farm, the drive began. A cattle drive required lots of help.

The hogs and calves were loaded on a large farm wagon, which was pulled by a four-horse team. When the cattle saw the other livestock on the wagon, they had the tendency to follow and not wander off onto the property along the way. Men walked in front of the herd and checked for open gates or crossroads where the cattle may try to break away. Some of them stopped and stood guard at those spots. Men followed by the side of the cows and some drove them from the back.

Not only was there some fear in the hearts of these strong men regarding the control of these animals, but homeowners along the way had no desire to see the herd break away and come onto their property and cause destruction. Folks helped when they heard them coming. It was a rainy, cold, windy day; not the kind of weather you would choose for a cattle drive. But that did not dampen our spirits—they were high.

Bond of Love

There was something different about people's spirit and attitude in those bygone days. It was obvious there was such a bond of love and goodwill. None of us had much of the world's wealth and folks were happy for the good things that came into each others' lives. We helped one another and truly wished them well. Regardless of the circumstances we faced, people shared whenever and whatever possible.

The Green Durante

Russell and I were still driving a horse and buggy, although many people had purchased the new machines—cars! Russell's Uncle John P. Grossnickle and his wife, Aunt Bessie, owned a green Durante car. She and Uncle John spent the day helping us move. John Peter Grossnickle and Flora Grossnickle Wiles (Russell's mother) were half sister and brother. Peter Grossnickle was both children's father.

Aunt Bessie drove me and the little children to the new home in Myersville. Besides this hen and her little chicks (referring to me and the children), Aunt Bessie carried one of my old clucks and her little peeps in a coop in the trunk of the car. Now that is not all, for she also had the children's rocking rooster and scooter. Quite a load she carried. Women, kids, clucks and chicks arrived safely, but a bit flustered!

The Rocking Rooster and the Scooter

We had to cross a small stream to get to the farmhouse. I cannot recall everyone who met us at Aunt Bessie's car upon our arrival. Folks picked up items from the car to carry into the house. Someone was carrying Marie's rocking rooster. Marie saw the water she must cross to get to the house, and she put up a fight to regain the possession of her treasured rooster. She had long learned that toys came few and far between, and she felt compelled to take care of the rooster herself. Russell Jr. held tightly to his scooter as he crossed the stream. He, being a more adventuresome child, probably wondered if he dared to ride through the water to the other side. But little Marie felt that if anything was going to happen to her rocking rooster, it would be she who would make the blunder.

Prisoners in the Privy

What a day! Pauline had taken her sister, Marie, to the outhouse. Somehow the doorknob turned while they were inside. They were trapped out in the old wooden privy on that cold spring day. Pauline stood on the seat shouting for help from the hole cut in the shape of a star in the side of the outhouse. No one heard her.

Pauline was wearing a sweater and she took it off and wrapped it around her little sister's shoulders. She knew Marie was cold. Jumping back up onto the toilet seat, Pauline shouted again for help to no avail. She began beating and kicking on the door with all the strength in her wee body. The knob was mounted with a spike. Finally, it bent enough to allow the knob to slip around. The door burst open, freeing the little prisoners.

I will confess there was so much going on around the house that day that I did not realize they had not returned. Sure enough, they opened the kitchen door and here the two little ones stood hand-in-hand weeping and cold. Pauline said she heard the men talking as they came in and out of the house but the wind was blowing so hard they could not hear her calling for help.

Marie Wants to Go Home

I had worked many days to get ready for this move, and the responsibility of getting the family home situated and in order was mine. Evening came and the realization that this was the new home for us finally became real. When Marie saw Aunt Bessie putting her coat on and getting ready to leave, she began to cry and wanted to go with her. Guess it was a traumatic day for everyone, but it was really taking its toll on this little one. With whatever comforting words I said to her, I managed to get her to realize she was staying.

I did not have just my day's work laid out for me— I had a lifetime of work laid up and waiting for me. But as faithful as each morning came, likewise the strength to accomplish it followed.

Aunt Bessie probably never knew the value of her help that day. Once again, the love that was showed to us during those difficult days shall never be forgotten. We loved Aunt Bessie and Uncle John Peter Grossnickle.

CHAPTER 28

AIRPLANE CRASH ON TOMS FARM

A Plane Falls From the Sky

We lived at the George Toms farm for two years, 1930-31. One time, about four o'clock in the afternoon, Callie Long, our farmhand at the time, and Russell were out in the barn working when suddenly they heard a loud, strange noise. They went to the barn door, glanced up to the sky, and spotted a small aircraft. Out in the country, we did not see planes often. Taking a moment from their work to watch the plane, they commented to one another that perhaps it was having a problem.

The men watched in amazement as the plane fell to the ground! It came to rest in our wheat field, very near the barn. Rushing to the crash site, Russell and Callie found the pilot, Captain John Mills Sterling, unharmed. This young, tall, slender man walked toward them and was most grateful to be alive and uninjured. Russell offered to do whatever he could to help, and invited him into the house to make necessary phone calls and report the accident. Little did I know that I was about to meet my house guest who would spend the week with us.

Borrowed Plane

Sterling, who was from Selfedge Field, Michigan, had borrowed the plane from a friend. He was on his way to Philadelphia, Pennsylvania, to see other friends. We had a dense fog that afternoon that caused him to lose his way and run out of fuel before crashing.

Janice Mae, the New Baby

I did not realize the plane had crashed until the men came into the house. Austin was very ill with tonsillitis. My sister-in-law, Maudie, came to help me and care for him. Janice, who was born June 21, 1930, was just six weeks old; I had my hands full without being worried sick.

Maudie made a "poilus" and applied it to Austin's neck. A poilus was nothing more than bread soaked in warm milk, tied in a cloth, and placed on the neck. It surely was a messy treatment. This was to aid the healing by scattering the infection in his throat. Maudie constantly stayed by his bed, caring for him. The doctor made a home visit and he told us if Austin was not better by the following morning, we would need to take him to the hospital for treatment.

I had tucked the other children in for the night and laid down on the bed with the baby. I remember Maudie coming into our bedroom saying, "I think Austin will be all right. His throat is beginning to open and drain."

As far as I was concerned, my sister-in-law had been an "angel of mercy." I declare, she certainly helped us through "troubled waters." I was so worn from all that was happening and caring for the new baby.

Trouble and Work

There was so much to do—in addition to having the pilot (and a stranger at that)—to feed and bed down everyone for the night. The family's needs were pressing. There were times when life appeared to be "just too much for me to handle." Trouble and work was coming in from every side. But as meager as our home was in furnishings and splendor, there was always plenty of love. We gave a welcome to all, and now especially to the one with such an urgent need. There was no doubt that Captain Sterling knew what an imposition he was to us with our household of problems. Perhaps he wondered what a mess he had gotten himself into!

The military authorities came and completed their investigation of the plane crash. Within a few days, trucks hauled the pieces of wrecked plane away. Captain John Mills Sterling said good-bye with his pleasant and polite manner. He was most grateful for our hospitality.

By the end of the week, Austin was feeling on the mend, and once again, we all could begin to see the sun was truly shining.

"Jockey Sticks"

There were fragments of the plane left on the field after the military did their cleanup job of the wreckage. Russell found some light metal poles, just the right size to use as the jockey or "G" stick which was part of the horses' gears. For years, we used these rods from the airplane and often thought of Captain John Sterling. The only contact we ever had with him since he spent that week with us was a letter. He included a picture of him standing with his mother and two friends. It was taken while he was in Hawaii.

CHAPTER 29

THE CAR

Driver's Education

We knew the children needed transportation to get to the Grossnickle church since we were now living on the south side of Myersville. We purchased our first car—a maroon 1930 Chevy for $800.

Callie Long decided to take on the task of teaching Russell how to drive the new vehicle. That evening after supper, the instructions were to begin. I decided I was going to ride along and try out the new auto as well. What harm could it bring? Russell got behind the steering wheel, Callie sat beside him on the passenger's side, and I took a back seat. We drove toward Middlepoint and, as we were returning, driving across the bridge at Summers' Store in Ellerton, Russell lost control due to speed. Not being used to driving something going so fast, we narrowly escaped hitting the bridge. I was scared. Callie laughed and said, "Pete, you just about didn't make it." A more truthful statement than that had never been spoken.

Whoaaaaa!

Well, we made it back to the farm. I was about to breathe a sigh of relief when Russell pulled up to the shed.

He hollered "whoa" but the machine did not stop. Oh, I thought we would crash—and we did! Russell momentarily forgot he was not driving a team of horses. He drove the car through the end of that weatherboard building! By now, all of us were anxious to get ourselves out of the horseless carriage. What an experience! I declared I would never ride with Russell again.

Beulah, Wade and Maudie's daughter, who was working for us, had her driver's license. She drove us to church on Sundays until Russell mastered his driving skills.

Driver's Test

At last, the day came when Russell was ready to take the Maryland state driver's test. He was not comfortable driving this fast-moving vehicle. Russell and Callie went to Frederick to the testing station at the Armory. For part of the exam, he had to drive around the city block.

The officer got into the car. Russell started driving and never shifted out of low gear. The officer noticed this and inquired, "Does this car have a high gear?" I do not know the answer Russell gave, but that cop was probably fortunate he never used it! Well, he came home that day with a license to drive. Practice helped and, indeed, the car proved to be a luxury for us.

No Heater

This 1930 Chevy did not have a heater, so we piled comforters on top of us. Since we always had a carload of people, our bodies created heat as well. Think of it—no horse to gear up, we were comfortably seated out of the rain, and a mere turn of the key started the engine!

CHAPTER 30

CHRISTMAS MEMORIES

Russell Jr. Brags

It was a day or two before Christmas. Austin was about fourteen years old and enjoyed seeing his younger brother and sisters excited about the season. It seemed we never had extra money for lots of gifts on Christmas morning, but we managed to get each child something. Every day for weeks, Russell Jr. bragged about what he would say and do if he met Santa in person. He was really excited. Santa was on his mind day and night. He was saying how brave he was and that he was not afraid of him. You see, Russell Jr. really was not afraid of much.

It's Santa

Austin felt Russell Jr. may have been exaggerating. He whispered a suggestion of his to me and I did not see any harm in him having some fun. In fact, I thought I might enjoy seeing the show this stunt may bring.

Austin had come upon a Santa Claus costume he borrowed, and so he proceeded with his plans. This evening after dark, he went outside and attired himself as Santa. Austin was ready to enjoy his act.

He stood on the cellar door that was under the window

near the kitchen table. He had asked me to make sure the children were nearby when he gave the signal.

The stage was set. As Austin quietly approached, he knocked on the window and pushed his face close to the glass. Russell Jr., who was sitting at the table, caught sight of him and quickly dropped to the floor. Like a flash, he crawled behind the stove, and said, "Tell him I don't want anything." His eyes popped open and I can still see the expression on his face. The little fellow was scared out of his wits. Russell Jr. was proven not to be what he had bragged—brave.

Speechless

Later in the evening, after Austin removed his disguise, he came back into the house. He told Russell Jr. he had been down to the woodpile a few minutes earlier and found Santa out there with his sleigh turned over. He said presents were spilled everywhere and that he helped Santa pack up so he could go on his way. Russell Jr. had little to brag about at this point. He was speechless and he certainly did not want to discuss Santa. It does not matter how much or how little of life's wealth you obtain, where there is love there will be joy.

First Christmas Tree

We never had a Christmas tree until 1926. You see, you can never imagine how poor we were back then. If we had not done without and saved the way we did, we never would have owned a home. I tell any young couple today, save and cut out the luxuries until you have a place of your own to call home. It is the only wise thing to do.

Anyway, we had plenty of pine trees on the farm along the fence rows or out in the woods, but we did not have decorations. Well, Austin asked his dad if they could go out and cut a Christmas tree this year. We all talked and decided we would order a few ornaments from the Sears, Roebuck and Company catalog. The ones we purchased were nothing more than a cardboard picture of angels trimmed in tinsel. They had a little string and tinsel hanger. They were the cheapest ornaments in the book!

This day, Russell agreed to go out with Austin to search for the perfect tree. As they walked along together in the freezing cold, Russell suggested several small pines they came upon. No way, Austin wanted a big one! With the saw in hand, his dad decided to let him choose. Austin found a nice big pine and was determined this was the perfect one. So they cut it down.

The two headed back to the house. Austin walked a short distance and looked up at his dad with eyes of despair and said, "Daddy, I just can't go any further. It's too heavy." Russell helped him. When they brought it into the house, Austin was beaming with pride. He had his tree! The children had so much fun making popcorn and paper chains. After adding our new ornaments, we had trimmed our first Christmas tree.

CHAPTER 31

NEVER A DULL MOMENT

Horse Dies

Russell and Callie were down in "Little Egypt" along the creek, working to widen the creek bed. "Little Egypt" was the lowland down over the hill at the Toms farm. Heavy rains had forced the creek to split into two streams. By widening its bed, the men hoped it would continue to flow in one direction.

While working, one of the horses slipped down into the creek and pulled the whole team into the water. One horse hurt its shoulder, never recovered, and died. There was a statement we shared when such mishaps occurred. "As long as the tragedy stays at the barn and leaves our household alone, it is okay." But, nevertheless, it was a financial loss we could not afford.

Tramp and a Lesson Learned

It was a cold, damp and stormy evening in 1931. Russell and Callie had been down below "Little Egypt" cutting firewood. They where coming from the field when a homeless man appeared on the farm. The fellow asked to spend the night. Russell, thinking it was too cold for man or beast to stay outdoors in the barn, decided he should be permitted to sleep in the house on the couch.

When morning came, Russell was up and outside working while the tramp was still asleep in the living room, or at least he was pretending to be sleeping. We trusted people, but a lesson was to be learned this day!

Razors, Knives & Watches?

Beulah Grossnickel, who was working for us, and I were busy with the housework and little ones. The older children were off to school. Marie and Janice were just babies. I was making bread that morning. Beulah was upstairs making the beds when the tramp, who was now awake, proceeded to talk to me.

Suddenly, he began to tell me how many people he had killed with the sharp weapons he had attached to a wide leather belt he wore strapped around his waist. His face was stern. He opened each button on his jacket and pushed the sides back to expose in full view the many razors, knives, and watches attached all over his garment. As he talked, he fumbled and played around with what appeared to be the "most deadly" of the knives. His eyes caught mine and he never blinked. There was a sharpness about his eyes I had never seen before in any human being. He caused every nerve in my body to jitter. I listened to his stories and heard every word he spoke. He had a captive audience.

My heart was running wild. He left no detail unspoken for me to use my imagination to figure out. After a time, I could not contain myself. I had to do something. His conversation was going too far. Somehow, I managed to carry those children in my arms as I walked to the steps that lead upstairs. I called for Beulah to come down. In a matter of seconds we met in the stairway. I knew she was afraid and

I only confirmed that fact. I whispered to her that if he made a break for us, she should grab Marie and I would take the baby and we would run. Beulah nodded. I tell you, if that man had so intended to harm us, we were "sitting ducks" waiting to be had. I know for sure when we live and when we die depends on God's order.

The Telephone Call

I have never lived when an hour was so long! The time absolutely stood still. Finally, Russell came into the house. I was so relieved to see him. I went to his side. Softly I told him what the tramp had been saying. Russell said not a thing to me, but went to the phone to call the feed supply store to ask them to deliver him a load of chopped grain for the cattle. When he picked up the handset to make the call, the tramp must have thought he was calling the police. He hurriedly jumped up, hastened out of the house, and down the road he went. Thank God, that tramp never returned. I never forgot that day. I was absolutely a prisoner in my own house.

Asleep in the Barn

After that, the tramps never came into the house to sleep. It did not matter what the weather was like, we could not take another chance. From that time on, we made available an old quilt and horse blanket for these unannounced visitors to wrap up in as they stayed in the barn. Russell always helped them dig a hole in the loose hay, then lined it with newspapers. The man laid down and covered up with blankets and more hay.

These tramps and their stories were not for me. The

193

fear of them set my last nerve on edge. It makes cold shivers run over me just thinking about these past experiences.

The homeless men never left our home without being served a hearty, hot breakfast. Through my fear, deep in my heart I always felt so sorry for them. I had so much compared to these poor souls.

Gasoline Washing Machine

Right before we moved to the Toms farm, Russell bought me a gasoline motor-driven washing machine. My, what a help this was to me! We put the machine out in the wash house since the exhaust pipe needed to be routed outdoors. One day, while doing the laundry, the strings of my apron got caught in the motor as I turned around. The force started to pull me backwards. I grabbed for the window sill and held on for my life. The apron string finally broke and I was set free.

CHAPTER 32

THE GREAT DEPRESSION YEARS

Stock Market Crashes

The Great Depression of 1929 and the 1930s had come. Everyone realized the devastation this brought to the economy. What a crisis!

On October 29, 1929, known as Black Friday, the stock market crashed on Wall Street. It was a disastrous financial collapse. Businesses that had been quick to achieve were now just as quickly folding.

On September 3, 1931, Central Trust closed its doors. Banks all over the country were folding, one after another, but the Myersville Savings Bank stood firm. People who had worked and saved all their lives lost whatever money they possessed as so many savings institutions closed their doors. Millions of workers were unemployed during the depression.

Dry

Not only did the years of 1930-31 bring depression, but they also brought the worst drought to the Middletown Valley I have ever lived through. Every farmer's crops burned from the intense heat. The lack of moisture and rain for over so long a period of time caused the riverbeds to appear as if they were sponged dry.

There was so little water available for our cows to drink that their milk supply nearly dried up. Cows need plenty of water to make milk and there was none; there was no supply that we could have carried to them. We prayed for rain and our hopes were encouraged if the sky so much as looked as if a cloud could form. The days and nights dragged by as we waited for a shower. We wondered what would happen to us if our farming business failed. What would we do?

God always had His plan in effect. He never left us for a moment of time. I know beyond a shadow of a doubt that if we had not put our trust in Divine strength, we never would have made it through those depression years. Every family suffered, not just ours alone. Anxiety was the word of the day! At times, "hope" almost lost its meaning. Why not give up? Because we managed to bring our thoughts in line and count the many blessings we did have to enjoy!

Liberty Car

Mr. Toms, our landlord, often came by the farm to check on how we were doing. Since we were farming on shares, he had an interest in the prosperity of the crops. I remember he drove a Liberty car. It definitely caught my attention when he drove up.

We Need a Farm

Again in 1932, Russell and I discussed our need to purchase a farm of our own. To delay seeking was no longer an option. We needed to get into business for ourselves. Moving in faith of finding this new home, the first of the year we gave George Toms notice that we did not wish to renew

196

our share-farming contract for another year.

We began searching. Time slipped away and we did not find a farm to buy. Not having much time before having to vacate, we met with a dilemma. It was early March 1932. We had no idea where we would go. I spent many sleepless nights. Russell always appeared to be able to fall asleep, but not me. Maybe he was just too worn and tired to stay awake, or maybe he had more faith in the help of our Lord than me. Anyway, I cried myself to sleep more often than not. Come morning, I would look at the faces of my young family and wonder what will happen to them.

We needed a farm large enough for all of us to live on, food to feed us, and money to purchase some necessities just for survival. The problem was big, but it appeared even bigger when I looked into the eyes of these sweet ones. I wondered, if we fail, who might hire the older children, Austin and Doris?

Austin was just about to turn 15 years old. The girls were a couple of years younger. Maybe Pauline could help someone but she looked so young and tiny. No one will ever begin to know the feeling of despair that filled my heart or the amount of prayers I prayed. The time had come when I tried to feed my faith so my doubts would vanish.

God knew and heard our cries for help. Just as He supplied the needs for the children of Israel in their wilderness, so would He supply us in our wilderness.

Wade's Daybook

My brother Wade kept a daybook, or diary, for many years. Some notes in it tell us that Austin, Clyde, Russell, and he attended farm sales together in 1931. No doubt Russell was trying to buy some second-hand farm equipment.

197

Wade recorded wheat selling for 56 cents a bushel, 55 cents a bushel for cattle corn, 14 cents a pound for crackers.

To hire a thrash machine to come to your farm to thrash the wheat kernels from the stalk was 34 cents an hour. Wade writes that he bought twelve pounds of fresh herring fish for one dollar. Gasoline sold for 13 cents a gallon. In 1934, death notices published in the newspapers were free and the obituary cost five cents per line to be printed.

CHAPTER 33

PURCHASING A HOME

Leighter Farm

It was late winter of 1932. The possibility of Russell and me buying a farm seemed bleaker than ever. But you see, we never gave up. I prayed for God's help as the days and nights flew by, and I believed He would help us.

We kept our ears open for any prospective purchase. We liked the appearance of the Lorenzo Leighter farm at Middletown, just from what we saw when driving by. After we learned it was for sale, Russell visited with the Leighters and looked over the land and buildings. For various reasons, he thought the soil would produce good crops, and to be located close to Middletown would be an advantage. The Middletown/Myersville Road (Route 17, north of Middletown) runs through the middle of the farm, but we decided that we would like to purchase this property since it was an attractive homestead.

While many local banks were going "belly-up" due to the Great Depression, we knew it was only by the protection and grace of God that our meager savings were still safe at the Myersville Savings Bank.

Public Auction

On March 17, 1932, the Leighter farm was to be sold at a public auction held on the property. On the thirtieth day of March, we had to move from the Toms farm. The deadline for us moving was upon us, just thirteen days away. That is what I call "cutting it too close."

Desperate to Buy

Most of the local residents knew Russell needed a farm. Fearing folks may think we were desperate to buy, and we were, Russell became concerned that other interested bidders might run the price up on him. So, with his wisdom, he felt his chances of purchasing the farm were better if bids were made by a friend and, hopefully, a stranger to the area.

Russell asked his good friend, David Mong, to come down from Ringold, Pennsylvania, and make the bids and purchase for us that day.

Sold! To Pete Wiles

The morning of the sale, Russell and 15-year-old Austin, drove down to the farm alone since Dave did not arrive in Myersville at the promised time. We feared something must have happened to him. Upon their arrival in Middletown, Russell and Austin looked through the crowd to make sure their friend was not already there.

We had ourselves a predicament. At 12:00 sharp, the farm was to be sold. The auctioneer started to chant. Russell began bidding as the sale had started. Austin recalls he and his dad were standing at the middle post on the bank barn floor. From that spot, they could look out over the crowd and onto Route 17.

Dave had an emergency. Before leaving his place in Ringold, a bull attacked him, pinned him down, and hurt him while doing his morning work. The animal broke Dave's arm and he had to go to the hospital to have the bone set before he could come.

Finally, they spotted Dave walking toward them. Their hearts were leaping with excitement. They saw his broken arm and a few words were quietly exchanged after Dave reached them. Russell, along with Austin, quickly walked away, but Russell whispered as he left his friend, "Buy it at whatever it takes." It took $14,170! The farm was auctioned to David Mong from Ringold on that 17th day of March.

When the auctioneer asked, "Sold to whom?" Dave said, "Sold to Pete Wiles." No one knew who in the world the man was who just spoke, but plenty of people knew the man who owned the name Pete Wiles. Most of Russell's friends referred to him as "Pete." He was so relieved to have succeeded in buying this home. Soon the news of the real owner spread through the crowd.

How faithful the Lord God Almighty had been to Russell and me during this period of extreme necessity. *"The righteous cry and the Lord hearth and delivereth them out of all their troubles." Psalms 34:17*

Dad Was Worried

My dad was worried about what was going to happen to us if we failed to purchase this farm. He was at the sale and, just as soon as he heard the auctioneer "knock off" the bid to Dave, and being certain that Russell was truly the owner, he started to walk back to Myersville to give me the message.

I stayed behind at the Toms farm that day because I could not get away from the little ones. Dad knew what a burden would be lifted from my mind when I learned the good news. I am sure he must have walked briskly, as his heart's desire for his "Girly" had come true. I was sewing Marie a little pink dress when Dad arrived at the door. He was so happy to tell me we had a place of our own to call home.

We had been weary and worn, but new strength and joy came. It is easy to give up, but it takes strong men and women to stand the tests life brings to us. I do not doubt that to be in God's presence brings liberty to the believer from problems and difficulty.

In spite of the inclement weather that day, a crowd of more than six hundred attended the Lorenzo Leighter farm sale. Mr. Leighter had purchased the farm from Jesse O. Bussard.

I have an old article taken from *The Frederick Post*, the daily newspaper. I think you will find it interesting. It is from the files of April 5, 1911:

> Jesse O. Bussard has sold to Lorenzo C. Leighter several tracts of land in Middletown Valley, aggregating about 194 acres, one tract being a farm of 132 acres, the consideration being $15,000.

Ben Clark

Ben Clark, a local bachelor farmer who attended Grossnickle Church of the Brethren, was at the sale that day. He was aware of the financial need we were facing. Talk about pennies from Heaven—Ben walked up to Russell and asked if he would like to borrow some money from him. You know the answer he gave to that question. This was just the kind of help we needed. The remaining amount we owed was borrowed from the Myersville Savings Bank. I will never forget and will forever be so grateful to the Lord God Almighty, our friends Dave Mong, Ben Clark, the Myersville Savings Bank and its president, George Bittle.

Moving In

I had not unpacked all of the boxes from our previous move to the Toms farm. We made do with as few household items as possible since we had not planned to stay at that location for a long time. When the last day of March came, we were ready to go farther south to Middletown, and we were one excited family. In fact, Russell and Austin started to move some farm equipment the next day after the farm was purchased.

Transporting by Wagon

It seemed March was truly "going out like a lion" that year. Blistering winds, rain, and bitter cold was the weather forecast for moving day, and it held true. Heavy rains fell all night. It was difficult to go to sleep thinking that we might be moving in the pouring rain the next day. But, come morning, we were up and hustling about and, yes, it was still raining and cold.

At that time, most of our belongings had to be transported to the new farm by wagon and a four-horse team. It carried our beds, kitchen pots and pans, household furniture, tools, small machinery, and maybe a few treasured items like the rocking rooster and scooter. When looking back, I recall a horse was tied to the back of a wagon and there he followed along to his new home at Middletown. The wind was blowing so strong that the men had a hard time tying the straw ticks on the wagon.

Cattle Drive

Again, as we moved to Middletown, we drove the cattle down Route 17 to our new home. Russell and the men loaded the hogs and calves onto a large farm wagon. It was pulled by the four-horse team and Russell asked my dad to drive. I guess he thought it might be easier on Dad than walking with the cattle down the road. Dad felt he did not know the horses and was reluctant. He hesitated but, upon Russell's insistence, mounted the saddle horse of the team and made ready to start out ahead of the herd.

Small Delay

The men and animals were all assembled and prepared to leave the Myersville farm. With Grandpap on the saddle horse, he gave the command to go. Immediately the horse knew a stranger was mounted, gave a big lunge, and broke a gear. The hame strap broke! Right now, my dad became quite upset. He said to Russell, "You see, there it is. I told you this would happen since the horses aren't used to me." Their keen sense caused them to buck and shake at a strange driver's commands. Anyway, the problem was solved and Grandpap tried again. Then they continued on their way to Middletown.

Our Friends and Family Help

Wade Grossnickel, his son Clyde, John P. Grossnickle, Callie Long, Bruce Palmer, Austin and Russell drove the cattle down Route 17. (Again, I am sure others I cannot recall helped us.) Oliver Hooper, our new neighbor, offered to be at the farm at Middletown that day to head off the cattle into the barnyard when they arrived.

Charlie and Jerry Gaver Moved My Organ

Charlie and Jerry Gaver had an old Plymouth truck and offered to help us move. They agreed to haul my organ down to the farm, and they moved it without a scratch.

Dad bought the organ for me around 1912 when I was a young girl. He purchased it from Mr. George Everhart's Music Store in Frederick. Mr. Everhart had a grown boy, named Mulligan, who helped him around the shop. Dad paid forty dollars for this second-hand organ and stool. He had it delivered to the farm and they brought it in a durrey wagon pulled by two horses. A durrey wagon is a covered wagon, with a bench across the front end. In front, a board hangs out over the top forming a sun visor. I remember Malon Barton coming to Mother and Dad's house to tune the organ. Our daughter, Janice, bought it at our farm sale in 1966.

Electricity

I often wondered if we would ever see "light at the end of the tunnel." We hoped, maybe, just maybe, things would get easier for us soon.

We had electricity in the new house at Middletown. Lights came on with a flick of the switch. How easy can it get? No more lanterns to fill and clean.

The children were fascinated with the light switch. When folks visited our home, the children loved to show how it could be flicked. Most people were already acquainted with switches, but we were certainly excited with the convenience.

Soon after moving to Middletown, we purchased our first electric Maytag washing machine. How little most of us appreciate modern appliances. And to think of the wonderful technology I take for granted today. Often, I think of how these inventions could have helped me if I had them when the children were small!

CHAPTER 34

SOBERING FACTS

Tough Days

Russell and I concluded that we had left tough days behind, but tough days were still ahead for all of us. Every penny had its place and not one could be used foolishly these days. Bills, taxes, and mortgage came as regularly as the sunrise and sunset.

There were happy times with our friends and family, but we always returned to the sobering reality of our debt and the work facing us. The hurt was not looking at our own needs but of those of the children. It gave me that hollow feeling in the pit of my stomach that you get when in despair.

Sometimes it seemed we were "the poor, the poor called poor." We tried to keep the children in decent clothes for school and church, but the "home" clothes hardly met the need.

Shoe Repair

Austin tried to find ways to make his clothing last as long as possible. Once he went to the pigpen and used hog rings to attach the sole back onto the shoe. That did not keep the gravel or moisture out, but at least it helped protect the bottom of his foot! Hog rings are made of heavy gauge wire.

They are pierced through the gristle in the hog's nose to discourage the animal from routing. Hopefully, it hurts the nose while boring into the dirt.

John Wise was the local cobbler and could have repaired the shoes, but that cost money we did not have. No one complained.

No matter how bad things got, we were never hungry, but we did live on very little money. Never did we sit and cry or complain, but we went on with our life making the best of the situation. When I think back over our lives, I remember all the rivers, valleys, and hills my feet have passed over just to get to the top of the mountain. Let me tell you, there was no way for us to succeed without relying on each other and the Lord.

Child's Advice

Doris was about 13 years old. She recalls how she tried to advise her dad when to sell the wheat crop. If she heard anyone say anything about the price of wheat or, if she heard her dad say anything to me about it, she would run to him and say, "Daddy, let's sell the wheat. Then we'll have plenty of money to pay for the farm."

You know she was too young to know anything about prices, but she and the other children talked as if we would be rich if they could just get their daddy to sell the crop immediately. Doris could not understand why he did not listen to her advice. Little did she realize it would have taken many good wheat crops to pay off our debt!

Hail Storm

In the summer of 1932, we had a terrible hailstorm.

First the drought and then the hail came.

This year we had fields of wheat, along with other crops, looking prosperous. Right before the harvest, a storm came and completely wiped out the wheat and ruined most of the other crops. Since the wheat was almost ready to be gathered, the hail knocked the kernels from the stalk to the ground.

What a loss, but every farmer faced the same destruction. Here we were, a struggling young family and we were to the point of wondering what to do next. Many days our eyes were heavy caused by sleepless nights and lack of rest. At times, we felt as if we were "down for the count." I know God sees tomorrow more clearly than I can see today, but the pressure was on. And again, I know it was He alone who carried us through those anxious years.

Chicken House Roof

The chicken house roof was leaking like a sieve and, if not replaced before long, the floor and the building would be ruined. It was useless to try to repair the old one. Somehow, we purchased tin for the roof. When looking back, I wonder how we managed to do that—such lack we were going through. However, we could not give up even if we were momentarily in despair. We must endure no matter what came our way. Believe me, plenty of disaster was aimed right at us.

John Smith Repairs the Roof

John Smith, a wonderful, generous neighbor, came to our farm and, as he promised, put the roof on the chicken house. He took nothing we offered for doing it. Buying this

209

tin was the only thing we could afford to do other than survive that whole year.

I have heard it said that "Christians are like tea bags." The "best" of them comes out when in hot water. Well, Russell and I have been in lots of hot water—truly tested!

My Sweet Niece

My brother Wade's daughter, Beulah, 21 years of age, was a wonderful and attractive girl. She had a great attitude and a love for life. For her, life had purpose! She had a heart of gold. Her willingness to help and do whatever she could for others showed in her daily living. She had worked for us a few years and we loved her. She was a beautiful person.

Beulah became very ill and, not knowing the problem, Wade and Maudie took her to visit the doctor. She was admitted into the Frederick Memorial Hospital and an appendectomy was recommended. Surgery then was not as refined as it is today. It was a dangerous procedure, due to lack of knowledge and experience. Everyone was concerned and afraid. Again, folks were praying for Beulah.

After the surgery, the family knew things were not progressing as rapidly as hoped. She had peritonitis. Beulah's life ended at 2 a.m. on July 4, 1933, short of her marrying and having a family of her own. She never saw her own life reach maturity. What sad days were ahead for Wade, Maudie, and Beulah's sisters and brothers.

How often I have thought of her. Even unto this day I remember her so vividly. The moment of death seems as endless as time, but somehow, we have the strength to get through these storms in our life. *"...Weeping may endure for a night, but joy cometh in the morning." (Psalms 30:5)*

210

CHAPTER 35

OUR HOME

A House Becomes a Home

We loved our Middletown home. The rich soil in the fields showed signs of the bygone Civil War battles. We often came upon bullets, arrows, buttons, and metal parts from horses' gears in the freshly plowed soil. One field had a strong spring. There, between those two little hills and that source of water, an abundance of reminders of heavy battle and its lost have been found.

The old farmhouse was built in 1837. That date is carved into a wooden beam in the attic. The house was used during the Civil War as a hospital. Through the years, the girls and I kept the inside walls papered and painted. A bathroom was added, windows were replaced throughout, and finally, a new kitchen was installed.

From March 1932 to March 1966, we lived in this house. I think of the crisp lace curtains waving at the windows in the warm breeze. So many times I stood and looked from the kitchen door towards the beautiful South Mountain. Here I watched the rainstorms wipe out the view of its peaks. I saw the fields stand in their bounty and again barren after the harvest. Lots of grass passed under my feet while living on this homestead. Home, sweet home, it is!

Pretend Church Services

There is an open stairway in the house. The children held pretend church services on the steps, which became their pews. All of them wanted to preach and lead the song service. Whoever was in the congregation held the dolls. The children saved empty corn flake boxes and used them for purses. Buttons became their money and an old tin plate was used to collect the offering. One of the children always pumped the old organ until he/she was hot, sweaty, and worn-out. Usually, the service ended because someone was sick and tired of listening to the "thoughtless and boring" sermon!

Pants Leg

The Christmas excitement was too much for Russell Jr. this year. It was in the early 1930s and Christmas morning had arrived. Russell Jr. was so excited about going downstairs to see what Santa brought for him. In his haste to dress himself, he got both of his legs in the same pants leg and fell from the top to the bottom of the stairs. Not that I enjoyed seeing him fall, because I know he hurt himself, but times such as these give us some of the treasured moments I still enjoy sharing today at the age of 95.

Death in the Early 1900s

In the early 1900s, when death occurred in the home, the undertaker came to the house to get the body. He placed a crepe on the door. A crepe is black veil or tulle, either draped on or around the door. Some crepes were long sprays of black cloth flowers. It was a sign of mourning.

The body was embalmed, placed in a casket, and

carried in a horse-drawn hearse back to the home. Here in the living room, the body laid in state for three sunrises. Three neighborhood men came to the home of the deceased each night and sat with the corpse until the day of the funeral. The family, tired and worn from stress, went to bed. Around midnight, the neighbors ate food that had been prepared by friends. Each morning, when daylight came, the men went back to their home.

Friends and family members came to the home to visit and express sympathy. On the day of the funeral, again a horse-drawn hearse carried the corpse from the home to the church for graveside services and burial. They determined whether the service would be held in the home or in the church by the number of people expected to attend the funeral.

The coffins were buried in a "rough box" instead of vaults like we use today. This heavy wooden box was placed in the ground before the coffin was lowered. Some folks made their own box.

The Board

When my grandmother (Dad's mother, Salina) died, she was laid out on a broad board. I do not know how the board came into my possession after Salina's death, but we had it. I needed a place to iron, so I sewed blankets around it and used it for a ironing board. I placed it between two chair backs, forming a table.

Years later, I purchased a manufactured ironing board and the "board" sat against the wall in a closet in the farmhouse at Middletown. Some of the children recently admitted that seeing it gave them an eery feeling. They were afraid to open that closet because they knew the board had

213

been used by a dead person.

More From Wade's Daybook

Wade's daybook says that in January 1941 eggs sold for 76 cents a dozen, butter for 20 cents a pound, and gasoline 13 cents a gallon. Banks were paying one-and-a-half percent interest. A five-month-old colt sold for $37.50. Wade bought a pair of pants for $3.50.

Just look at some interest rates today in 1995; not much better!

No Bathroom

The "Saturday night bath" is no joke! When we were living in the houses that did not have bathrooms, we took our baths in a metal washtub in the living room by the chunk stove. And they were definitely not taken every day. I heated the water on the kitchen range and filled the tub by hand. The little ones were always bathed first. Each family member continued to get in line until all had a turn. In the summertime, we heated water in the iron butchering kettle out in the wash house. We had more freedom to splash when we were not in the house.

Frozen Pipes

In the early years of living at Middletown, the pipes in the farmhouse occasionally froze during the wintertime if we had an unusually cold spell. One dark, cold, icy night we had a real problem. It seemed everything that could freeze that night did! Not one drop of water flowed through the pipes in the house.

Spilled Water

We had a spring of fresh running water in the meadow here on the farm. This water was clean so we could consume it. I asked Austin, Doris, Pauline and Russell Jr. to carry some water to the house. They all dressed warmly and off they went out into the cold, icy night. The wind was blowing around every corner. Each took a metal bucket. They lowered them into the spring. The sleet was thick on the ground that night and it was almost impossible to keep their footing. With their buckets filled, they were on their way back to the house.

All at once, Pauline's feet shot out from under her and she fell down in a flash. She landed on the bucket, bent it, and spilled the water. Austin was laughing so hard at the sight of Pauline that he fell too. I knew it was dark and cold, and I hated having to send them back to the spring for more water, but I did.

Dad Never Drove a Car

Because our home was located at Middletown, I seldom visited with my parents back in Ellerton. That could be explained by the fact that so much work had to be done every day on the farm and for my family.

Since my father never owned or operated a car, he would start walking to Middletown to attend the bank directors' meetings. He also visited with us on those days. Folks driving by invariably gave him a ride, either all the way to our house, or at least to Myersville, where he caught the trolley. If he happened not to catch a ride and the conductor saw him walking alongside the road, he stopped the trolley car and picked him up.

Dad came in the morning, ate the noontime meal with us, then walked into Middletown to the bank for the meeting. He loved seeing the children and, of course, his own little girl—the busy mother. I often wished, as the visit ended and the time for him to leave approached, that I could have stopped my work and spent the time just with him. What a shame—we so often miss the "good things" because of the "cares of life."

As I have reached this "ripe old age," I have learned that giving of your time is truly a wonderful and priceless gift. Time is precious when spent with those you love. It is one gift that only you can give.

The Slop Barrel

We raised swine on our farm from 1932 until the last few years before we retired in 1966. Farmers kept a "slop" barrel in the pigpen. It was a large wooden barrel filled with chopped grain and water. This mixture was called mash. When we peeled vegetables or fruits, or if we had any leftovers from the table we were not going to use, we took it to the slop barrel and mixed it in as well. The slop fermented and the mash turned sour. Believe me, the pigs loved it.

Kittens

The pigpen had a half-loft over the top of the building. Austin, Doris, Pauline, and Russell Jr. had gone out to the barrel with some table scraps. Once they entered the pigpen door, they heard kittens crying and decided to investigate. They suspected the noise was coming from the loft. They climbed to the top by putting their feet on the log frame, and then between the cracks of the wooden sides of the building.

All of them made it up except Russell Jr., who was not making headway. He began to fear he was going to be left out and began to cry. Austin and Doris decided they were going to be loyal. They grabbed hold of his arms and began to drag him up. It was going well until, all of a sudden, Russell Jr. slipped from their grips and splashed right down into the slop barrel. Somehow they rescued him and brought him to the house. I took a look at these children, listened to their story, and thought to myself, "Wonders just never cease around here!"

Mumps

Doris and Austin were teenagers when an epidemic of mumps was going around in school. We had not been living at Middletown for very long. When one of the children came down with a childhood disease, we could be assured all of them were going to catch it. Doris heard that rubbing one's neck on a pigpen feeding trough prevented or lessened the severity of mumps.

So, one day she took all the children to the pigpen and gave them the treatment. They each kneeled by the trough at her instructions, and then she made sure their little necks made contact. Austin went along to witness this, laughing and poking fun all the while, but Doris was quite certain she was doing a good deed and paid no attention to him. She had convinced herself no one would get sick. Within days, everyone came down with the mumps, but you can never guess who had the most violent case—Austin!

CHAPTER 36

MOUNTAIN STORIES—HAZARDS

Daddy, the Wagon Rubbers Broke!

Russell drove from Middletown to the Gravel Hill mountain lot to cut wood for the stoves in our home. We were still cooking on the kitchen range. Russell no longer sold logs because it was too far to travel with horse and wagon, and he did not have the time to spare. The farm at Middletown had more acreage and he had more fieldwork to do.

One day, Russell decided he would go to the mountain and cut some wood for the stove. He took Russell Jr. along to help. He was a young boy but he rode the lazy board of the wagon and pushed down on the wagon rubbers (brakes) while going downhill from out of the woods and down Route 17. The brakes were nothing more than blocks of wood that pushed against the steel wheels of the wagon when someone pulled on the big steel lever.

As Russell and Russell Jr. were returning home from the mountain with a heavy load of timber loaded on the wagon, the rubbers broke. They were coming down Bidle's Hill, which is very steep. Russell Jr. managed to jump off and run ahead of the team to the side of the saddle horse his daddy was riding. He shouted to him, "The wagon rubbers broke!" His daddy could not hear what he was trying to convey so he kept shouting back to Russell Jr., "Get on the wagon. Watch the rubbers." The horses' metal shoes, the chains on the gears, and the steel wheels made lots of noise on the cement road. Finally, the look on Russell Jr.'s face told his daddy something was terribly wrong and he listened more carefully.

Russell started pulling back on the line and hollering "Whoa," with a stern and loud tone to his voice. He was able to get the horses to pull the wagon off the road and into the ditch.

Having such a heavy load, they could not continue on without brakes. The weight of the wagon and its load would push on the gears of the team of horses. With so much force, the gears would break and allow the wagon to roll away. There beside the road Russell unhitched the team from the wagon. He and Russell Jr. both came riding home and hooked up another wagon to the horses. Back they went up the road to transfer the load of wood.

Come night, can you imagine how tired these fellows were after being out working all day? Sleeping was seldom a problem unless aches and pains were nulling on us. Everyone worked hard and our bodies were ready for rest by nightfall.

Wildcats

Many residents of the mountain areas surrounding the Middletown Valley can tell you stories of hearing and seeing wildcats. There were times when Russell and our young boys, Austin and Russell Jr., worked into the night on the wood lot. Many times as they traveled down the dark mountainside, they heard the scream of wildcats in the distance. As the shriek came through the night air, it sent cold shivers down their spines and caused the hair on the back of their necks to stand straight up!

The little boys' hearts beat faster as they peered into the woods trying to catch sight of the cat as they passed by each tree. The team of horses hitched to the log wagon pulled to the side, trying to shift away from the noise. They jerked and bucked with fear. Russell knew the children were scared as they pushed closer to him. He told them, "Everything is all right. Those cats are far, far away. They won't hurt us." But the truth was, he hated to hear that cry as well. Perhaps he wondered how close they really were to them. He, too, wished that he and the children were home. Needless to say, this was dangerous work and I feared for their safety when they did not arrive home at the expected time.

CHAPTER 37

OUR FRIENDS

Albert and Bertie Nirkirk

When we first came to Middletown in 1932, Albert and Bertie Nirkirk lived up toward the Myersville end of the farm in the house Paul Routzahn and his wife own today. They stopped in and paid us a visit now and then. They were up in years and drove a gray, rumble seat, Model T Ford. Bert started the car by stooping down in front of the engine and turning the crank. Bertie sat in the driver's seat, giving it gas. When the engine turned over, he ran to the door, and jumped into the car as Bertie quickly slid over to the passenger's side. Off they drove as they waved good-bye to us.

Thinking of this reminds me of how I would hate to count the many times I have waved good-bye to my friends and family. For so many years, I have seen the leaves burst crisp and green from the tree boughs and then within months die and fall to the ground. Time does not wait for any of us!

Would You Like a Ride?

Once Janice was going to the field with a bucket of water for her Dad to drink. Bert was driving up the road and approached Janice as she walked along. He slowed down his

Model T and asked if she would like to ride. Janice thought it was a good idea so she answered, "Yes." The problem was, Bert never brought his car to a complete stop and she had to get in as it was coasting along. When they reached the upper field, Bert only slowed again to let her out. Janice decided after that ride she would rather walk.

Newspaper Article

A newspaper article from *The Middletown Valley Register* on November 18, 1928 reads:

> Albert W. (Bert) Nirkirk, a farmer near Middletown, narrowly escaped being killed by an infuriated bull on the farm of Lorenzo Leighter. Mrs. Nirkirk, who stayed in the car while her husband went to the barn, went to her husband's assistance and was also hurt. Miss Estelle Leighter drove the bull off with a pitchfork.

The local news was truly "local" in those days!

Asbury Hoover

Asbury (Tuck) Hoover, from Wolfsville, was a traveling Witmer Products salesman. He came up the steps and into the house at Middletown whistling, and carrying his basket of products. A chair always sat right inside our kitchen door. There he sat down and began his sales pitch.

He recommended his line of Witmer products: extract, talcum powder, and a liniment named Black Diamond. I always purchased the Black Diamond, since we used it for bruises on the children, cattle, and horses. I shall never forget this jolly man with the snow-white, curly hair, and bright blue eyes.

Not in My Garden!

We had a white wooden picket fence that edged the garden and Route 17. One day, Tuck was in a hurry while driving down the road. He was going too fast. All of a sudden, he lost control of his car.

I was working in the kitchen when I heard a noise. It sounded like a crash. Looking out, I saw Tuck sitting in his car in my well-groomed garden. I opened the back door and said, "Asbury Hoover, what are you doing in my garden?" Tuck replied, with an understated wit, "Lady, that is just what I'd like to know." Tuck's car rammed through the fence and spun and dragged onions, cabbage, and red beets everywhere as he hit the dirt.

Edward and Mary Stevens

Our friends, Edward and Mary Stevens, visited in our home often. I knew Ed from the time I was a little girl. Back in the early 1900s, he was a blacksmith and operated what was known as old man Butcher's Blacksmith Shop in Ellerton. The shop was located just down the road from my home. He was a single man then and lived at my parents' house. They rented him a room and he ate his meals with our family.

Sweet Cider Barrel

In the early- to mid-1900s, most families had a barrel

of sweet cider from which they drank freely. At home, the barrel laid in the yard in the sun until it worked, or fermented, and became vinegar. Then we used it for seasoning and preserving foods.

I had a little bottle with a long string tied to the neck. Ed helped me fix this rig. Each evening, when he came home from the blacksmith shop, he asked me if I would like to go out back and get some sweet cider. He knew I was going to answer, "yes." I would grab my bottle and out of the house we would go. Ed could drop the bottle down through the hole in the top of the barrel, and bring me up the best drink of cider I have ever had. When I lowered my bottle into that barrel, it floated on top. I could not get a drop to go into it.

My brother, George, also loved the taste of sweet cider. He would go to the barn and get a clean wheat straw, put it down into the barrel, and use it for a drinking straw. The wheat stalk was hollow and had plenty of room for liquids to flow through. Here, beside the barrel, George helped himself to the "juice." We had to enjoy drinking it while in season. We had no way to preserve its sweet flavor in those days.

George was pretty clever using the straw, as long as the cider barrel was full. When it got low, his straw did not reach the bottom. But Ed and I had it made. We could still get my bottle filled. You see, Ed made certain I had a long string!

Later, Ed married Mary Alexander and they had two girls and two boys.

Robert Ridgely

The doors of our home have welcomed so many friends. Robert Ridgely was a tall Native American with high cheekbones and a ruddy complexion. He lived alone in Myersville and was also known as "Buffalo Bill." When he was young, he rode a horse, but in the later years of his life, he walked wherever he needed to go. He never owned a car.

After we moved to Middletown, on days Robert came to town to take care of business, he periodically stopped by our house to rest and get a drink of fresh water. Robert was an antique dealer. Occasionally, he walked to my old corner cupboard and there he stood. After admiring my beautiful old dishes for a few minutes, he offered to buy some of them. Of course, I could have used the money, but here were a few treasures I had accumulated through the years. I am sure Robert knew what my answer to his offers would be before I could speak. My wealth was my family and the investment I have made in their lives.

This corner cupboard was made by Uncle Charles Gaver, a wood craftsman. Uncle Charlie married Dad's sister, Effie. One day, he was showing my dad an oak corner cupboard he had just finished constructing. Dad liked it so he purchased it for me. He paid thirteen dollars for it. It still stands in my house and is just as beautiful as ever.

"Vaseline" Basket

Certain dishes caught Robert's eye but no money could have taken them from me. A clear, light green glass "Vaseline" basket that Net Harshman (Nettie Harshman's mother) gave to Marie when she was a little girl was the "charm." He inquired about it most often. He already knew I would never break down and part with it.

I was visiting Net on March 24, 1929, and had taken Marie along. It was her second birthday. When Net learned it was her birthday, she wanted to give her something, so she went to her china cupboard. She carefully took out this glass basket, filled it with red cinnamon berry candies, and gave it to Marie. I could never have sold something given as a gift to my child.

After resting, Robert continued on his way home. I have to admit, it was fun to know that I had something among my meager household items that someone admired and wanted.

Robert's Sunday Ride

On Sundays, we often gave Robert Ridgely a ride in the car from the Grossnickle Church to his home in Myersville. Our car was already packed with people but we "double-decked" and Robert sat on the edge of the back seat. The children were quiet and, after a few minutes, he would look at them and say, "Don't everyone talk at once." This broke the silence and made them giggle.

Edison Bere

On our way to church on Sunday mornings in the early- to mid-1930s, Edison Bere and his mother were sometimes walking along the side of the road. They lived across the Middle Creek in a log cabin. We stopped since we knew they were also headed to church. Edison stood on the running board. Mother Bere somehow always managed to squeeze into the car. She was a tiny woman and wore a little dark hat with a bunch of artificial bright red cherries attached to the band. Janice was a tiny girl and always reached for those cherries. I had to really watch she did not make a grab while I was looking elsewhere. We were all packed so close together.

228

Mr. Sharrer

Door-to-door salesmen were popular from the 1930s to 1950s. Mr. Sharrer, who lived in Woodsboro, Maryland, stopped by regularly to sell me his products. Rosebud and Cloverine Salve were his popular items. He carried his small line of merchandise in a little black leather bag. I most often bought a little tin box of salve since it seemed useful to have in the medicine cabinet.

Mr. Sharrer needed a place to stay overnight. Since he walked his sales route, he routinely asked if we could give him a room and a few meals. There were no nearby motels, restaurants, or fast-food chains, and it was too far to return to his home each evening. I had to cook for my family so I accommodated him most often. It seemed all the peddlers wanted to eat and stay all night at our house.

"Home Comfort"

The "Home Comfort" is the old brand name of a coal and wood-burning kitchen range. Mr. Lane was a supervisor in his door-to-door Home Comfort Sales Company. When he was working near our house, he stopped in to board with us. Often joining him were at least one or two younger men who were trainees.

The Home Comfort salesmen stayed with us while living at Middlepoint, Myersville, and Middletown. They found us no matter where we moved. Mr. Lane drove a little-featured driving horse and buggy. They carried a small-scale range that was used to give demonstrations.

Most of the time, Mr. Lane paid me fifty cents for a breakfast. A bargain, I would say, for ham, eggs, potatoes, toast, plus the extras I served. We treated people right.

Gear Up the Horse

Mr. Lane taught the young men in his company how to gear the horse and hitch him to the buggy. This was part of the training. One day, it was Mr. Michael's, the young trainee, turn to demonstrate what he had learned. Due to his lack of experience and knowledge, he decided to put the crupper, that goes in back of the tail, up around the horse's head. At the expense of Mr. Michael, Mr. Lane had himself a good belly-shaking laugh that morning.

Apple Fights

On one occasion, the salesmen were waiting for me to serve supper. The two of them walked out into the yard and under the green apple tree. One picked up a summer apple and, with a wind-up of his pitching arm, threw it at his partner. It was a direct and hard hit. That was all it took and the fight was on. Those guys had the green apples flying, hitting one another as they yelled, but neither one backed off.

Reverend Irving Stottlemyer and Annie

For many years, Reverend Irving (Eb) Stottlemyer and his wife, Annie, pastored at the Grossnickle Church of the Brethren. He preached hellfire and brimstone, but also the love and goodness of God. Solid as a rock was the Reverend. He was a very tall, thin man with a meekness about his personality. Annie was jolly and a happy soul. Occasionally, we invited them to our house for dinner. While eating, once in awhile, someone in the family would try to "cut a shine or two" and get punished, even though they were all warned to be on their "good behavior."

CHAPTER 38

MORE FAMILY NEWS

Stillborn Daughter

The next little one to come to us was another daughter. This baby girl was born March 14, 1934; she was stillborn. Our hearts were broken again. It did not matter how many children came, we always had plenty of love for another. The only shortage for me was time.

Cal and Lola Gladhill

We made another trip to the graveyard on that lonely, still hill. Calvin and Lola Gladhill were the funeral directors in Middletown. Lola heard the news from Dr. J. Elmer Harp and came out to the farm. As she entered the house, she carried a blanket draped across her arm to wrap the baby in. She sat in a chair she pulled close to my bed, and in her soft, soothing voice she tried to comfort me. Lola asked me to please get well. She said that she and her husband would put the little one to rest. She told me Cal was making a wooden box or casket to bury the baby in, and we did not need to worry about anything. You cannot image how kind she was. She was simply a wonderful lady and I will never forget her.

The death was hard for us. The heartache was worse when we had to explain it to our young family.

Burial

Austin was about seventeen years old, and much too young to assist in the burial of his little sister. But he was willing to do whatever he could to help. The next day, Cal came by our house to pick up Austin, and together with the baby, they rode in Cal's car to the top of the silent hill at the Grossnickle Church of the Brethren Cemetery. Here the two dug a small grave. They laid our precious little daughter and sister to rest.

Dad Dies

So much happened from day to day and from year to year. In late March 1935, I was very ill and Dr. Elmer Harp came on a house call. The illness caused my face to turn a fiery red. I looked a sight and felt even worse. The stress of my family and life itself was taking its toll on me.

Dr. Harp left our home in Middletown that day and drove to Ellerton to my parents' house to visit my dad. The doctor found him critically ill. While at his bedside, Dad passed into eternity that Friday morning, March 29, 1935, at 11:30. Dr. Harp stopped at our house again that day on his way from Ellerton back to Middletown. He told me Dad had died. I was feeling so poorly and was not able to attend the funeral. Instead, Russell took me home to visit, as Dad was lying in state there. It was a sad time for me. I loved Dad with all my heart—I was his "Girly."

Dad's Funeral

My dad, Charles Webster Grossnickel, was 76 years old when he died. He was born on December 9, 1858. My mother, as well as all four of their children, were still living. His sisters, Lee Gaver and Effie Gaver, and two brothers, John D. Grossnickel and Harry M. Grossnickel, remained. He had been a member of the Old German Baptist Church in Waynesboro, Pennsylvania. The Old German Baptist Church was also known as the "Price House." The funeral services were held in the meeting house of the Grossnickle Church of the Brethren. Elders D.S. Flohr, Charles N. Freshour and Irving Stottlemyer conducted the service. More than 800 people attended. I truly wish I could have been there, too!

Regean Phyllis is Born

Regean Phyllis was born March 18, 1936. She arrived in the early morning hours. This March had been especially wet and stormy. We had days of rain, and the Potomac River, at Harpers Ferry, West Virginia, had risen out of its banks and caused severe flooding. An old article from *The Frederick Post* stated that the river peaked at 32 feet above its normal level at Brunswick. The bridge between Maryland and Virginia on U.S. 340 at Harpers Ferry was wrecked and swept away by the swift water. The Brunswick railroads were flooded. Water almost touched the eaves of the railroad station. The Point of Rocks area was hard hit by the flood. Approximately two hundred people were temporarily driven out of their homes. Austin and Russell drove down to Brunswick to witness the high waters. They came home and told us that they saw a straw stack with a pitchfork stuck into it going down the river. They saw drowned hogs and cattle floating downstream in the swift water. Small buildings and all kinds of debris were swiftly washed away.

233

No TV

The evenings were long on the farm during the winter. There was no TV and it was not until 1936 that we purchased a radio for home entertainment.

Beauty Parlor

Russell loved to have his hair combed. In the evening, he coaxed the children to sit on his shoulders or on the back of his easy chair, and then he would pass them a comb. He offered to pay them. They bargained until they struck a deal. The children borrowed the older girls' curlers and bobby pins to give him a "professional" hairdo. Each child had their money in a cup in the corner cupboard. It seemed that cupboard was the "keeper of our treasures."

Out on the Town

When Austin was a teenager, he enjoyed going into Middletown on Saturday nights. There he met his friend, Grayson Wise, and the two sat on a bench outside Main's Ice Cream Parlor. They chatted and either treated themselves to ice cream from Main's parlor, or they walked down the street to Jimmy Koogle's Soda Fountain, where they had a cola float. Roy Bussard worked at the fountain and served the customers.

Summer Concert

The Middletown Band performed summer concerts on Saturday evenings in town. They blocked what is now Alternate 40, near the Middletown Lutheran Church, and the band members were seated in the middle of the street as they gave the concert.

The country life was quiet and much different from today's hustle and bustle. At the present time, there is so much for the young people to do outside the home, that some forget they could have a home life.

Yvonne Fay is Born

Our last daughter, Yvonne Fay, was born May 5, 1938. She arrived early in the morning and by noontime I was very ill. I was faint, and Doris, who was caring for me, called for Dr. J. Elmer Harp to make a house call. Russell and Austin were in the field planting corn. That morning, the wind was blowing hard and it was cold with more snow than just flurries in the air. From the field, Russell saw the doctor's car coming in the driveway. He suspected something was going wrong. He left Austin with the team of horses and corn planter, and came running to the house.

Get the Clothes Basket

Dr. Harp asked Doris to get a basket to put the baby in. He was afraid if Yvonne remained in bed with me, I would roll on her because of the medication I had been given. Doris brought one of Charles Phleeger's willow clothes baskets. She lined it with a pillow and blankets. Carefully, she placed the baby in the basket, hoping she would stop crying. But when she continued to cry and the doctor was gone, I asked Doris to put her back into my bed. As soon as she got warm she fell fast asleep.

The birth had not been easy and had taken its toll on me. I remember as the doctor left that day he said to Russell,

"Take good care of her, she is a sick lady."

Let's Pray

Austin did not stay in the field. The weather was turning for the worse, and he, too, was wondering what was happening in the house. He brought the team and corn planter to the barn. He removed the gears from the horses. His dad consistently put on, in order, each part of the horses' gears and expected them to be taken off in the same fashion. Today, nothing seemed to matter but getting those gears on the knob in the barn behind the horse stalls. Mom was sick and there was a new baby sister in the house.

Austin hurried from the barn to the kitchen, grabbed Doris by the hand, and beckoned all the children to come into the parlor. The children were very frightened and alarmed. They were never allowed in the parlor room without me and now their brother said they were going there to pray.

With a little time and rest I did get well. I was so thankful to be able to care for my family again.

My Babies

A few years ago, Yvonne brought home the sweater and cap she wore as a baby. Upon seeing the set again, it brought back so many memories. As I held it in my hands, I kissed that little cap and wept as I thought of the many times I had held my sweet little ones in my arms. But to think I have lived to see my great-great grandchildren is indeed a blessing from God. I have been granted so many privileges over my lifetime. Without a doubt, God's hand has been protecting me. He has shielded me from so much pain, worry and grief.

CHAPTER 39

DAYS AT THE MIDDLETOWN FARM

Peanuts and Bananas!

Periodically, Austin drove Doris, Pauline, and me to Frederick to shop. He made certain we knew where he parked the car. Then he would go buy himself bananas and peanuts in the shell. This was before littering laws were in effect. He sat in the car dumping his rinds and shells to the street as he enjoyed his treat. Because horses traveled through town, a man with a horse-drawn, two-wheeled cart was hired to clean up the manure. He also picked up the other trash on the street with his shovel and brush.

By the time the girls and I returned, we found it not to be a surprise that Austin had enjoyed himself. And he definitely was not suffering from hunger.

One Hot Fire!

One day, Russell Jr. stayed home to help his dad haul manure from the stables while we shopped. I asked him to keep wood on the fire in the kitchen stove and instructed him not to let it burn out. While helping to load the manure spreader, his father also asked him to be sure to open the gate when he returned to the barnyard after going to the field to spread the manure.

237

They were working along when, suddenly, his dad reminded Russell Jr. to check the fire. He ran to the house and found it nearly burned out. Russell Jr.'s first idea was to hurry to the pantry for the kerosene can. And so he did, after pushing more wood into the firebox. Then he turned the can up and poured a drenching amount of kerosene onto the wood and hot coals. Instantly, a minor explosion occurred. The force blew the lids off the cast-iron kitchen range and he had a leaping, ripping, hot fire on his hands.

All of a sudden, Russell Jr. heard the noise from the steel-wheeled manure spreader and the horses' iron shoes. Then he remembered his dad's command, "Be sure to be at the gate. You need to open it for me." Russell Jr. did not know what to do first. He decided to stay by the stove. He made a good choice! The oil burned quickly and things came under control. Children living on the farm learned to handle responsibility early in their young lives.

Doing the Laundry

One day, Pauline was doing the laundry. We starched the dress shirts with a boiled flour and water mixture we made. When the laundry was finished, we disposed of the mixture.

A yellow stray cat that had been appearing at the wash house door every laundry day showed up just as Pauline was pouring the starch out. The cat got in the way and got drenched. His fur stood up over his body for days.

The Skunk

Day after day, we noticed a skunk coming and going as it pleased, in and out of the runoff drain pipe that ran under the wash house, and out the other side of the building. By taking the shortcut, the skunk discovered he could eliminate crawling underneath the fence to get to the meadow. We were all afraid of taking it by surprise and getting sprayed.

Russell Jr., now a teenager, decided he was going to catch the skunk. Since work was slow around the farm this damp day, he waited for the skunk to make his daily show.

Hold the Bag!

Meanwhile, Russell Jr. coaxed Doris to be his accomplice. He needed someone to hold open a burlap sack "to bag" the skunk after he caught it. He told her it was safe since he was going to hold its tail up, thus making the skunk defenseless. Doris agreed to help.

At last, seeing the skunk coming out the drain, Russell Jr. bent low from behind the pipe's opening and caught him by the tail. He knew what he was going to do with his catch. "Open the sack," he called to Doris. In the excitement, and without much thought about what was going to happen when he let go, hurriedly Doris helped him with the bag. When the skunk hit the bottom, it gave its revenge, and, oh, what "sweet revenge" it was.

With the skunk in the sack, Russell Jr. opened the gate by the woodshed and ran into the meadow. Behind the privy stood a peach tree. Here he tied the "bagged skunk" from a limb to wait for the junk dealer. I was upset that they had messed around with the skunk, and I did not find the tree an appropriate "waiting cell." After all, it was too close to the outhouse. I insisted Russell Jr. move him.

Russell Jr. had planned to sell the fur and hide. He had talked with our neighbors, the Adams boys, and now he knew the prices: A skunk hide brought seventy-five cents to two dollars; and a "number one" hide had just a little dot of white on top the head and was worth two dollars. A "number four" was completely white down its back and was of less value. Some farmers caught the skunks, threw them in a pit or dried up cistern, and sold them to the junk dealer alive.

Since Russell Jr. had not thoroughly planned this act, he and Doris ended up in big trouble. Russell Jr. had discussed with the boys the "ins and outs" of the trade, but somewhere he missed the odor issue! They scrubbed and bathed but with little results. Even the lye soap did not help! After washing their clothes and finding they still smelled of skunk, they hung them on the clothesline to air.

The Milk Inspector

The excitement was about over and here came the milk inspector to make an unannounced check on the dairy that same day. He routinely stopped to check that all health rules were being followed. The wash house and dairy was a duplex building. Really, it is a wonder the man stayed around to do his job. With the stench of skunk and the sight on the line, I often wondered if he figured out what had happened. For days, the air anywhere near the farm reeked with the odor. And the "brave ones" could be whiffed long before they ever appeared in front of you.

Within a couple of days, the junk dealer came and Russell Jr. made the sale he had so earned. He collected ninety cents for the hide.

Solitary Confinement

There were other students at school who also tried their hand at the trade. Those who came to class with the

240

"scent" were escorted to the furnace room for the day. They did their lessons in solitary confinement, unless some other student in the classroom had also recently been on a "wild hunt." Often, a few students showed up for class on the same day wearing the identical fragrance!

The Weasel

Russell Jr. decided trapping was a fairly easy method to earn himself some cash, so he set three traps down along the branch in the hollow by the Coblentz farm. He checked every day in hopes of being successful. One day he caught a weasel. Now this critter was odorless! The weasel was a nasty one and was not going to give up even if he was captured. It was ready and willing to fight for his freedom. The electric or telephone company workmen were along the road working on the lines and they noticed the boy had been successful. One of the workmen saw the struggle between "man and beast" and came to the branch to help. He killed it. Again, Russell Jr. anxiously awaited for the junk man to return so he could sell the fur and hide.

CHAPTER 40

THE BLACKSMITH

"Black Johnny"

We farmed with workhorses until the early 1950s, when Russell purchased our first Farmall tractor from H. B. Duvall's farm equipment establishment in Frederick. Over the years, Russell had repeatedly made the comment, "No tractor wheels will ever press down the soil on this farm while I own it." But time changed things.

The workhorses' feet required to be shod with the proper steel shoes. This task was done for Russell by a blacksmith named "Black Johnny." I say the name affectionately. He was a well-known man and was kind hearted. His niece, a single lady, was addressed as Mae Johnny. She was heavyset, friendly, and wore a big smile on her face. They drove up the road in their little black Ford pickup and parked it under a shade tree beside our blacksmith shop.

The Blacksmith Shop

The shop was a little white weatherboard and log building with a red tin roof. It had large black wrought iron hinges on the wide door. It latched with a metal hasp and a wooden pin through the loop. The building sat close to the

243

road.

Its contents were the same as every farmer's blacksmith shop: an anvil, hammers, forge, coal for fueling the forge, and a pile of "junk." The drill press was fastened to the right side of the log frame as you entered the building. A bull's horn was mounted on the left side. The building had a sod or dirt floor, and the interior, as a rule, was messy. Once every year or so on a rainy day, Russell cleaned. No—maybe he just moved things from one side of the building to the other.

Tie the Bull

Sometimes in the summer, if the grass in the pasture fields was low, Russell tied the bull by a chain and the ring in his nose to a heavy steel stake that had been driven deep into the ground near the old blacksmith shop. Here the bull grazed for the day. He preferred to be left alone and, since he could not be trusted, we had to keep our distance when passing by him.

Johnny would begin the preparation in the blacksmith shop. As he started a hot fire in the hearth, Russell headed for the barn to bring the horses, one at a time, for their new shoes.

There was a large tree that stood just to the side of the shop door. On hot summer days, Johnny tried to stand in its shade while he worked. He wore a heavy leather apron and held the horse's foot between his legs, just about at his knees, as he nailed the shoe to the hoof. Once in awhile, the horse might try to get away, but most of the time it was content as Johnny worked. The children liked to watch him but we preferred they did not go near the shop. We were afraid they might burn themselves on the forge or, we thought, perhaps a horse may try to break away or kick them.

244

Mae Johnny

When the blacksmith arrived at the farm, Mae Johnny got out of the truck and slowly made her way to the house to pay me a visit. Of course, I could not afford to take the time to sit down and talk but I pulled a chair close by for her to rest, and we chatted while I continued along preparing the meal.

Mae liked to visit and she was treated with the greatest respect. She knew she and her uncle would be invited to stay for the meal. I did not mind the company for dinner and they took their places around the farmhouse table with the rest of our family. Russell and I always felt if a man was good enough to work for us, he was good enough to eat at our table!

This was during the days when black and white folks did not share the same table. This was never the case at our house—race did not matter. God loves all of us! Russell and I each sat at the ends of the table. He always seated whomever was working for him on his left side. He made certain this person was served and felt welcome to eat plenty. Russell believed if you were going to work you need a full tummy. The children sat to his right on a high bench so they could reach the table. We all ate together.

When I asked Mae if she would like another serving, she often answered, "Oh my, Mrs. Wiles, I can't eat it now."

When the meal was over, I cleared the table. I packed anything I thought they might enjoy reheated for another meal. Mae was my friend and I enjoyed giving to her. She appreciated my food, and always made a nice comment.

Now my family was also used to eating leftovers, but I had learned that to share not only gave me satisfaction at the time, but also proved the Word of God. *"Give, and it shall be given unto you; good measure, pressed down and shaken together, and running over, shall men give into your bosom. For with the same measure that ye mete withal it shall be measured to you again." (Luke 6:38)*

Scrap Iron

A junk dealer from Frederick came by the farm a couple of times a year to buy old scrap iron. When Russell accumulated a pile of broken plow points, used machinery parts, and old horseshoes, the dealer came, weighed it, and bought it. He also bought clean rags. I saved the "remains" of worn-out clothes until I filled a burlap bag. When we first moved to Middletown, the junk dealer came to the door singing or humming softly this little tune: "Any rags, any bones, any old gum shoes."

Dead Animals

A man from a business establishment in Frederick came to the farms to remove our horses, bulls, and cows that died. The animals were processed for fertilizer. There was no charge for pickup, and they gave us a box of soap powder with each visit.

CHAPTER 41

WORLD WAR II

The War Days

Now I know that war has always been a story to be told from the homes of most Americans. In fact, few homes have been missed by the sting of death and the lonely days and nights spent worrying over loved ones' safety and well being. War is so cruel. It is a thief that robs a nation and its people. Many families around our home suffered the loss of sons, brothers, and husbands to battle and strife.

None of our sons were called into the military, but three of our sons-in-law served: Janice's husband, W. Kenneth Hawkins Sr., during peacetime; Yvonne's husband, Darius Georg, served in the Korean Conflict; and Doris' husband, Ralph Grossnickle, during World War II. All served in the U.S. Army.

Ralph U. Grossnickle

Ralph U. Grossnickle was a very special young man to Russell and me. Ralph enlisted in the U.S. Army and spent three years in the field artillery at Fort Hoyle in Baltimore.

Ralph returned home from serving that tour on April 3, 1941, and soon after, started dating Doris. In a short time, he knew he was going to serve again since he was drafted back in the U.S. Army.   Our country was at war—World War II.

Tears

I shall never forget the day Ralph left to return to Fort Bragg, North Carolina. It was on Good Friday. An hour or so before leaving, he, his sweetheart Doris, Pauline, Russell Jr., Marie, Janice, Regean, Yvonne, Russell and I gathered in the living room of our old farmhouse. The walls of that room could tell of so many happy times together, but now the air itself was filled with sadness. Nothing like this had ever been experienced in our home. Ralph was not our son-in-law yet, but we thought of him as a son and we loved him. He and Doris were planning to marry when he returned from the war. Not much was being said by any of us that morning except by the youngest of our children at that time.

Yvonne, who was about four years old, was busy going from lap to lap asking everyone, "Why are you crying?" She remembers Ralph picking her up, hugging her closely, and telling her he would give her some coins if she would promise to stop asking that question. Yvonne agreed to stop and he gave her the money. Several quarters was a lot of money then. To keep Yvonne from losing them, before Ralph left, he carried her to the corner china cupboard, opened one of the big glass doors, and helped her tiny hand deposit the quarters into a small antique crystal saltcellar (salt cup). I wondered what he was thinking as he held this tiny one there?

The Dreaded Moment

The minutes left to spend together were rushing away like water spilling over a dam. Tears were flowing down our cheeks. Finally, that dreaded moment had come, and it was now time for Ralph to leave that farmhouse and his sweetheart. Must he really leave again, we thought?

Drive to Frederick

Russell Jr. pulled our 1940 brown Pontiac out from the garage and parked it in the driveway ready to take Ralph to the National Guard Armory in Frederick. From the armory he departed along with another hometown young man, Austin Kuhn, from Wolfsville. From Frederick, the U.S. Army provided transportation to Fort Bragg, North Carolina. He left North Carolina with a group of soldiers to go to Shreveport, Louisiana, and then on to Muskoogee, Oklahoma. Then he went back to New York to the Port of Embarkation, and from there, overseas. Most of the soldiers traveled to foreign soil by ship. He served in North Africa, Italy, and in the PO Valley.

Never Looked Back

Russell Jr. can never explain the long drive that short eight-mile trip to Frederick became that day. Ralph constantly stared from the passenger's front-seat side window as they drove. It was as if he was taking in every last memory of the Middletown Valley he could catch and store in his mind. When they drove up in front of the armory, and almost before Russell Jr. had completely stopped the car, Ralph quickly opened the door and jumped out. Without saying a word, he briskly walked toward the building showing only the wave of his hand. Without so much as a glance backwards over his shoulder, he entered the building and disappeared out of sight.

No doubt many American hearts were aching as these brave soldiers left their families and loved ones to journey to foreign soil. What a waste war brings to mankind. It shows no respect to the rich or the poor. The young and old wept due to the emptiness in their hearts created by the battle.

Waiting for News

It was difficult to keep our minds on what we were doing in the days that followed Ralph's leaving home. Every day, we listened faithfully to the news on the radio in hopes of hearing that some miracle to end this war would be announced. All interest and attention was on Europe, Africa, and Asia.

V-Mail Letters

Time passed slowly as everyone anxiously awaited the daily U.S. Mail delivery. It seemed Doris received either no letter for weeks or a handful of letters in one day. Between times, we worried.

The letters were called V-mail letters. Each was microfilmed and scanned by the U.S. Military to avoid any leak of secrets that might damage the security of the United States. Now the battle and most details are viewed on television in our homes. Sometimes I wonder if our nation has security today.

Some letters were so vague by the time they had been censored that they made very little sense to us. But, we tried to tell ourselves, at least a note means he is still alive and able to write. It remained a fact, however, that he was constantly in immediate danger. The war was the first thing that came to our minds at the dawn of each day. From the beginning to end, we put our faith and trust in the Lord for protection of our soldiers and our country.

Newspaper Article

I have a local newspaper article from *The Frederick Post* from the World War II days, which reads as follows:

> With 5th In Italy: Cpl. Ralph U. Grossnickle, son of Upton Grossnickle, Myersville, Maryland, Route 1, is a wireman with the 173rd Field Artillery Battalion of the Fifth Army in Italy, according to an announcement from the Fifth Army headquarters. This outfit recently completed its 400th day in combat and has fired 110,000 rounds into German positions on the Italian front.

There were no sophisticated weapons used to fight this war!

Air Raids—Blackouts

World War II brought air raids, rations, death, and more worry and fear than one could imagine. The radio warnings of air raid alerts were often. The smaller children were frightened by the sound of the whistle warning us of a "blackout."

A "blackout" was a period of time at night when all lights were turned off or concealed so no light would be visible to enemy air raiders, if they were in the sky. Often, during the blackouts, we heard airplanes flying low over the buildings checking if people were obeying the "lights out"

251

rule. The noise always sent a hush and a chill over us. We had no way of knowing for sure if it was friend or enemy in the plane.

Russell, the children, and I always sat in the living room during the blackouts. I pulled the dark green shades and tacked a heavy dark comforter up to the farmhouse windows to ensure no light could be seen from the outside. Then I lit a small candle and cuddled the little ones close to me. They were so afraid, and so was I! We all were extremely quiet. I prayed for the lost, the sick, and the safety of the world. Such a time of concern and so little I could do but continue to pray.

The Great Depression years had flattened the economy. Now with World War II raging, the manufacturing business was stimulated to new growth. Business was booming!

Running Home

Janice was attending the Middletown Elementary School during the World War II years. The school required practice air raids for their students. The children were instructed to run home as quickly as possible and then return to school.

Janice was out of breath and excited, with a bit of fear in her voice, as she entered the farmhouse kitchen door. She tried to tell us what was going on.

She remembers how concerned she was that Mr. and Mrs. Dodd would be on the porch or that Oliver and Tissie Hooper might be working in the garden when she ran home during a raid. They always stopped the children to ask how their parents were doing. Janice was afraid this would slow her down. She knew for sure that they were not aware of the crisis she was in and that this was not the time for them to be asking questions. She was on a "mission!"

Because Janice made it home and back to school so quickly, the teacher doubted that she had come all the way. After convincing her she *had* made the complete journey, the teacher queried the students from down in the Canyon. The Canyon was down by the Gladhill Furniture Store at the lower end of Middletown. She asked the other students, "Where were you fooling around?"

At school, the children practiced taking cover under their desks should sudden disaster strike. I believe it was God's protection that kept the fighting off the soil of our homeland.

Because the farm was located less than one mile from the school, our children were not permitted to ride the county public school bus. However, it was too far for them to walk in cold, rainy, winter weather, so we drove them to school much of the time. During these war years, we were still farming with horses so we did not need to conserve gas for a tractor.

Lloyd Stine's Jitney

When the gas shortage became more severe, Lloyd Stine drove his family and our children to school. He lived nearby. Lloyd drove an old Ford panel truck. He installed seats for the children; they called it the "jitney."

Milk Truck

Gerald Kline, Frank Brandenberg, Asa Harshman, and Paul Harshman were milk truck drivers who picked up our milk cans and delivered them to the commercial dairy. Sometimes Gerald offered Marie and Janice a ride to school in the truck. The steel milk cans held ten gallons and were hard to lift up and out from the milk cooler, which was approximately three to four feet deep. It was a nasty job in the winter, as their clothing got soaked from the cold water dripping off the cans. These milk coolers were large tanks filled with water that was cooled with an electric cooling unit.

The early, old-fashioned milk cooler was also a metal chest-type box, and it had a compartment on both sides which held fifty-pound cakes of ice. This was anything but convenient since we had to go to Middletown to buy the ice every day.

Coupon Books

Coupon books for rationed items were given out by the government to each family by a fixed portion. The amount of coupons distributed to each household to buy sugar, shoes, tires, gas, chewing gum, and rubber shoes was established by the number of dependents in each household.

Dr. J. Elmer Harp exchanged his sugar and shoe coupons with us for our tire coupons. He needed the tires for traveling to the hospital and making house calls, and we always needed shoes for someone.

During the war years, some shoes were manufactured from a paper and cloth fiber. These were not rationed since no rubber was used to make them. We bought them for the children. They did not wear well, but the little ones outgrew shoes quickly anyway.

Sunday Dinner

Each Sunday after church I invited our married children to bring their families and come along home for dinner. I needed sugar for cakes and pies, so our "coupon swap" with Dr. Harp helped both of us.

Never was a crumb of cake wasted. Pauline's husband, Carroll Grossnickle, enjoyed the crumbs that accumulated on the cake plate as each person removed their slice. No one ever noticed them. But I fondly remember him gathering these broken bits of cake and icing onto his plate. Families were taught not to waste anything in those days.

Who's Wearing My Apron?

A sun parlor joined the back of the kitchen and living room at the farmhouse. We used it as our dining room. I can still envision Carroll taking one of my aprons that hung on a hook in the wall behind the back door. He would smile as he put it on each Sunday, wearing it during the meal to protect his dress clothing. What love and happy times were exchanged around the table that seated fourteen or more people. Here, each Sunday, Doris shared the news received from Ralph, who was still away at war.

Ralph is Coming Home

In late summer 1945, Doris heard Ralph would be coming home after serving another three years in the Army. We all tried not to get our hopes too high until we actually saw him home on American soil. So much could happen. Finally, on August 12, 1945, he arrived. What a happy day!

Brush With Death

Ralph told us about some of the daily incidents where he brushed alongside death. He found shrapnel beside his bunk upon awaking after a few hours of rest. He was so fortunate to come home carrying that metal in his suitcase, and not imbedded in his body. He and Doris were married seventeen days later on August 29, 1945, her birthday.

I remember our hometown boys coming back to the states with their war brides. Young men from the Grossnickle Church came to the service on Sunday mornings in their uniforms, walking with their sweethearts close by their side. These young men had somehow aged while away from home. They had no doubt attached a new value on life! I will never forget the local men we knew who lost their lives. Their families were heartbroken and I could not help but let those sad thoughts keep returning to mind. I too had strong feelings about war—just like Grandpap Leatherman had during the Civil War. I hated the bloodshed and the devastation it caused.

During World War II, Americans planted vegetable and flower gardens in a "V" shape. "V" for victory! Indeed it was a victory if you served our country and came home alive.

CHAPTER 42

ARMY WORMS

Invasion of Army Worms

In the mid-1940s, the army worms traveled across the Middletown Valley. These worms were from the caterpillar family. The larvae got their name because they had a habit of traveling from field to field in a "host" or "army."

When the news of the outbreak came, many farmers dug ditches or a trench around their crops, and covered that fresh soil with Paris Green and lime in the hope that the chemicals would kill the worms as they crawled through it. But the volume of worms was so great, there was no control. So many worms were smashed by cars on Route 17 along our farm, that the road was black with debris. They created a putrid odor.

Crops Lost

We had a full-grown barley crop and the worms cut it to the ground as they crossed the fields. The whole crop was lost. Russell cut the hay crop early in order to salvage whatever was possible. As we brought the crops in, additional worms were carried into the barn. They were already so thick on the floor that we could not walk without squashing them under our shoes. I tell you, it was worm next

257

to worm. When we looked across the wooden barn floor, there were so many worms crawling that it looked like the waves of the ocean. It is hard to conceive this thought without being a witness. I have never seen anything like it before or since.

Heat in the Barn

The volume of worms was so great it created a tremendous amount of heat in the barn. Russell was concerned that this condition would cause a spontaneous combustion. Long after we retired for the night, he sat by our bedroom window looking out into the dark towards the barn. He would say to me, "I tell you that barn is hot." There was a long moment of silence and then he repeated those same words dozens of times. Both of us were upset and had very little rest or sleep for a few nights.

As the Army worms destroyed the vegetation in their path, they traveled to the next neighbor's fields. What destruction! One might think of Pharaoh and the plagues.

CHAPTER 43

ELEVENTH BABY IS BORN

Thomas Mitchell is Born

Seven years following the birth of our tenth child, Thomas Mitchell was born. The thirteen day of March 1945, brought us our ninth living child and third son. What a surprise! I suggested to Dr. Harp, that since I was 45 years old, perhaps I should go to the hospital for the delivery. He smiled and remarked, "You will only get the baby into the world and you will want to go home right away. You might as well stay there."

So this baby was also born at home. Upon his arrival, all the children wanted to hold him and everyone was keeping track of who had held him last. By now, the family was helping me so much that I could afford to hold this baby myself. So often, as I sat in the rocking chair by the kitchen window rocking him to sleep, I wondered if I would live to see him grow up. I have not only been blessed to live to see him grow up, but married, and have grown children of his own.

Derr's Grocery Store

After we moved to Middletown, about a week before Christmas, Russell went into town to Derr's Grocery Store and purchased "pounds" of Christmas candy. All of us eagerly awaited his return so we could sample the varieties. He sat the big box of candy bags on the kitchen table and we allowed all the children to eat as much as they wanted. Then it was set on top of the top pantry shelf, not to be tasted again until Christmas morning. Russell always tried to please everyone by bringing them their favorite kind. He even brought me a few chocolate drops. Maybe I had never made it clear how much I hated the things!

Buying the Groceries

Marie was too young to have a driver's permit so she walked into Middletown to the Derr's Grocery Store for groceries. The older children were married and gone from home. Marie was tall and ever so thin. I have never figured out how she managed to carry such large bags of groceries home.

Mother's Death

It was on May 16, 1953, that my mother became ill with pneumonia. She was 92 years old. She was born on June 6, 1861. She died three days later, on May 19, 1953.

Mother's funeral was held at Grossnickle Church of the Brethren. Reverend Samuel D. Lindsay and Reverend Basil Grossnickle conducted the service. They were assisted by Reverend Earl Mitchell. Mother was buried beside my dad, her loving husband.

Remembrances of Mother

Mother had discontinued housekeeping after Dad died

in 1935. She held a public sale of their personal property on April 13, 1935, at 1 p.m. She privately sold the six-room house to Elroy Leatherman, a local farmer. It was advertised as having ten acres of land, good spring water running in the kitchen, a good well in the yard, electricity available, bank barn, and all the necessary out buildings in good shape. It was located between Myersville and Ellerton on State Road.

Aunt Melissa Harshman

After the public sale, she lived with my Aunt Melissa Harshman (her sister). Both were widows. After Aunt Melissa died, Mother was a guest at the Lamar Nursing Home in Middletown, and she also spent extended visits with her family. The last years of her life were spent at the Fahrney-Keedy Nursing Home, located outside Boonsboro in Washington County.

Dinner

While Mother did not live with us, we invited her to come along home after church every couple of Sundays. She ate dinner and spent the afternoon visiting with the family. Come evening, one of the children drove her home. On many of these visits she rehearsed her life stories of the Civil War to my children.

Candy in an Envelope

When Mother opened her letters, she cut the envelopes across the end with scissors. She saved them and used them for candy bags. Before leaving for church on Sunday mornings, she filled one with an assortment and folded down the top. She placed a rubber band around the envelope and tucked it into her purse.

Mother's Simple Attire

Mother always wore a floor-length black dress with a white pin dot. She made these dresses and they were all from the same simple pattern; long sleeves and buttoned to the neck with a small collar. She wore laced high-top black shoes, black stockings, black shawl, black gloves, and carried a simple black purse. She wore the black dunkard bonnet with a white, thin prayer covering underneath.

As we drove home from church in the car, the children could hardly wait for her to open her purse and get out the envelope. She passed it to each child and they searched for their favorite piece. Then she gave it to the youngest child to hold and share until it was empty—this did not take long!

Room for One More

Nearly every Sunday, as we were driving home from church, we approached someone walking along the side of the road. We never passed anyone by unless we were carrying enough passengers in the car to pack the inside and fill the running boards as well. There seemed to be no limit to how many could fit inside that car! We would carry folks from a family for awhile and then they would purchase a car. But there was always someone who needed a "lift." Families did not own a couple of vehicles. In fact, you were lucky to have one.

It was safe to pick up anyone and it was a common courtesy to stop. These folks hopped onto the running board and there they stood holding onto the doorpost. With the windows open, we could hold a conversation as we drove along.

Wrong Car

One day, between 1945 and 1950, Russell drove the brown Pontiac to the Middletown Valley Supply Company, operated by Mr. Raymond Cashour. He had gone to town to buy farm supplies. In those days, hometown folks left their keys in the ignition. You seldom met a stranger in town, and if one was spotted, everyone watched him. He would never have had a chance to do anything wrong without having a witness.

Well, this day Russell was in a hurry, came out of the establishment, opened the car door, started the auto, and drove on home. He pulled the car into the garage and back to the barn or field he went.

A little later in the day, I got a phone call from Francis Summers, an employee at the supply store. He was laughing as he asked if Russell would mind returning his car! You see, Francis and Russell each owned identical automobiles, and it seemed, in Russell's haste, he got into the closest vehicle and came home.

Bang!

Once in awhile when Russell returned home, and if the garage doors were open, he would drive with full speed into the garage. We had a vinegar barrel that sat on the right-hand side in the building. Without fail, we heard a bang as he rammed the car's bumper into it. He never damaged the car, and a mark on the wooden barrel was the extent of damage made by this maneuver.

CHAPTER 44

WILL THE ENDS MEET?

Little Peeps

While farming at Middletown, each spring I purchased 200 peeps, either from the Maryland Chick Hatchery or the Middletown Valley Supply Company. The chicken house had a room for the hens and one for the new chicks. It was located beside the road. I fired a coal burning brooder stove to keep the peeps warm. Years later, we purchased an electric brooder for heat.

Car Horn

A lady, who regularly traveled the road, consistently blew her car horn as she neared the curve in the road on Route 17. Right about the time she got to the chicken house, she laid on the horn. At the sound, the little chicks ran and huddled on a pile in a corner of the room. Then, one of the children or I had to go to the chicken house to make sure that they scattered out or else they smothered themselves.

Saving Money

Since money was tight, when the chicks matured, they supplied us with plenty of eggs for our family's use, as well as cash income to help run the household. I sold the surplus eggs to the huckster, Gilmer Hawkins, as he made his weekly route through the valley.

I tried to save some of this money to buy the children clothes. As I saved a few dollars here and there, I put them in an old cardboard box from Doll's Jewelry Store in Frederick. Then I stuffed it under my clothes in the corner of my bedroom dresser drawer. I saved and counted until I had enough to go shopping. I especially liked the children to have nice things for church. I remember getting them dressed on Sunday morning and then they all had to take a seat in the living room. No one was allowed to run around or go out the house once they were "shined up."

Henry's Clothing Store

I remember Henry's Clothing Store on North Market Street. Mr. Henry usually greeted me and the girls as we came in the door. He would say, "What do you need today?" I would tell him I needed a dress for all of them. God bless the man—he would mark down the prices and always work out a deal so I could get something for everyone. Little did he ever know how much he helped us.

Thomas Haggerman

Thomas Haggerman, from Hagerstown, had a taste for home-cured country ham. Our acquaintance came by my brother, George, who had a farm feed and supply store in Myersville. Mr. Haggerman was a salesman and stopped in at George's place to promote his products.

I was so delighted when he came to the kitchen door puffing on his cigar and asked, "Are the hams ready?" I stopped whatever I was doing since I was anxious to make the sale. We walked down across the yard, ducking under the clotheslines filled with clothes drying in the wind. I unlocked the little white weatherboard meat house. He looked over the hams and chose one.

I liked to do business with Mr. Haggerman since he always came with a handful of cash. I never sold the food away from the family. We butchered hogs a couple of times during the winter months to give us plenty of pork. We had chickens and beef cattle to slaughter.

CHAPTER 45

DANGER!

The Scythe

Russell hired men by the day to help on the farm. They came to work in the early morning and worked until evening. Jack Brunner was helping one day and was out in the field cutting weeds and briers along the fence row. Russell and Austin each had a horse and plow. Russell was working old Florrie. She was a sorrel and a good horse. I remember Russell saying that her former owner told him he rode Florrie in the Boonsboro parades. She was a very disciplined horse. The men were plowing, preparing the ground for seed. They were in the field along Adams' lane.

I sent Russell Jr. to the field to tell the men that dinner, the noon meal, was ready and they should come to the house to eat. Often I rang the dinner bell on the tall pole at the edge of the garden, just outside the back door. When the horses were in the field and they heard the dinner bell ring, they whinnied and, if standing still, they pawed their feet in the soil. To them, that signal meant a fresh drink of cool water and a few ears of corn as well. It was as if they were letting me know they heard the call. After Russell Jr. delivered the message, Russell and Austin unhitched their horses from the bar-shear plows. Austin started to the barn to feed and water his horse.

Russell hopped onto Florrie's back and rode side-saddle over to the fence row where Jack was working. "Jack, it is time to eat," he announced. "Hop on!" Jack said he was going to walk to the house, but Russell replied, "Oh, come on and jump up here and ride with me." This time he accepted the offer. He asked Jack to hand the scythe to him and he told him he would take it to the shed and sharpen it. Russell always wore heavy high-top work shoes on the farm. He placed the scythe on the toe of a shoe as he so often rode along holding a tool. A scythe has a long, slightly curved sharp blade about 20 to 30 inches long on a four- or five-foot handle.

As Florrie was walking on the plowed ground, suddenly and without warning, she switched and walked over on the sod. As she shifted, she got too close to the fence row and rammed the blade of the scythe into her side!

Russell and Jack were shocked to see what happened so quickly right before their eyes. With his heart nearly fainting, a few seconds later Russell carefully removed the blade from her body. Florrie managed to walk to the barn. He removed her gears so she could lie down.

Russell came to the house with a look of grief and horror on his face as he told me what happened. He was distraught, to say the least! He called for Dr. Frank Ryan, the Middletown veterinarian, to come examine her, hoping to save her life. However, what had happened was quite clear to us, and we knew death was most certain. The doctor did not give us much encouragement.

No Appetite

Russell finally came to the house and sat down at the table, but he could not eat a bite of food that day. His eyes were filled with tears—his heart was sick to think of what had happened to Florrie. Perhaps he was thinking it could have been Jack or himself injured instead of the horse. We kept a close check on Florrie day in and day out. There was nothing we could do. Within days, she developed gangrene and died.

Florrie meant so much to Russell. She always did a good day's work for him. I recall that before we moved from the Middlepoint farm to the Toms farm, he rode her every night for a week to Myersville to see his mother, who was deathly ill. The night Flora Maria Wiles died, old Florrie made the trip with great speed.

Baker

At another time, our horse, Baker, had a heart attack and died while hitched to the hay wagon. Russell purchased this horse from a local man.

Russell was making hay that day. It was evening and the men where unloading the hay from the wagon on the upper level of the bank barn. Harold Harshman, our son-in-law, had come home from his public job and was helping in the hay maul when, all of a sudden as he looked down, he saw Baker fall to the barn floor. He was still hitched in the team to the wagon. Baker's heart had stopped and he just fell down as he died.

Jaws of Death

Many jobs on the farm were dangerous—silo filling was one of them. The corn fodder chopper was the very jaws of death sitting before you. None of the young children were allowed to be near the barn when this job was in progress, especially if the chopper was running. In the field, each corn stalk was cut off at the ground and set up in shocks by hand. The hired men carried it to the silo with the horses and wagon. Once the strings on the bundles of fodder were cut, it was thrown into the chopper. This machine cut and blew the chopped corn stalks up into the silo.

Callie Long

Callie Long was working for us in the early 1950s, and it had been a long, hot, late summer day. He had gone up the inside ladder to the top of the silo and was stumping down the corn and filling any hollow spots created by the blower. Callie was working with a pitchfork. In the rafters of the roof hung an electric light bulb without a wire cover. The silo was full and, as he moved around, the handle of his fork hit the light bulb, breaking it and sending electricity through Callie's wet and sweaty body. He was knocked out cold.

Thinking it was taking Callie a long time to come down from the silo, Russell began to wonder if he was all right. So he called up the shaft to Callie. Not getting an answer, Russell quickly climbed the ladder to the top. There, before his eyes, Callie lay, face down and unconscious. He started mouth-to-mouth resuscitation. When Callie began breathing, Russell shouted down into the barn and demanded help. The bank barn and silo stood side by side. They were connected by a walkway so the silage could be carried out into the part of the barn where the cows were milked.

Someone Get Help!

Marie heard her dad calling for help and ran out of the barn to the road and frantically waved her hands, trying to signal the cars going by to stop. People thought she was just "fooling around" and drove on by. By this time, I was aware of what was happening and called the Middletown Fire Department. Within minutes, the firemen arrived. They tied ropes around Callie's shoulders, waist, and ribs; then guided him down the thirty-foot shaft. We made him comfortable and soon Dr. Harp came to examine him. With a few days of rest, he was up and around the farm working again. As such accidents occurred, we were more assured than ever that God's protecting hand spared our lives so many times.

Children Loved Callie

The children all loved Callie. Some of the little ones liked only the crust of the pies, but I insisted they eat the whole slice, fruit as well.

When Callie saw the children stalling, he would ask them to pass their dish to him and then he scraped the filling off onto his plate. The children knew I would never scold Callie for anything that he did at the table, so they sheepishly smiled, sort of looked at me, and quickly passed their slice of pie.

When Austin was young, one day he was sitting next to Callie at the dinner table. I had made potato chips and Austin was passing the bowl around the table. He said, "Callie, watch out for this. It is really heavy." Believing him, Callie placed his hand under the glass bowl and gave it a hefty lift as though Austin was telling him the truth. The chips shot out all over everything. Callie did not get upset; he was a good-hearted soul.

Callie worked for us while we farmed both at Myersville and Middletown. He was a faithful farmhand and a very good friend. Long after he retired, he and his wife, Eva, often visited us on a Sunday afternoon.

Blood Streaming Out

Since the children spent so much time in the barn, Russell had the local veterinarian cut off the cows' horns. They were dangerous for the family and, if the cows got into a fight, they could injure each other.

One day, Dr. Thomas Clark, from Middletown, came to the farm and performed the procedure on a cow. For some unknown reason, when the veins were tied off, the blood did not clot. Instead, the blood squirted out in a constant stream. I was in the kitchen when Russell came into the house and told me he did not expect the cow to live. He said she was showing the strain and was so weak from the loss of blood that she could not stand.

I always kept my Bible in the kitchen cabinet on an open shelf. Upon hearing the bad news, I quickly picked it up, grabbed my coat, ran to the barn, and prayed for the bleeding cow. I read Ezekiel 16:6, *"And when I passed by thee, and saw thee polluted in thine own blood, I said unto thee when thou wast in thy blood, Live; yea, I said unto thee when thou wast in thy blood. Live."*

No need to pray if you do not believe God will answer. So I prayed and came back to the house to continue with my work in the kitchen.

That evening, when I went to the barn to help with the evening work, the cow was up chewing her cud and was doing quite well.

Yvonne was small but she remembers what an impression this made on her. She thought, if God would do this for a cow, what would He do for her? God knows when a sparrow falls, and just as surely He knows and cares for us when we fall. What a mighty God we serve!

CHAPTER 46

FARM WORK FOR EVERYONE

Hoeing in Corn

The children all worked hard on the farm. They still talk about how much they hated some jobs such as hoeing in corn. This was done to catch all the spots where the corn planter malfunctioned or where the birds ate the seed. Other times it just did not sprout up. We walked down the long rows across the cornfield and stopped wherever we saw a spot without a stalk of corn. Using the hoe we carried, we dug a hole, dropped in a kernel of seed corn taken from our pocket, covered it with soil, and then we moved on down the row to the next vacant spot.

It was a hot, early summer day. Russell Jr., who was not very old, decided he had it. He had dropped his last piece of corn for that day. He waited until no one was looking, dug a big hole, emptied his pocket, and then placed a rock on top.

Now, finding a large rock on the Wiles farm was a chore in itself. Russell always picked stones from the fields to provide the best growing conditions possible for his crops. Weeks after Russell Jr.'s "corn burial" the kernels spouted into a hearty bunch of stalks. He knew right then and there that trick would not work for him again.

Picking Stones

Another dreaded chore was picking stones off the plowed fields. The children all participated. A two-horse team pulled the small, flatbed wagon, and all the family piled on and headed for the field. The weather was usually hot and dry and, when the wind picked up the fresh harrowed soil, it was a miserable job. And with all the stooping, come evening, our backs ached from the strain. If a stone was missed, Russell called to the person nearest to him, "Get that big one over there!" A "big one" to him seemed like a mere pebble to the children. It seemed Russell always lagged behind to get the last one.

Once the wagon was loaded with stones, they headed the horses toward the meadow to the banks of the branch and behind the pigpen. There they picked up each stone again and tossed them off the wagon. Sometimes they pitched them into an open ditch in a field. This helped to stop washing problems during heavy rains.

Leon Gouker

Leon Gouker also worked as a farmhand. He came nearly every day but Sunday for many years. When he saw the stone-picking job dragging, he quietly called the horses to move on. The children were delighted when Leon was around to help because they knew their dad would not say anything to him if he was the one whistling for the horses to move on.

Thomas A. Edison once said, "Opportunity is missed by most people because it is dressed in overalls and looks like work." Well, I tell you, the children did not miss "opportunities" very often.

Charles Wise

Charles Wise, who lived in Middletown, also worked on the farm for many years. If Charlie said he was going to help, we could depend on him. He kept his word. He was quite a fisherman. He lived to fish, or at least to have the opportunity to talk about it. Charlie caught lots of carp and brought them to the farm. Here he gave them a temporary home in the cattle's water trough until he was ready to use them.

Husking Corn

By the end of the summer, much of the fieldwork was done. The last big job before the bitter cold weather came was gathering the corn crop. Before the corn picker was invented, the corn stalk was cut by hand and put on shocks. Russell hired local women and men to work shucking the ears of corn from the stalk.

They removed the husk from around the ear, then threw the ears on a pile. Later, Russell, the hired hand, and the children drove the two-horse team hitched to the large corn wagon down the rows of corn piles. They picked the ears up into a willow bushel basket. Then Russell or the hired hand dumped them into the wagon to bring to the corncrib for storing. The fodder was pitched into the barnyard or field for the cows to eat the leaves. With time, the stalks rotted and decayed.

In the fall of the year, the teenagers would often light a few shocks of corn on fire as a prank. The temptation was too great when the cornfield was so close to the road. No one ever got caught in the act.

Stop Looking!

Our daughter, Marie, and her husband, Harold Harshman, were married on October 22, 1947. Not finding a home to purchase by the time they married, they lived with us on the farm for two years.

Harold was young and worked hard at a public job. When he came home, he was hungry. If he arrived before we finished the barn work, he helped us. Then we all ate supper together. Yvonne's place at the table was beside me, and across from her was Harold's seat. He piled the food high on his plate and, having a good appetite, did not waste time eating.

Yvonne propped her elbows on the table, rested her head in her hands, and there she sat staring straight into Harold's plate and face. It appeared that nothing got her attention but a hard tap on her toes with my foot. This happened time after time. It is a wonder the child had any leather on top of her shoes after my constant tramping on them. She was so intrigued by watching Harold. I tell you, that girl would have rather watched than eat her food. I was afraid she would stare at him until she managed to capture his appetite.

We never talked about this until years later. It seems Harold was enjoying his food so much he paid little attention to her big brown eyes.

Slave Quarters

The old dairy and wash house were under one roof, and on the second floor of the dairy portion of the building was the slave quarters. I often wondered about the quality of

278

life for the people who lived in these quarters during the years of slavery. So many of those dear people had such horrible lives.

The children set up a playhouse here. Tom and Yvonne spent many hours playing house and pretending they were canning. Any old jars they could find were a treasure. They canned anything from red beet tops, grain, fertilizer, salt, or whatever they could scrounge up. Then they forgot about it. With time, these jars became "time bombs" as the food spoiled, fermented, and blew up.

I had an old black Girard Novelty wood-burning kitchen range in the slave quarters. We used it for heat if we wanted to work in the building in the wintertime. I often put a quilt in the frame and we worked as time permitted.

Butchering Day

Butchering day was a big event on the farm for all the family. We usually butchered four to six hogs after Thanksgiving and that many again in February. The girls and I prepared food for a big noon meal.

First the hogs were herded to the meadow and shot in the head using a rifle. Then their throats were cut to drain the blood from the animal. They were dragged to the outside of the wash house by a farm horse, scalded, scraped, hung on a tripod, gutted, washed and then cut into pieces.

The wash house had running water and a concrete floor. The fireplace had two fixed hinged bars, or cranes, on the side wall. They could swing in and out from over the open fire. The bars held the bale of the cast iron kettles we cooked in. We all worked to get the wash house in order; knives were sharpened and tables were cleaned.

Outside, the scalder was set in place. It was a large

flat, rectangular metal tub. In the early days we used a big barrel. The pig was placed in this tub to scald, making it possible to scrape its skin clean. The wood was gathered nearby so it would be ready in the morning to build a fire for heating the water to the boiling point. The tripod poles used to hang the pigs on were also set up ahead of time.

We invited family, neighbors, and friends to help with the butchering. The head butcher was usually Alvey Delauter or Arthur Flook. These men would oversee the amount of ingredients added to the meat and the butchering products. They were the "head cooks."

Faithful Helpers

Oliver and Tissie Hooper, along with Willie and Annie Wiles, seldom missed a butchering day at our farm. They worked hard and were loyal friends. All of our family enjoyed the time shared with them. I guess we could have called butchering day, "homecoming day." Dr. J. Elmer Harp was always our guest for dinner on this day.

Sugar Curing

We preserved the meat by curing and canning. The sugar cure ingredients are brown sugar, black pepper, salt, and saltpeter. This mixture is rubbed on the meat until each piece is covered with a thick coat. We laid it on a wooden bench in the smokehouse for a few weeks. When ready to smoke it, we hung it from hooks in the rafters.

The smokehouse was a small building with a concrete floor. When we smoked the meat, we started a fire in the middle of the floor using hickory wood. We added damp sawdust so the fire would smoke for a long time. This allowed the smoke flavor to draw into the pork. A damp, rainy day was excellent for smoking meat since the dampness in the air made it more difficult for the smoke to seep and escape through the cracks in the weatherboard sides of the building.

Hams took approximately seven days per inch of thickness to cure. A side of bacon needed about sixteen days to cure the whole piece of meat. The hams, shoulders, and middlings are the cuts that were salted and sugar cured. Red pepper and Borax were used on the meat to keep the "skipper flies" off. "Skippers" are the larvae of the skipper fly. If the larvae got on it, the meat would have spoiled.

We were smoking the pork one day and, as I looked out the kitchen window, here came the fire engine in the driveway. The firemen quickly got out of the truck and headed straight for the smokehouse. I hurried to the door and told them everything was fine; I was just smoking meat. It seemed they were passing by the farm on their way back to the station from a call. Noticing the smoke, they decided to check it out.

The Scrapple

The ingredients in scrapple are cornmeal, flour, salt, pepper, and the broth from the head meat. Head meat is exactly what it says—the meat from the hog's head. The head is shaved with a sharp knife and cleaned. The ears, eyes, tongue, nose and brains are removed, and then the head is cooked in a large iron kettle of salt water over the open fire. When done, the meat is picked off the skull and ground to use in the scrapple. As the scrapple mixture cooks, it thickens. It is poured or dipped into flat pans. Hot lard is poured on top to seal and preserve it. When stored in a cool place, it will keep for weeks. To serve, it is sliced, rolled in flour, and fried in fat until crispy.

The Lard

Lard is rendered from the waste pieces of fat discarded from the cuts of pork. The fat is cooked in the large black iron kettle until it becomes liquid—then it is poured into a sheave and press. The liquid runs through and the membranes of the fat are pressed until it forms a cake called "cracklings." Cracklings can be used to season food. We gave them to the chickens to eat since they are very greasy and our family did not care for them.

The Stomach

The stomach of the hog is called the maw. The maw is cleaned and scraped to remove all the waste. When ready to eat, it is filled with potatoes, sausage, onions, celery, salt, and pepper—then it is baked until brown and crispy. Some country cooks add different seasonings, but those mentioned are the general ingredients.

The Bladder

The bladder is turned inside out, cleaned, and laid in salt water to soak. It is stuffed with sausage meat and tied to look like a bowling ball. These are smoked along with the other cuts of pork. When ready to eat, the whole bladder is boiled, then sliced and served as a cold bologna or sausage roll.

The Souse

We also made souse from the pig's feet. They were soaked, washed clean, and cooked until the meat came off the bones. Then I chopped it very fine. Salt, pepper, and vinegar were added and the mixture was poured into a dish to mold. After cooling, it jelled and was ready to serve. I tell you, very little of the hog is wasted! Something can be made of most parts.

Thrashing

Russell planted large crops of wheat and barley. Before the combine was invented, the farmers cut the grain crops with a binder. This machine could be pulled either by horses or a tractor. We used a five-horse team. Three were hitched next to the binder, and two pulled in front of them. The binder cut the stalks off at the top of the soil and tied them into a bundle. Then it pitched the bundle out onto the ground. The men followed the binder and set the bundles on shocks with the heads of grain up. A bundle of the stalks was fanned open and placed over the top of the shock to protect the kernels from shattering in the weather. This was called a "cap." It could be weeks from the time the wheat was cut until it was thrashed. The farmers waited their turn for the thrash machine to come to the farm.

Tom Arnold and Wilbur Kline ran thrash machines from one farm to another to thrash the farmer's grain crops. The machine was pulled into the upper barn floor.

Russell hired enough men to help get the harvest done. Out in the field, they loaded the sheaths of grain on wagons to carry it into the barn. The wheat was run through the thrash machine to beat the kernels from the heads on the stalks. A large pipe shot the straw out of the barn into the barnyard on a pile or stack. The grain poured from the machine onto the barn floor. The men bagged the kernels and placed them on the barn floor or carried it to the grainery in the barn.

The men worked hard and were hungry so I needed to prepare lots of food. These were long days for everyone.

Blizzards

There was always lots of excitement of one kind or another on the farm. Our farmhouse was located on a sharp curve and right up next to the edge of the road. Winter snow and ice storms caused the road to become treacherous and turned the drive around that bend into a "dare devil" track. People absolutely lost total control of their cars and knocked down the concrete block wall that edged the lawn. Sometimes the cars ran onto the front porch. After hearing a noise in the night, most often we would look from the window only to see a car continue to drive away and leave us responsible for rebuilding. Occasionally, someone was honest or got hurt and came to the door for help.

The winters brought blizzards; sometimes snow blew and drifted until Route 17 became impassable for days. The county did not have the heavy-duty equipment like that of today to keep the roads cleared. The milk trucks could not get through the snow to come to the farm and pick up the milk. Most farmers had no way of storing it once their cans or milk tank was filled. The cows were milked but the milk had to be poured away.

Feed Sack Clothing

On days when the weather was bad, I would catch up on my sewing. The chicken feed came bagged in printed or flowered cotton sacks. Many farmers' wives, including me, washed the sacks and used the cloth to make clothing, dish towels, tablecloths, etc. Our children wore lots of clothes made from the bags. It was not always the color or print we liked, but we used the fabric anyway. It seems we were easier to please in those days. It appeared we did not shop on Fifth Avenue!

"Kline's Best Flour"

We bought flour and cornmeal from Kline's Mill at Keedysville, Maryland. It came bagged in a cotton cloth sack. The manufacturer's logo was printed with dye on the white or unbleached muslin. That did not matter—we used the cloth anyway. I bleached and washed until some of the dye was removed. I made slips and "bloomer" underwear for myself and the girls. I tried to lay the pattern on the fabric and cut without getting the remaining logo on the garment. But once in awhile someone got a "Kline's Best Flour" on their designer undies!

CHAPTER 47

HOMETOWN FOLKS

"A Little Something for the Children"

One day, each year as Christmas neared, we would look outside and see Tissie and/or Oliver Hooper walking in the driveway. As they entered the house, they would tell me they were stopping in to bring "a little something for the children." Again they carried a basket. They never forgot us. Our family loved the Hoopers.

Quilting

Tissie Hooper loved to quilt in the wintertime. The girls and I occasionally went to her house to give her a hand with the project. They lived at the edge of town. Years later, she and Oliver moved into Middletown on Green Street.

Oliver was a quiet man who always spoke softly. He came to the room where we were quilting and visited with us as we sewed. The younger children sat near me. After we had been there for awhile, Tissie would say, "Oliver, please get the little girls something to eat." Slowly, Oliver would go to the kitchen and return with a treat for all of us. It was usually ginger ale served with cookies and always a can of candy for us to choose a few pieces. We never heard a cross, mean word come from the mouth of either of them.

I remember Oliver and Tissie walking out from town to their farm that was located off Pete Wiles Road. They were retired and living in town but they often spent the day hoeing out thistles from their pasture fields. Both wore straw hats and carried their hoes. Usually, they had a basket of food and a little tin bucket of water to drink.

As I talk about all the "bygone days" my thoughts keep returning to how God has blessed me with a mind to remember all this at the age of 95.

Charles Phleeger, the Basket Weaver

Charlie Phleeger was the basketweaver and broommaker from Middletown. Russell offered him the use of the "hollow" to grow his willows and broomcorn. The hollow is a long narrow strip of land that joins the Charles Coblentz farm at the end of town.

Charlie drove out to the farm and spent days cutting willows by hand for baskets and broomcorn for the brooms. He hauled it to the barn on a trailer pulled behind his car. He cleaned the seed from the stalks of corn with a small machine but most of the work was done by hand.

Charlie was well known throughout the valley and today his baskets bring high bids at sales and auctions. Most of the children still have baskets made by Charlie Phleeger.

Main's Ice Cream Parlor

Main's Ice Cream Parlor was a high spot of Middletown. The business was owned and operated by Charles Main and his sons. The ice cream was coined the "best ice cream you ever ate" and had rightfully earned that reputation. Our family and friends consumed many gallons of this "delight." Usually, on a Sunday after we returned home from church, one of the children drove into town and purchased a drum of their favorite flavor of ice cream. Most of the time, one of the Main brothers, Doc Shank, and in later years, Harry Bussard, was the salesmen.

Our Ice Cream

Not only did we go to Main's to buy ice cream, but in earlier days, Marie or Russell Jr. drove the car down Main's alley to the back door of the establishment to buy ice. We purchased fifty-pound blocks of ice to make our own ice cream. Pete Shank, who worked at Main's business, came to the side door with the heavy steel ice hook in hand and asked, "How much ice do you need?" Pete carried the ice to the car and positioned it on the shiny steel bumper of the car for the ride home.

While someone went for the ice, I was at home gathering the ingredients for the mixture. I was waiting to pour the concoction into the ice cream maker upon their return. If it was summertime, we had to hurry so the ice did not melt away before we got the ice cream made. On hot days, it took forever to freeze and set. Whoever in the family was around at the time took turns turning the crank on the freezer. Once the mixture hardened to the point that we could not turn the paddle, I dipped it into pans and stored it in the deep freeze.

Deep Freezer

We stored our food in an ice box before we purchased an electric refrigerator. An ice box was a metal insulated cabinet. Again, we went to Main's to buy ice every couple of days.

Yes, the deep freeze was a treasured investment. With a freezer, many hours of standing and canning food near a hot stove were now saved. Our friends, Ivan and Olive Gladhill Routzhan, came to the farm to visit often. Ivan worked for the electric company and he gave us good advice as we purchased our first freezer.

Really, Russell and I were careful not to "waste," as it causes "want." We tried not to waste money or anything else. We always shopped for the best bargain.

Today, Olive still comes to see me or we talk on the phone and chat about the good times we have had together. God has blessed me with such wonderful friends; both young and old—new and those dear from long-standing relationships.

Preserving

I have always canned fruit, vegetables, and meat for our family's use. Today, at 95, I still can green beans, tomatoes, fruits, and mincemeat for pies.

Years ago, as I sat down to eat at the table in my spattered apron, Russell often looked my way, smiled and complimented me on setting a nice table. He told me how much he enjoyed certain foods I prepared. He would push back from the table and straighten his suspenders. He rubbed his tummy as he got up from his chair and again repeated that he had thoroughly enjoyed the meal.

I knew each one's favorite dish and I aimed to serve it as often as possible. One of Russell's favorite desserts was gingerbread. He could sit down almost anytime and eat a pan of warm gingerbread, but he especially enjoyed it when he came in from outdoors.

Delauter's Ice Cream Cones

During the summer, we made trips across the mountain to buy fruit from the orchards in Smithsburg, Maryland. We took any of the children who wanted to go along. On our way back home, Russell stopped in Middlepoint at Lee Delauter's Store. Pauline, Lee's wife, dipped big cones of ice cream for the family. Lee worked for us on the farm for a short time when he was a very young man.

Home Delivery Bread Man

I think of how modern and blessed we finally became when we could afford to have a bread man deliver bread to our door. He delivered bread door-to-door in the rural homes. No more baking bread a couple of times a week. We saved time and enjoyed the taste of bakery bread for a change.

In the summertime, occasionally Mr. Jones from Boonsboro stopped by the farm to sell fruits and produce. Russell and I especially liked to get the cantaloupes because they were the best.

CHAPTER 48

LIFE GOES ON

New Cow Barn

In 1959, we decided to build a new dairy barn. In order to sell milk to a Grade-A milk market, it was mandatory to move from the bank barn to a new facility. We hired George Wiles, a local building contractor, to begin the work. This was a great improvement to our farm and it made milking so much easier. We had come a long way from when Russell and I were first married and we milked cows that were tied with a rope or chain around their neck to keep them in place!

Fires

I remember tragedy striking the neighbors' lives, such as the fires on the Ellsworth (Johnny) Wiles farm and on the Charles Coblentz farm where Donald Keller was farming. I recall when death and accidents happened in families living nearby. I have seen storms and lightning rip through the valley.

Russell Jr. was in the barn during a thunderstorm once and was struck by lightning while holding a pitchfork in his hands. Marie was struck while standing in the house by the telephone. Their lives were spared but the jolt stunned them momentarily. Most often, during a thunderstorm, I sat in the living room with the children. If Russell could make it into the house, he too, often waited with us until the storm passed.

Presidents

I have lived under seventeen United States of America presidents. When I was born in 1899, William McKinley was in office. He served the country as president from 1897 to 1901.

Next to hold the office were Theodore Roosevelt, William Howard Taft, Woodrow Wilson, Warren G. Harding, Calvin Collidge, Herbert Clark Hoover, Franklin D. Roosevelt, Harry S Truman, Dwight Eisenhower, John F. Kennedy, Lyndon B. Johnson, Richard M. Nixon, Gerald R. Ford, Jimmy Carter, Ronald W. Reagan, and our current president, Bill Clinton.

When I think of all the presidents I have lived under and the great and the horrible situations that developed under their leadership, I become more thankful each day that God is in control.

I recall our nation's tragedy, the day President Kennedy was shot and died, and the wars and conflicts on foreign soil.

"Pete Wiles Road"

I recall Russell coming into the house one day telling me he had a conversation with an employee who was working with the Frederick County highway road crew. This gentleman informed him that they would soon be placing a sign on the little road that turned off Route 17 at one end of the farm. It would read "Pete Wiles Road." Russell commented that he considered it an honor.

Miss Flora Wiles Dies

On July 26, 1963, Russell's other sister, Flora, died in Catonsville, Maryland. She was born June 4, 1895. Russell was now the only surviving member of his immediate family. I am thankful that our three sons have boys to keep the name alive.

I am the last surviving member of my immediate family. My youngest brother, George, died in 1963.

CHAPTER 49

THE CHILDREN

Behavior

Most of the time, our children got along well with each other. Marie was notorious for teasing Janice with the mice she caught in the barn or the corncrib. Poor Janice was scared "out of her wits" of them! I threatened Marie with the fact that Janice did not have to help her with the work if she continued to tease. And Tom loved to push Regean and Yvonne into the water puddles.

Through the years, our family has laughed and cried together, but always with love. The force of love binds hearts with a long, lasting bond as nothing else can do. We tried to teach our children to have courage and faith in themselves. The children knew their daddy and I were depending on them to behave. None of them caused us shame, but maybe some embarrassment from time to time!

Off to the Chicken House

We had one child who sneaked off to the chicken house to play with the chickens. It is a wonder Yvonne bothered the hens as they tended to peck at her hands when she came near. Anyway, she would go to the henhouse and catch a few of my laying hens.

Never underestimate the imagination of a child! As she caught each one, she swung it around until it was too dizzy to walk.

On the farm we have a branch that runs down through the middle of the meadow. Here she laid the dizzy, "out cold" hens on the bank to wait for their turn to be submerged into the water. Of course, when their heads hit the cool water it brought them to themselves again.

As they shook and ruffled their feathers to shed the water, she laughed to herself and had a good time—until I caught her—or her sister, Regean, came to tell me what was happening. I need not say that I punished Yvonne.

Mommy's Little Saint

Regean was always a good child. When Yvonne could not entice her to join in her "fun," she became annoyed and insisted on calling her sister, "Mommy's little saint." Then she got punished again. She had a hard time learning I would not tolerate name calling.

The Rooster

As I reminisce, I remember a story I must tell you from back in the late 1940s or early 1950s. Maybe this will shed some light on why Yvonne loved the chickens.

Mother was ill and staying with my brother, Herbert, and his wife, Mary. I went to their house to visit. Since there was no bathroom indoors, I told my sister-in-law I was going to the privy. She warned me to watch out for the rooster who stayed out back. "He is cross," she said. She added, "He flogs me as well as strangers." The rooster did not like anyone to enter onto his territory. I replied, "Well, I am going and I guess I'll just take care of him when I get there."

Mary was right! I opened the gate and started down the path. The old rooster came strutting up to me as if he was "king of the grounds." I kept walking and he kept coming toward me. We met and he was ready for action. I reached down to grab his neck and my aim was on target. I had his feathery neck in my hand. I flung him in circles and pitched him away. He struggled to get up on his feet as he landed. When he did regain his footing, he was aware of this fact: He no longer owned the world or the path to the outhouse!

Vines for Mother

Edward and Mary Dodd lived in Middletown in a little yellow house on the present site of the Model Garage showroom. Their home stood beside the old trolley tracks. The Dodds often sat on the front porch. They were elderly. Mr. Dodd was a thin man who nearly always wore a black suit jacket. Ms. Mary was heavyset, had a full face, and wore tiny round eyeglasses that slipped to the end of her nose. Her thick, white hair was pulled to the top of her head in a bun. She often was seen wearing a floral dust cap and apron. Mary was always smiling and ready to hold a conversation with anyone who was interested in sharing. They were a kind couple.

I sent Tom to Middletown one day for something I needed from Derr's Grocery Store. He had just grown tall enough to ride a full-sized, two-wheel bike. He had a new red bike with a wire basket and streamers attached to the handle bars. Indeed, he was proud of his "two wheeler."

When Ms. Mary saw him passing by on his way back home, she caught his eye and he stopped. She was working in her garden, pruning vines. She then proceeded to come to the street and instructed Tom to take the bundle of cuttings she held in her arms along home for me to plant. His eyes were filled with concern as he watched her place the cuttings in his new wire basket. Before she could gather up the second handful, he said "good-bye" and pedalled toward home. He was wondering just where she found her nerve to mess up his new bike that he gave such special care. All the way down the hill he wondered how he could dispose of the vines. Then he had it—he knew exactly what he was going to do! Just prior to arriving home, he stopped by Phleeger's willow patch and pitched the vines into a ditch.

As Tom came in the kitchen door, he disgustingly told me about his encounter with Ms. Mary. He said to me without catching his breath, "Mommy, Ms. Mary gave me some flowers for you to plant, but I threw them in Phleeger's willow patch because they were nothing but weeds. And she made my new bike dirty." Just what could I say? Really, there was no harm done!

Horseback Riding

It was a Sunday afternoon. We were still living on the farm and Marie and Tom decided they were going to go horseback riding on old Kate. Tom was just about 14 years old. Together they went to the horse stable in the barn. They were just going to ride around the meadow so who needed a saddle? A bridle was all they would use. They led Kate to the watering trough. Standing on the narrow edge, and being careful not to slip into the water, Tom mounted in front and Marie hopped onto back of the horse. All was wonderful—Kate was trotting along ever so gracefully for a workhorse. What more could they expect from her?

Then, all of a sudden, Kate caught a glimpse of

300

Dr. Clark's racehorses running along the fence that surrounded their pasture field across the road. These racehorses boarded at the neighboring farm. Just so quickly and without warning, Kate gave a frolicking kick and started off jumping. Too late to gain control, she was off and running. As quick as a flash of lightning, Marie was on the ground, and a second later Tom was following down over Kate's rump. Kate was gone! The two gathered themselves up, decided only their pride was hurt, and determined maybe this was not the best afternoon for riding.

Healthy Crew—A Blessing

Our family was a healthy crew, thanks to our Heavenly Father. However, concerns ran wild when childhood diseases broke out, especially the whooping cough. The children were so sick when they became infected. This was in the days before vaccinations. The coal bucket sat in an open fireplace behind the stove, and I recall one of the children coughed so hard and long that he/she fell into it.

And yes, it seemed each year, pink eye came in time for Easter Sunday morning! Back then, there were no medications to help clear the infection, and to bathe the eyes was the only comfort we could find.

Broken Bones

With the nine children, only once did one of them suffer a broken bone. Russell Jr. and Janice were in the yard playing with a ball one day and, as both were chasing after it, he fell on her leg and broke it. He heard it snap when it broke.

CHAPTER 50

NO ROOM IN THE INN

Humbug

From the time we moved to Middletown in 1932, unannounced visitors (the traveling homeless, known then as tramps) stopped in to visit us more often. This was probably due to living close to town and because the farm buildings were near the road. One gentleman, named Humbug, appeared regularly. He would ask to spend the night in the bank barn on the hay maul. These men who came regularly never went into the barn without getting Russell's permission.

Humbug talked very little, but when he did, he used a robust, rough, deep voice that bellowed. When he did not want to answer or comment on what Russell was saying to him, he would say, "Ah, Humbug." Not ever giving us his real name, he got a title anyway. He never shared any information with us regarding his background, other than telling us he was from Germany. Some folks suspected he may have been a spy during the World War II years. We often wondered what life was like for him during his youth.

In almost any season, Humbug appeared in a long, black overcoat. He wore one built-up shoe and carried all his life's wealth in a bundle. He was polite but never smiled. He seemed to know when supper was being served at our house. If he happened to be late arriving and we had finished the meal, Russell took a plate of food to the barn for him. In nice weather, he enjoyed dining on the porch. Seldom, unless it was extremely bitter cold outside, did he come into the house to eat, and never to sleep! Russell stayed with us until the man consumed his meal and then he showed him to the barn.

Russell asked these men to give him their matches. He never allowed anyone to smoke in the barn. They gave him their matches and we wondered how many they kept in another pocket. We never saw any indications that they had been smoking during the night.

Humbug never harmed anything and it seemed safe to have him around. But after the dreadful experience I had with the homeless man who recited such horror stories to me years earlier, I never liked being left alone with these people.

Humbug Has a Need

Most of these men were truly trustworthy. The only items we ever missed after Humbug's stay with us was a few cakes of homemade lye soap. I made soap and placed the cakes on the porch to dry. He helped himself and I really did not mind. I guess he needed it. Perhaps he heard the statement I often made to the children: "Cleanliness is next to godliness." I so often repeated that statement to them, and with such authority, they thought it was Scripture from the Bible.

In the morning, I always served breakfast to the homeless guest and then he was on his way. His set of metal tableware—utensils, plate, cup and bowl—was cleaned thoroughly and neatly placed in a box on a shelf behind the pantry door to wait for his next visit.

It can truthfully be said that we never turned anyone away who was in need. I always had a bite of food for everyone. Who knows how many angels I served unaware? Everyone needs a lifetime of love. Humbug was alone and perhaps needed our kindness. In his own way, he seemed to appreciate our hospitality.

Another homeless man who sometimes visited us asked if he could have lots of the "thick stuff" when I was serving him soup. Guess he wanted to ensure having a hearty meal under his belt. I would offer the homeless men seconds, and one man always answered, "Full and plenty," when he had all he could eat. I never had much to share but I always had plenty of food to give away.

As the years passed, these homeless folks visited less frequently, grew old, and soon never returned. I often wondered how they spent their last days on this earth. One never knows the circumstances that causes another to make the choices that have determined their lifestyle. Or was it ever a choice?

Sleepy Visitors

During our last years of farming, it was not unusual to find local men sleeping in the barn without getting our permission. These were most often men who had too much liquor, happened to be walking our way, and wandered into the barn for the night. Sometimes, they decided to sleep off their alcohol lying down beside the cows in the straw.

It's Only Jimmy

Once a fellow stopped without our knowledge during the night and took lodging in the bank barn in the cow stable. As he laid down in his drunken state, he hit a water facet by the cows' feeding trough. The water dripped on him all night.

He was soaking wet and probably sober by early morning when we found him. As we turned on the lights and were about to walk into the barn, we saw him lying face down beside the cows.

At the sight of the man, Regean let out a scream of fear like I had never heard before in my life. He never moved or raised his head but kept repeating, "Don't be afraid, it's only Jimmy. I won't hurt you." No doubt he was afraid of us at that point. It seemed to make no difference if it was Jimmy or whomever the "unexpected stranger," their presence always startled us, to say the least. Jimmy would not have harmed us or anyone. But there was something about someone suddenly appearing before us in those early morning hours that did truly send cold chills down the spine!

Lassie

We had a collie dog named Lassie. He was a good farm dog. After we moved into the new cow barn and started to milk there, Tom took Lassie along with him when he went into the old bank barn in the early morning to feed the young cattle. Lassie barked and warned him of any intruders before he walked right up on them.

CHAPTER 51

THE SUNSET YEARS

Retirement

In the spring of 1966, with farm help so hard to find, and Russell at age 74 and me at age 67, we decided it was time to stop farming and retire. It was not a welcomed thought! Russell and I had been dedicated to each other and farming was the only lifestyle we knew.

During the busy seasons, Austin came home to help as much as possible with the fieldwork. Russell Jr., who was farming, came home to help as well. Then he took a public job. The older girls had been married and gone from home for years. Regean had married and left home. Tom had been working at the Middletown Valley Bank for a few years and was helping with the milking morning and evening. Yvonne was the only one left at home. We decided to sell out and rent the farm.

Russell and I had a new house built in the corner of the old apple orchard. We contacted a local building contractor, Calvin Shafer and Son, to begin building our new brick rambler. Never in all my dreams could I imagine having such a nice, comfortable house in which to spend our retirement years.

Our Farm Sale

Our farm sale date was set for March 10, 1966. It was a splendid, sunny, early spring day—perfect weather. We hired Doty Remsburg to be the auctioneer at the sale. Our livestock, machinery, and a few household items I no longer needed were to be sold. The family came back home to help us get the cattle ready to sell. The cows were clipped, tails bleached, and groomed. That morning, the animals seemed to look straightforward into our eyes. It was a sad day for us. This lifestyle had provided our living for fifty years. Farming was our life!

Change was here whether we were ready for it or not. Things sold well and the day went by without mishaps, but not without tears. God blessed our life of hard work with a monetary reward. We had been successful in so many ways even in the midst of our trials. God had given us the courage not to give up even though situations along the way looked hopeless. The Lord truly will lead thy way through the wilderness and all we have to do is follow!

We moved into our new home not long after the farm sale. It was "homey" but our hearts were still with the farm life we loved. Maybe we missed walking through the cool green grass in the early morning. Or was it the rising from bed before dawn and before the sound of the rooster crowing? Perhaps it was the hard work we knew for so many years of our life that we longed for. Whatever, an adjustment was going to be needed and it was no surprise that it would surely come. To anyone who has ever left the homestead, you understand.

The notice of our Public Sale appears in the back of the book.

308

CHAPTER 52

RUSSELL IS ILL

No, So Soon

Russell had been healthy his entire life. His only serious illness was an appendectomy when he was 55 years old. We had good years of retirement beginning in 1966. In May of 1970, Russell began to develop a shortness of breath and many days he did not feel well. His condition gradually worsened and he was hospitalized. The doctor decided to implant a pacemaker. The surgery was successful. Soon he mended, felt much stronger, and could do light work again.

This all happened in the early days of using the pacemakers. The batteries needed to be changed about every two years from time of implant. Each time this battery replacement operation took place, it left him in a more weakened condition.

After his last battery replacement in 1977, he did not respond as rapidly as before. Toward the end, gradually, it grew clear that everything was taking its toll on him. He had problems with fluid accumulation and, in general, had breathing difficulties.

That June, he returned to Frederick Memorial Hospital, and this time, he knew he was tired of it all. I, too, was certain things could never be the same for us. I knew him better than anyone else. He fought a good fight! He did not have a heart attack, but his heart was so worn and weak it could not continue. Gone was his strength. Nevertheless, to the end he never once complained. He never suggested that life had "short changed" him anywhere along the line.

Russell left us on June 13, 1977, after being very ill for only two weeks. That night was the longest night I have ever lived through. As I and some of the children and their spouses stayed by his side in that hospital room, our hearts were broken. We all loved him and hated to see him suffer.

I suppose no matter when death comes, we are stunned and not fully prepared. I gathered myself together in the days that followed. But God had been kind to us even in the midst of the storms of life. I did not know how I could bear the loss. At times I wondered if I really wanted to go on. We had been together forever, it seemed. I have learned to trust the unknown future to the Lord! *"My presence will go with you and I will give you rest." (Exodus 33:14)* That promise has been proven to me, for surely He has been with me, and yes, He gives me rest. Perfect peace! God has never taken back a promise from His Word.

Funeral

Over my lifetime, I have followed many loved ones and family members to their graves on that old hill back of the Grossnickle Church. On the day of the funeral, the sun was high in the sky and we could feel the warmth.

This time, Thursday, June 16, 1977, was different. This was the love of my life, the father of my children, and the head of our household and home, my beloved husband, Russell Peter Wiles Sr. Our grandsons, Charles A. Wiles, Wayne L. Wiles, Robert A. Wiles, Monroe F. Grossnickle, Ellis E. Grossnickle, Gary L. Grossnickle, Richard E. Wiles,

310

and William K. Hawkins Jr., carried their grandfather to his grave.

All the children were together for the service and the church was filled to capacity with our relatives and friends. The entire service seemed "unreal." When the graveside service was over, I thought, could it be that it is here on this little plot of ground Russell and I would part? How could my grief be so heavy and I still live?

Lonely Days

In the days that followed, I remembered all the tragedy and problems God had brought us through together. He touched our lives so many times. Knowing that the Lord recognized I needed a brand-new touch, I, too, realized I would have the strength to carry on. At this point, I decided that no matter how lonely I became, Lord willing, I would be determined to hang onto my independence. Without Russell by my side, loneliness filled my heart. At times, I was distressed and wondered what was really happening.

The table with all the children gathered around had been empty for some years, leaving Russell and I to eat together. Now, with him gone, I eat alone. My mind races as I try to recapture thoughts of him during our years together. The good and the bad times flash by me like lightning during a storm. Our married life seems like such a short span of time in my long life.

CHAPTER 53

THANKFUL

Oldest Member of Grossnickle Church of the Brethren

I am now the oldest member of the Grossnickle Church of the Brethren. All of my brothers, their wives, and most of our dear friends are gone. In the meantime, God, being so good to me, has given me the most healthy years of my life in my old age. Some of my best years have been from 80 years old until the present.

These days, at 95 years of age, I find myself in my rocker on Sunday morning listening to the Christian broadcasting. I have attended church services all my life with my family, but it is harder for me to get there these days. We never gave a second thought about whether or not we were going to church when my family was home.

I am so thankful for this well being and God's wonderful keeping power. I have a healthy mind and I give God the glory, honor, and praise. I do enjoy living, but I remind the children not to be sad when I leave this old world and go home. Nothing happens by accident when your life is in God's hands.

Daughters Widowed

I have lived to see two of my daughters widowed.

Doris' husband, Ralph Upton Grossnickle, and Janice's husband, William Kenneth Hawkins Sr., are deceased. I loved these men; they treated me with the same respect and love as my sons. Their death and absence from our family has been most difficult for me to endure.

Still Baking Doughnuts

I am still working at whatever I can do for myself and others. On Shrove Tuesday 1994, I baked 50 dozen doughnuts at age 93. I gave most of these to the employees of the Middletown Valley Bank and the branch offices. My alarm was set for one o'clock in the morning. I got up, and went down to my "work kitchen" in the basement to start my task. (I have a kitchen on both floors.) I did not have to bake, but again, I had that desire in my heart to do something for others. To me, that is what life is all about. I knead the dough, roll and cut it, and fry it in the deep fat. I am sure my house would not hold the amount of dough I have made in my lifetime. There is real satisfaction in seeing something raw and tasteless turn into something so delicious.

The result is I take great joy in seeing my family and friends eat my goodies. Seldom do my visitors leave without carrying a plate of something I have baked. If there is any truth in "idleness being the devil's workshop," I want to keep busy! I find it interesting that people talk so much these days of being depressed. Perhaps staying busy doing nice things for others would help them. We all need a reason to live, and the joy of giving is wonderful to me.

Ninety-Fifth Birthday

I wonder how many women can say they made nine

dozen doughnuts on their ninety-fifth birthday? Again on September 17, 1994, I was up before daylight and had the dough ready to roll and cut when Doris, my daughter, arrived to spend the day with me. She cut the doughnuts as I rolled the dough. Together we fried them in the hot deep fat. I was happy she came to help me since I am not as strong as I used to be. I wonder why!

Family and friends sent flowers and cards to help me celebrate, but do you know what I enjoyed most about my birthday? By my standards, it was being healthy and strong enough to work!

Christmas Day

From the day of our wedding, January 1, 1916, until 1994, I have prepared dinner and celebrated Christmas Day in our home with my family, no matter what was happening in our lives. In recent years, not all of my children and their families come home for dinner because I can no longer fit so many people in my house. However, as of December 25, 1994, I have cooked 78 feasts.

Austin and his wife, Ruth, have missed only a few Christmas days back home. They have been married since 1940. How I do treasure the fact that the day means so much to them!

Each year, and down to every second I spend with my family becomes sweeter and sweeter to me as time speeds by. As I look at my family, I think, what does life have to offer that could be better than this? With my work in life done, I ask myself, "What is success?"

It seems too many sunsets have gone down behind the mountains surrounding the valley and our home. Just one day after another slipped away and then year after year followed.

Family Picnics

Since 1949, on the first Sunday of August, as many members of our family as possibly can, gather for a family picnic. It is not often that one of the children miss the occasion, but sometimes, their family members have other commitments that keep them away. It is always a wonderful day to me. I have heard it said that "a great man is he who does not lose his child's heart." I believe that statement is so very true.

Director's Table

Today (1995) I look at my son Tom and think back on those many years ago in the early 1900s when I, as a little girl, walked through the Middletown bank doors to make my first deposit. I think of Tom now being the president of this same bank. I also think of Dad being a director years ago, between 1920 and 1934.

Now, so many years later, here my daddy's grandson, Thomas Mitchell Wiles, sits at that same old wooden table as the president with a board of directors. What would Charles Webster Grossnickel, whose picture hangs on the wall of that bank, think and say if suddenly he could see our lives today? I wonder what he would say about his little "Girly" living to be 95 years old, having nine living children, all who married wonderful Christian men and women, and who are living comfortable lives in homes of their own. God has blessed me and my family!

Worry can kill you and rob you of the joy that rightfully belongs to you. I am sure the good behavior of my children has added many happy years to my life. I have had someone to love me and someone to live for.

CHAPTER 54

MEMORIES

"Down Home" Love

Oh, at this point when I stop to think back over my life, it seems no mind should be large enough to hold all these memories. I have had a rewarding life.

When we moved from Myersville to Middletown, we soon made new friends. We had wonderful neighbors, Ross and Nora Adams, Edward and Elizabeth Flook, Oliver and Tissie Hooper, William and Annie Wiles, Russell and Nannie Stine, Bert and Bertie Nirkirk, and Mr. and Mrs. Herman Coblentz and all their families. Leroy Adams and Elvin Flook have been my neighbors for the past sixty-three years.

You know, I have come to the realization that family and friends are what really matters. I cherish the visits with the people I have loved for so many years. Recently, Tom Delauter, whom I had not seen in 40 years or more, stopped to see me. I was so happy he came.

I enjoy the visits of the Miller boys from Middletown. They liked the homemade ice cream and the cakes we made years ago. Ernie and Jeff come by and we still have ice cream, but not homemade! When these men were little boys, they came out to the farm and played with Russell Jr. I always made sure they ate at the table along with everyone else who was working on the farm that day. I like to hand out

317

"down home" love. Even today, I seem to constantly find new faces to be my cherished friends.

William and Annie Wiles

When we first moved to Middletown, we became good friends with Willie and Annie Wiles. We lived as neighbors from 1932 to 1994.

I had a gander that my brother Wade gave me. I was cooking corn one day and I had taken the pot from the stove and removed the corn. One of the girls went out the back door to pour the hot water from the kettle. The poor old gander was out in the chicken yard and, when he saw flowing water, he waddled right into the hot stream. It ran over his feet as he scampered away. It was too late! We noticed he was guarding his steps and, days later, all the skin peeled off his feet.

One day, when Annie was visiting, she informed me she wanted a gander for her goose and so we made a trade. I gave her the gander, she gave me a sideboard. I am still using that piece of furniture.

The passing of family and friends is very difficult for me. Annie and Willie passed from this life during the first part of 1994. We exchanged so many visits and phone calls in recent years. I miss them. I cherish my memories and will never forget them.

Each name I have lovingly mentioned in this book has their special spot in my heart. I love the "home folks!"

CHAPTER 55

CHANGE COMES

Everything Changes With Time

Many things have changed over my life. Our methods of farming turned ahead and the improvements made life easier; from horses to tractors, hand milking to electric milkers, horse and buggy to automobiles. What a convenience the electric refrigerator was! Ice, whenever we needed it, and cold water and food at any time.

I have lived through an era where so much has changed for both the good and the bad. I could go on and on when I think of my many memories created by my numerous trips around the sun. I often wonder what reason God, in his mercy, has in mind for me living here for so many years. What a gift to me!

Crow Rock Road

Recently, two of the girls took me out for a drive around the Myersville/Wolfsville area and we drove down Crow Rock Road. There along that road stood the same old rock I played under as a kid. It is shaped so that it makes a little "lean to." I played under and around that rock for many hours with my friends. Just seeing the rock brought back scenes from yesterday as clear to my mind as if they were happening this very moment. Living from September 17, 1899, to now, 1995, gives plenty of time for one to make memories.

I Still Own the Farm

In 1966, Russell and I started to rent the farm to young farmers. After his death, I continued. My present renter is our youngest son, Thomas and his son. I am pleased that, together, we have been able to tidy up around the buildings, fence rows, and fields. These days I do enjoy looking from any window of my home and seeing the soil Russell and I set our feet upon for so many years. It looks so good to me!

Though my feet have never been out of the United States, I am sure there is no place like home. The United States of America is one grand old country to me. I love this land and especially THE BEAUTIFUL MIDDLETOWN VALLEY.

It is said that Andrew Jackson referred to it as, "One of the most favored and delightful spots on the earth." I could not agree more! Today I still own our "favored spot" of the valley—the farm Russell and I purchased on March 17, 1932. I praise God!

I often thought when we were first married and the children were little, "How can I keep going on when what is going to happen tomorrow will be more of the same work and worry as today?" Well, now I clearly realize the fact that life is not a "bed of roses" for most people. Yet, having unburdened myself of past hardships has left my attitude toward life and the Lord richer. Everything that happened has helped to build a stepping stone ahead of me. Perhaps it is not surprising that some of those stones hurt my feet and frequently I was hopelessly confused.

Now, headaches are few—I have peace. Nothing can steal my happiness unless I allow it to happen. My flesh and bone may fail, but not my Lord! *"And he said, Certainly I will be with thee,...." (Exodus 3:12)*

I am so happy I had the persistence for the good things—looking for the good in family and friends, and having, through the grace of God, strength to conquer foes. *"...he did it with all his heart, and prospered." (II Chronicles 31:21)*

CHAPTER 56

TRUTHS

You see, this book holds only a few short moments of my long life. Time has disappeared as a vapor. *"... For what is your life. It is even a vapor, that appeareth for a little time, and then vanisheth away." (James 4:14)* I have seen so many sunrises as the dew or frost sparkled on the blades of grass.

I have thought so many times as I shed tears that crying only makes this world worth less to me and Heaven worth more. Time has proven my love, and my walk with the Lord is truly sweeter as the days go by.

So many of the truths I have heard throughout my life suddenly seem more factual to me than ever before. And yes, our children are truly on loan from God. We need to always keep in mind we do not own them, even though we love them so dearly.

And I am reminded that peace of mind truly comes from "letting bygones be bygones," or letting past offenses or disagreements be forgotten. To be "even" is not important.

As this story nears its end, I can say that when I got old enough to get by with saying whatever I wanted to say, and wealthy enough to buy some of the things I longed for all my life, I no longer desired to say it or have it!

The most cherished truth I must leave with each of you this side of Glory is that God in His goodness will always be near to those who choose to stay close to Him. I have never doubted His presence! You can tell Him your secrets and share every heartache. Always trusting, never forget to thank and praise Him for His goodness and grace. *"From the rising of the sun unto the going down of the same the Lord's name is to be praised." (Psalms 113:3)*

If you have God's presence, you have possession of His richest blessing. He is my Lord and friend! What I have in my heart I would not exchange for any treasure that money can buy.

I thank God for giving me for SO MANY MORNINGS!

THE END

APPENDIX

PHOTOGRAPHS

Letha Wiles in 1992.

Front row, left to right: Letha, Charles W. and Clara
R. Grossnickel (Letha's parents), and George (Letha's
brother). Back row, left to right: Letha's brothers
Wade and Herbert. Photo was taken out by the buggy
shed and goose barrel, probably on a Sunday.

The Martin Grossnickel farm. Letha grew up on this homestead. The farm is now owned by Steven Leatherman. (Photo courtesy of Neil A. Meyerhoff, Inc., Baltimore, MD)

Letha and her mother. Letha was one–and–a–half
years old.

Letha and her father. Letha is wearing a dark navy pinafore made from her mother's wedding dress.

Letha Alice Grossnickel, age 14 years.

Letha's father, Charles Webster Grossnickel.

Martin Grossnickel (Letha's grandfather on her
father's side of the family).

Front row, left to right: Flora M. Wiles (Russell Wiles'
Mother). Back row, left to right: Flora Wiles
(Russell's sister), Russell P. Wiles Sr. (my husband),
and Mary (Russell's sister). This photo was taken at
Grandfather Peter Grossnickle's farm.

Jacob E. Wiles (Russell's father).

House on Myersville Church Hill Road, where Letha
was born in 1899.

Wash house and summer kitchen on the farm in Ellerton that Martin Grossnickel owned in the early 1900s. On steps is Brandon Leatherman, son of Steven Leatherman. Photo taken in 1995.

Bittle's Store in Ellerton.

Summers' Store in Ellerton.

Peter Grossnickle, (Russell's grandfather and Maria's husband).

Maria Bittle Grossnickle. Peter Grossnickle's first wife. His second marriage was to Mary Harshman, my Uncle Caleb's sister.

Letha and Russell Wiles Sr., 1966.

Letha and Russell Wiles Sr., 1949.

Left to right: Russell Jr., Pauline, Doris, and Austin.

Left to right: Yvonne, Regean, Janice, and Marie.

Thomas Wiles, the youngest child.

The Wiles Homestead, taken June 13, 1956, from an airplane.

Russell husking corn in 1955.

Hauling field corn in 1955. Horses, Bob and Kate.
Left to right: Thomas, Yvonne, Russell Sr., and Leon
Gouker.

Russell hauling manure.

Janice and her dad cutting the wheat crop with the
binder in 1954.

Butchering day. Left to right: Marie Harshman, Tissie Hooper, Leon Gouker, Pauline Grossnickle, and Annie Wiles.

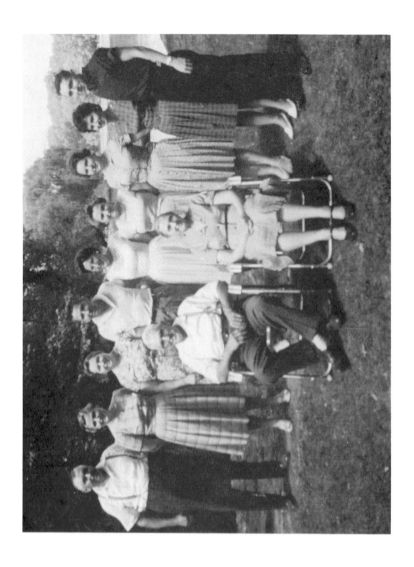

Front row, left to right: Russell Sr. and Letha. Back row, left to right: Austin, Doris, Pauline, Russell Jr., Marie, Janice, Regean, Yvonne, and Thomas. Photo taken in August 1963.

Sunday morning at the Grossnickle Church of the
Brethren. Built in 1899.

Mom and Yvonne at the August 6, 1995 Wiles family picnic. It was a cool, rainy day, but nothing could dampen Mom's spirits while spending time with her children.

CHILDREN
RUSSELL PETER WILES SR. &

Russell Peter Wiles
b May 10, 1892
son of Jacob E. and
Flora M. (Grossnickle) Wiles
d Jun 13, 1977

married

1. Austin Charles Jacob Wiles
b Mar 22, 1917
m Ruth Naomi Grossnickle
had 4 children

4. Pauline Alverta Wiles
b Oct 18, 1920
m Carroll Undrew Grossnickle
had 4 children

2. Kathleen Isabelle Wiles
b Jul 29, 1918
d Aug 29, 1918

5. Russell Peter Wiles Jr.
b Feb 21, 1925
m Betty Jane Harshman
had 2 children

3. Doris Eileen Wiles
b Aug 29, 1919
m Ralph Upton Grossnickle
d Jan 14, 1988
had 1 child

6. Marie Flora Wiles
b Mar 24, 1927
m Harold Leo Harshman

OF
LETHA ALICE GROSSNICKEL

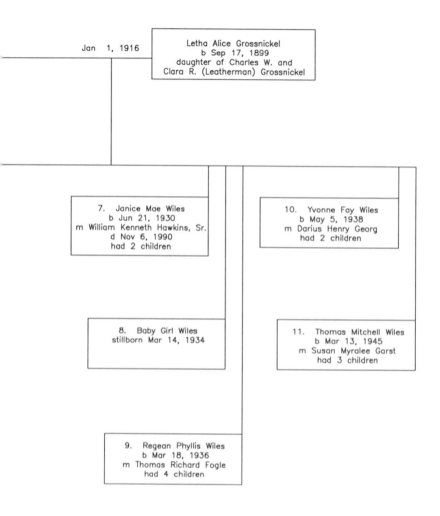

Jan 1, 1916

Letha Alice Grossnickel
b Sep 17, 1899
daughter of Charles W. and
Clara R. (Leatherman) Grossnickel

7. Janice Mae Wiles
b Jun 21, 1930
m William Kenneth Hawkins, Sr.
d Nov 6, 1990
had 2 children

10. Yvonne Fay Wiles
b May 5, 1938
m Darius Henry Georg
had 2 children

8. Baby Girl Wiles
stillborn Mar 14, 1934

11. Thomas Mitchell Wiles
b Mar 13, 1945
m Susan Myralee Garst
had 3 children

9. Regean Phyllis Wiles
b Mar 18, 1936
m Thomas Richard Fogle
had 4 children

FAMILY TREE OF
RUSSELL PETER WILES SR.

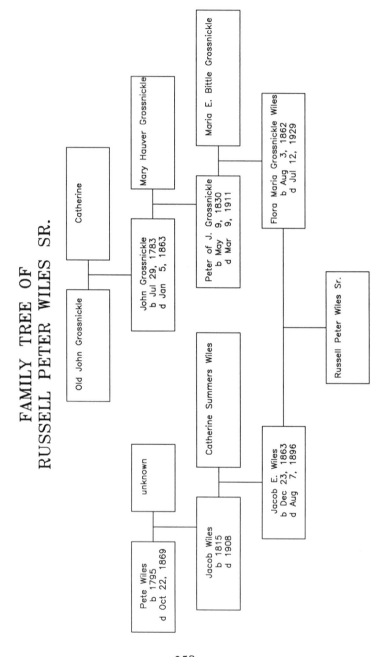

FAMILY TREE OF
LETHA ALICE GROSSNICKEL

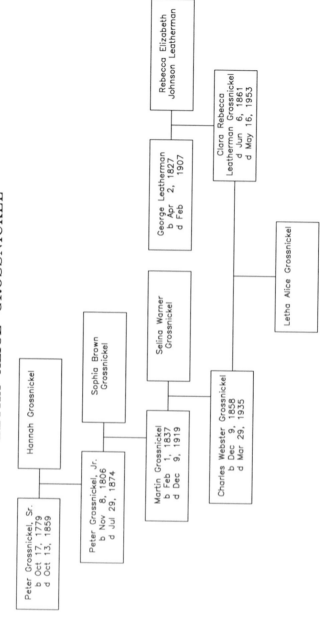

PUBLIC SALE

Having rented my farm and discontinuing farming, I will sell on the premises located just North of Middletown and Rt. 40A along the road toward Myersville in Frederick County, Maryland on

THURSDAY, MARCH 10, 1966

BEGINNING AT 9:30 A.M. PROMPTLY
TO-WIT:

60—HEAD REGISTERED AND GRADE HOLSTEINS—60
22 REGISTERED—38 GRADES

Forty-one are milk cows, seven bred heifers due in fall, eleven large open heifers. The herd is nearly 100% artificially sired by Maryland-West Virginia sires and bred now to these top bulls. It is a young herd with lots of dairy character and good udders. Foundation cattle were of Rag Apple bloodlines and several excellent cow families sell. Daughters of Champion, Posch, Supreme, Aim, Reward, Booster, Leader, Della, Em peror, Master Cross, Grand Master and Senator selling. The cows are bred to freshen throughout the year and sell in all stages of lactation. The heifers are well grown, all artificially sired from the top cows of the herd and exceptionally nice. An excellent opportunity to purchase quality Holsteins, either registered or grade. T.B. and Bangs accredited and Certified, and 30 day test.

FARM MACHINERY AND EQUIPMENT

McCormick-Deering Farmall Model M tractor recently overhauled, good rubber; McCormick-Deering Super C Farmall with fast hitch, corn cultivators; Model 600 New Holland field chopper with grass head, New Idea 2 ton rubber tire wagon and flat bed with racks, McCormick-Deering 4 ton rubber tire wagon with flat bed and racks, John Deere rubber tire hay rake, Model 606 New Holland hay crusher, Super 77 New Holland baler good as new, John Deere hay fluffer, JD 27 tooth 3 section harrow, 28 disc heavy duty McC-Deering disc harrow, Smoker 40 ft. grain and bale elevator, new Dunham 2 row cultipacker, tractor type wood saw, 12" Little Genius 2 bottom plows, JD fertilizer and lime sower, JD 7 ft. trailer mower, New Holland large size pull type manure spreader like new, Century field sprayer with drums and 2 wheel trailer, McC-D riding corn plow, Syracuse 30-78 barshear plow, single and double shovel plows, corn coverer, one horse dump cart good condition, corn sheller, bag truck, 1,000 lb. Fairbanks scales, line shafts and pulleys, cant hooks, 15 log chains, old broad axe, grain sacks, 2 buggy poles, single and double trees, hitchings, wagon tongues, hitches, yokes, jockey sticks, 2 sets good breeching, wagon saddle, leather lines, fly nets, pair studded housings, plow gears, log wagon, hay loader, 2 sets block and tackle, 2 sets dehorners, 2 screw jacks, 150 ft. hay rope.

Complete blacksmith tools—anvil, forge, vise, tongs, hammers, etc., horse shoeing equipment, lot old home made door strap hinges, etc.

Butchering equipment—scalder, 3 iron kettles, tables, hooks, 8 sets tripods, good grinder and stuffer, etc.

DAIRY EQUIPMENT: Majoinner 250 gallon tank, 3 De-Laval milker units, wash up tank, strainers, milker line in old barn for 18 cows, stall cocks, 2 sets electric clippers, feed carts, forks, shovels, scoops, hand tools.

FEEDS—All baled alfalfa and mixed hay, and silage left by time of sale.

HOUSEHOLD, ETC.—Large Advance heatrola, 2 oil heaters, electric brooders, poultry equipment, gallon milk pasteurizer, crocks, jars, pans, dishes, stands, electric heater, tin tub, metal wardrobe, porch furniture.

Antiques: 6 hardbottom chairs, walnut case Worcester organ and stool, spice rack, hand churn, butter bowl and print, old wooden safe, 2 section meal chest, 3 old poster cord beds, solid cherry bed, bureau and stand, chest of drawers, rockers, etc. and many items needless to mention.

TERMS—CASH on day of sale. Not responsible for accidents on premises. You are welcome to make inspection anytime before sale. Be on time as sale must start promptly at 9:30 A.M.

RUSSELL P. ("Pete") WILES

EMMERT R. BOWLUS
A. DOTY REMSBERG, Auctioneers
HORACE M. ALEXANDER, Clerk
Lunch by Ladies of Grossnickle's Church of the Brethren

DEATH NOTICES

These articles appeared in The Frederick Post and The Middletown Valley Register at the time of the death and funeral.

Russell Peter Wiles Sr. – Death Notice

Born May 10, 1892
Died June 13, 1977

Mr. Russell P. (Pete) Wiles Sr., 85, well–known retired farmer and husband of Letha Grossnickel Wiles, Route 2, Middletown, died Monday night, June 13, at Frederick Memorial Hospital. Born in Myersville, May 10, 1892, he was a son of the late Jacob E. and Flora Grossnickle Wiles. Mr. Wiles had farmed in Frederick County his entire life and was a member of the Grossnickle Church of the Brethren. He was the last member of his immediate family.

Surviving besides his wife are six daughters, Mrs. Ralph U. (Doris) Grossnickle, Walkersville, Mrs. Carroll U. (Pauline) Grossnickle, Walkersville, Mrs. Harold L. (Marie) Harshman, Frederick, Mrs. William K. (Janice) Hawkins, Braddock Heights, Mrs. T. Richard (Regean) Fogle, Cearfoss, Mrs. Darius H. (Yvonne) Georg, Silver Spring, three sons, Austin Charles Jacob Wiles, Middletown, Russell P. Wiles Jr., Frederick, Thomas M. Wiles, Middletown, 20 grandchildren and 12 great grandchildren.

Friends may call at the Gladhill Funeral Home in Middletown on Wednesday, June 15. The family will receive friends from 7 to 9 p.m.

Services will be held on Thursday, June 16, at 1:30 p.m. from the Grossnickle Church of the Brethren. His pastor, Reverend Ronald Beverlin, will officiate. Interment will be in the church cemetery.

Memorial contributions may be made to the Frederick County Heart Fund.

Russell P. Wiles Sr. – Funeral Service

June 16, 1977

Funeral services for **Mr. Russell P. (Pete) Wiles Sr.**, husband of Letha Grossnickel Wiles, Route 2, Middletown, who died Monday, June 13, at Frederick Memorial Hospital were held at 1:30 p.m. Thursday, June 16, at the Grossnickle Church of the Brethren. The Reverend Ronald Beverlin officiated.

Bearers were grandsons, Charles A. Wiles, Wayne L. Wiles, Robert A. Wiles, Monroe F. Grossnickle, Ellis E. Grossnickle, Gary L. Grossnickle, Richard E. Wiles, and William K. Hawkins. Interment was in the church cemetery. Arrangements by the Gladhill Funeral Home, Middletown.

Martin Grossnickel – Death Notice

Born February 1, 1837
Died December 9, 1919

Mr. Martin Grossnickel, an aged and prominent retired farmer, and one of the best–known residents of upper valley, died at his home at Ellerton last Tuesday about noon of congestion on the lungs, aged 82 years, 10 months, and 8 days. Mr. Grossnickel was a life–long resident of the vicinity of Ellerton, with the exception of a few years in his younger life, which he spent at Bladensburg, Maryland, Prince George's County. He was a successful farmer. He was married twice, but both of his wives preceded him to the grave. His first wife was Miss Selina Warner, of Ellerton, a sister of Mr. Elias Warner of Yellow Springs, this county, who died about 15 years ago. His second wife was Mrs. Eleanor Taylor, daughter of the late George W. Cartee, also of near Ellerton, she died about three years ago. Mr. Grossnickel was a gentleman of the highest integrity, honest to the cent, liberal in his dealings and friendly to the needy. Consequently, he was held in the highest esteem. He is survived by six children by his first marriage – Charles W. Grossnickel, Ellerton; Mrs. Nettie H. Toms, Wingertan, PA; Mrs. Mary C. (Molly) Gaver, wife of Lee Gaver, Middletown; John D. Grossnickel, North Manchester, Indiana; Mrs. Effie Gaver, near Ellerton; Harry M. Grossnickel, Highland. Two brothers also survive: John A. Grossnickel, Keedysville, Washington County and Richard Grossnickel of California.

The funeral will take place this Friday morning at 11:30 from Grossnickle Meeting House, near Ellerton, of which the deceased was a member for over 50 years. The service will be conducted by Reverend C. F. Ausherman.

Burial will be made in the adjoining cemetery. The pallbearers will be C. W. Rice, John F. Summers, Elias Shepley, Jacob L. Routzahn, Ord Stroup and Lewis F. Gaver. Bittle Bros. Funeral Directors.

Mrs. Martin Grossnickel (Selina Warner) – Death Notice

Born October 27, 1837
Died November 1, 1900

Mrs. Selina Grossnickel, beloved wife of Mr. Martin Grossnickel, who died November 1 at her home in Ellerton, this valley, was aged 63 years, and 4 days. She had been afflicted for several years with kidney trouble, but her death was due to diabetes and blood poison. She bore her affliction with patience and Christian resignation, believing in the goodness and wisdom of the Creator, who doeth all things well. She had been a consistent member of the German Baptist Church from her youth, and was a kind and affectionate mother and beloved wife. She leaves a sorrowing husband and family. The children are: Charles W. Grossnickel of near Myersville, John D. Grossnickel of North Manchester, Indiana, Harriet M. Grossnickel at home, Mrs. Tilghman Grossnickle, Mrs. John Shepley; Mrs. Elmer Toms, Mrs. Lee Gaver, Mrs. Charles Gaver, and Harry Grossnickel all of near Myersville. She is survived by one brother, Mr. Elias Warner of Yellow Springs, this county. The funeral services at Grossnickle's Meeting House on November 3 were conducted by Elder John F. Bussard, assisted by Elders George S. Harp, and Charles F. Ausherman. Elder Bussard's text was, "Thanks be to God, who giveth us victory."

Mrs. Martin Grossnickel – Funeral Service

Selina Grossnickel died on a Wednesday night at her home. She was held in the highest esteem by a large circle of friends. She was a devoted member of the German Baptist Church and her faithful and consistent Christian character had endeared her to all acquaintances. The funeral services were conducted by Elder John F. Bussard at the Grossnickle's Meeting House at 10 o'clock, last Sunday morning.

Charles W. Grossnickel – Death Notice

Born December 9, 1858
Died March 29, 1935

Charles W. Grossnickel, well–known retired farmer, died suddenly of a heart attack at his home near Ellerton, Friday morning at 11:30, aged 76 years, 3 months and 20 days. He was a son of Martin and Selina Grossnickel and is survived by his wife, Clara Rebecca Grossnickel, and the following children: Mrs. Russell P. Wiles Sr., Middletown; Roy W. Grossnickel, Herbert A. Grossnickel, and George M. Grossnickle, all of Myersville. Two sisters: Mrs. Lee Gaver, Middletown and Mrs. Effie Gaver, near Myersville. Two brothers: John D. Grossnickel, North Manchester, Indiana, and Harry M. Grossnickel, Highland.

Mr. Grossnickel was a member of the Old German Baptist Church. Funeral services were held Sunday afternoon from the meeting house of the Church of the Brethren, of Middletown Valley. In charge of the service was Elder D. S. Flohr, Shady Grove, and assisted at the home by Elder L. B. Flohr, Vienna, Virginia. At the church, Elders C. N. Freshour and Irving R. Stottlemyer assisted. More than eight hundred persons attended the funeral services. Interment was made in the adjoining cemetery at the Meeting House.

366

Charles W. Grossnickel – Funeral Service

March 31, 1935

Funeral Services for **Charles W. Grossnickel** were conducted at the Grossnickle Church of the Brethren, near Ellerton, Sunday afternoon, by Reverend D. L. Flohr, of Shady Grove, for Charles W. Grossnickel, one of the best known and highly esteemed retired farmers of the section of the Middletown Valley, who died at his home Friday morning at 11:30 from a heart attack, aged 76 years, 3 months, and 20 days. Reverend C. N. Freshour and Reverend Irving R. Stottlemyer, of the Grossnickle Church assisted in the services. Mr. Grossnickel was a son of the late Martin and Selina Grossnickel, spent his entire life in the northern section of the valley. He had been in bad health for about three years. About 20 years ago he became associated with the Middletown Savings Bank as a director and served in this capacity until 1933, when he resigned because of his health.

Pallbearers were Francis Easterday, William Shepley, Harvey Grossnickle, Charles Cartee, Charles Delauter and Charles Bussard. Gladhill Co. Funeral Directors.

Mrs. Clara Rebecca Grossnickel – Death Notice

Born June 6, 1861
Died May 16, 1953

Mrs. Clara Rebecca Grossnickel, widow of Charles W. Grossnickel of near Myersville, died at Fahrney Memorial Home, near Boonsboro, Saturday night after a short illness, aged 92 years. She was a daughter of the late Elder George and Rebecca Johnson Leatherman, of near Harmony, and was a member of the Church of the Brethren. Surviving are four children: Mrs. Russell P. Wiles Sr., Middletown; Roy W. Grossnickel, Herbert A. Grossnickel and George M. Grossnickle, all of near Myersville. 27 grandchildren, 40 great grandchildren, and one great–great grandchild also survive.

The body rests at the Middletown funeral home until Tuesday afternoon and will be taken to Grossnickle Church of the Brethren for services at 2:30, conducted by Reverend Samuel D. Lindsay and Reverend Basil Grossnickle.

Interment in the church cemetery. It is requested that flowers be omitted. Gladhill Company, Funeral Directors.

Clara R. Grossnickel – Funeral Service

May 19, 1953

Funeral services for **Clara R. Grossnickel**, widow of Charles W. Grossnickel of near Myersville were conducted Tuesday afternoon, with brief services at the funeral home in Middletown and final rites at 2:30 p.m. at the Grossnickle Church of the Brethren. Reverend Samuel Lindsay and Reverend Basil Grossnickle officiated, assisted by Reverend Earl Mitchell.

Grandsons of the deceased were pallbearers and included: Ernest, Richard, Eldin, Wilbur, Joseph Grossnickle and Russell Wiles Jr. Interment was in the church cemetery. Gladhill Company, Funeral Director.

Elder George Leatherman – Death Notice

Born April 2, 1827
Died February 1907

A well–known minister of the German Baptist Church –
Former resident dies suddenly.

Elder George Leatherman, one of the best–known and
most highly respected members of the German Baptist Church in
Middletown Valley, died at his home near Harmony at 1:30 last
Monday morning, from the effects of an attack of grip, aged 79
years, 10 months, and 23 days.

Elder Leatherman was born at the mill now owned by Mr.
Charles Johnson, near Ellerton, on April 2, 1827. He married
Rebecca Johnson on December 19, 1847, and to this union 12 chil-
dren were born.

Elder Leatherman became a member of the German Bap-
tist Church in 1854, having been connected ever since with the
widely known "Grossnickle Church," which was established near
Ellerton in 1847, meetings being held at the private houses previ-
ous to this. On September 23, 1858, Mr. Leatherman was elected
a deacon in the church and on February 19, 1855, he was elected to
the ministry. On October 22, 1867, he was advanced to the second
degree and on May 22, 1880, was ordained as Elder. During Elder
Leatherman's long ministry, 412 persons joined the church, 56 were
baptized, and 43 were married by him.

No man was better known in the valley than Elder George
Leatherman and no other was held in higher esteem. He was a
kind and gentle gentleman and made friends with all whom he
came in contact with. He had the interests of his church at heart
and he labored long and faithfully in its behalf. His life work was
an honor to him and he passed away loved and respected by all.

A widow and 10 children survive, as follows: Mary E.
wife of Joshua Summers, Myersville; Sarah C. wife of Scott Derr,
Feagaville; Clara R. wife of Charles W. Grossnickel, near Ellerton;
Julia M. wife of Daniel C. Harshman, near Church Hill; John C.
Leatherman, near Myersville; Charles T. Leatherman, near
Sharpsburg; George C. Leatherman, near Myersville; Alfred J.

Leatherman, near Harmony; William H. Leatherman, and David O. Leatherman, at home. One sister survives: Mrs. Elizabeth Ausherman, of Ellerton. The deceased was the oldest member of his family. There are 43 grandchildren living, and 17 great grandchildren.

Funeral services were held from the Grossnickle Church near Ellerton, on Wednesday morning and there was a large assemblage present to pay last tribute. There were nearly 50 vehicles in the funeral cortege. Reverend John M. Bussard preached the funeral sermon from Luke 23:28 "But Jesus turning unto them said, Daughters of Jerusalem, weep not for me, but weep for yourselves, and for your children." This text was selected some time ago by the deceased.

The bearers were Samuel Kinna, David Summers, Charles Coblentz, Samuel Brandenburg, Elias Stine, and Charles Cline. H. C. Feete of Middletown, Funeral Director.

Mrs. Rebecca Elizabeth Leatherman – Death Notice

Mrs. Rebecca Elizabeth Leatherman, of near Harmony and this valley, died last Saturday night about 8 o'clock from the effects of a stroke of paralysis received on the previous Wednesday, in her 81st year. Mrs. Leatherman's husband, the venerable and widely known Elder George Leatherman, died February 1907, in his 80th year. Mrs. Leatherman was a lady of most excellent Christian character and was held in high esteem by a large circle of friends and acquaintances. Ten children survive: Mary E. wife of Joshua Summers, Myersville; Sarah C. Derr wife of R. Scott Derr, Feagaville; Clara R. wife of Charles W. Grossnickel, near Ellerton; Julia M. wife of Daniel C. Harshman, near Church Hill; John C. near Myersville; Charles T. near Sharpsburg; George C. near Myersville; Alfred J. of near Harmony; William H and David O at home.

Mrs. Leatherman who was a Miss Johnson, was a consistent member of the Lutheran Church at Church Hill, near Myersville, but services were held from the German Baptist Church or Grossnickle Meeting House, near Ellerton, last Tuesday, of which her late husband was the officiating Elder. Mrs. Leatherman's pastor, Reverend G. W. Stroup, officiated at the funeral, assisted by Elder John M. Bussard. The pallbearers were Elias T. Stine, David Summers, Samuel Kinna, Charles C. Coblentz, Emory Castle, Charles T. Cline, H. C. Feete of Middletown was the funeral.

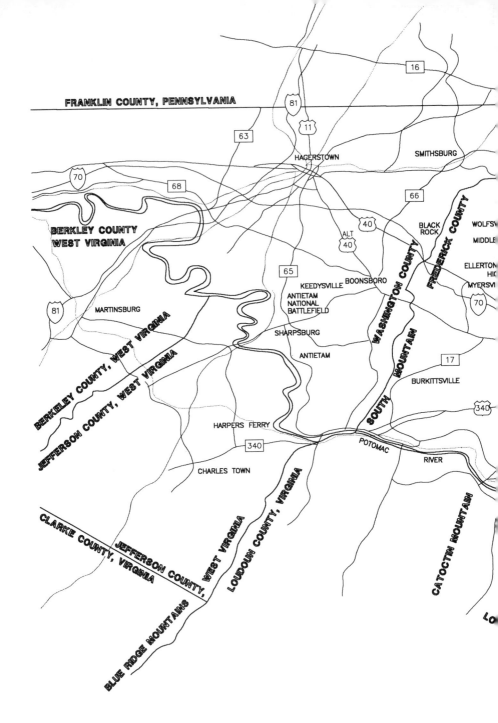

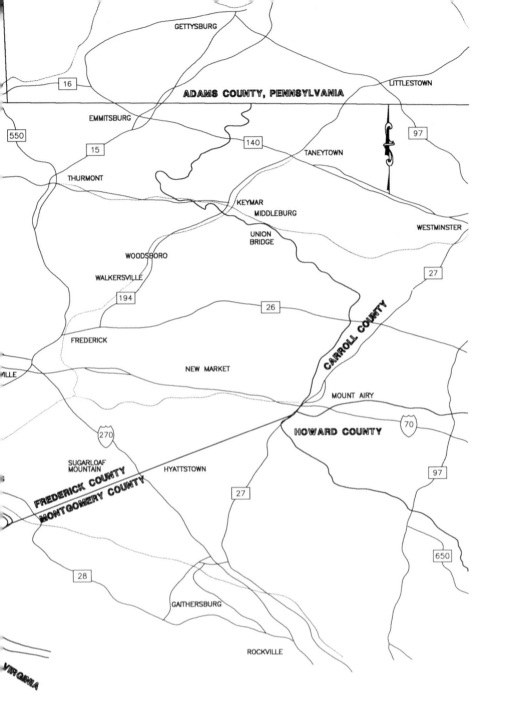

POEMS BY LETHA ALICE GROSSNICKEL WILES

These poems were written over the years by Mom. They have been tucked in her Bible on little pieces of paper and kept down through the years. They mean so much to her.

MY LIFE

I would not want to relive my life
I was a mother and a wife.
Some people think the job is small
But I don't think it's that at all.
I washed and ironed and scrubbed the floors
I cooked the meals and did the chores.
Out to the barn in the morning light
And, Oh, how tired I was at night.
I bathed the children and combed their hair
Tucked them in bed and whispered a prayer.
That God would keep them through the night
And then a kiss, sleep sweet and tight.
We sent them to school for someone to teach
I kept bread and butter where little hands could reach.
Maybe a cookie, maybe a pie
Maybe an apple as they passed by.
Out to the barn the boys would go
But the girls had the baby to keep you know.
They strolled to the window and there they'd look
With a pencil and paper and maybe a book.
The baby would scratch and pull their hair
But still they tended them with greatest care.
When evening shadows begin to fall
From the barnyard fence you heard them call.
Mom! How soon will you be done?
It seemed to me I had just begun.
So I'd hurry and often run, so the baby I could take
For I know many times that their arms did ache.

Mom

50 YEARS

50 years as a man and wife
  a golden span took from our life.
What kind of gold was in these years?
  Was it gold or was it tears?
What was the price that we have paid
  for this foundation we have laid?
A toll was taken every day
  while both our heads were turning gray.
And as each child would go their way
  that was the price I had to pay.
Now the homestead we must leave
  my hands grew weary and my heart did grieve.
To leave the place we loved so well
  and part with the things we had to sell.
We built a house and furnished it well,
  but it was not home we both could tell.
We missed the work we used to do,
  the dirty coat and the overshoe.
We worked so hard to pay the debt
  for money then was hard to get.
Now I leaf through my memory book
  and often stop and take a look.
Some things I see was not so good
  but then we did the best we could.

Mom

OUR WILLS

We made our wills today
I took time out to pray.
Afraid I'd do some thoughtless thing
And cause a heart to ache or sting.
I couldn't tell the man today
What I really wanted to say.
Things were so heavy on my heart
We were preparing now to part.
Many, many times we disagreed
While we brought up our family tree.
But either right or either wrong
God held our hand and made us strong.
We left these wills inside the courthouse door
For safe protection and nothing more.
Now these are worth their weight in gold
If we can live and just grow old.

Mom   May 3, 1962

MY FAMILY TREE

My family often reminded me of apples hanging on a tree.
They grew so close, when one would fall it seemed as though it bruised them all.
I like to see them grown that way and do for one another.
Whoever needs a helping hand, a sister or a brother.
Many, many times they disagreed and eye to eye they did not see.
But winds will blow in all the trees and cause the limbs to lose some leaves.
I sprayed my tree with plenty of love, and asked for help from up above.
When supper was over and chores all done, neighbors came in and that started the fun.
How fast they could run they all wanted to see when they were joined by a bumble bee.

OUR LORD

Who could make the sky so blue
Or be a friend to all more true?
Who could make the wind to blow
And make the lovely flowers grow?
Who could make the birds to fly
And sit in trees that are so high?
Who could make the rain to fall
And hear his children when they call?
Who is the one that holds our hand
When we grow weary and cannot stand?
Who is the one we must obey
And praise His name along the way?
The cross he bore, the crown he wore
The blood he shed, he bowed his head.
On the cross he cried and then he died
Father, forgive them, they know not what they do.

Mom

MY BIBLE AND ME

(This poem is in Letha's own handwriting at the age of 92.)

My Bible and Me

My Bible and me are best friends you see
When I open the book Jesus talks to me
Now listen to me every word that I say
For there is coming a great Judgement day
The road is narrow and straight is the way
Two words to be added and none took away
He says he is kind and very forgiving
Follow me and work for a living
He is coming in the twinkling of an eye
Watch he will be coming in the sky
Remember the stripes, thorns, and Blood that day
The cross and our sins that he took away
As the Cloud rose and took him up high
This same Jesus is coming back in the by and by
The graves will be open and saints will appear
And we who are ready will join those we hold dear
Not all will be going for they don't believe
You must ask forgiveness and his grace receive
How sad it will be for those left behind
For trouble and tribulation will be of all kind

Mami

THIS IS A FARMER

Farmers are found in the fields plowing up, seeding down, returning from, planning to, fertilizing with, spraying for, and harvesting it. Wives help them, little boys follow them, the Agriculture Department confuses them, city relatives visit them, salesmen detain them, meals wait for them, weather can delay them, but it takes Heaven to stop them.

When your car stalls along the road, a farmer is a considerate, courteous, inexpensive road service. When a farmer's wife suggests he buy a new suit, he can quote from memory every expense involved in operating the farm last year, plus the added expense he is certain will crop up this year. Or else he assumes the role of the indignant shopper, impressing upon everyone within earshot the pounds of pork he must produce in order to pay for a new suit at today's prices.

A farmer is a paradox—he is an "overalled" executive with his home as his office; a scientist with grease under his fingernails; a dietitian with a passion for alfalfa, animals, and antibiotics; a production expert faced with a surplus; and a manager battling a price–cost squeeze. He manages more capital than most of the businessmen in town.

He likes sunshine, good food, state fairs, dinner at noon, auctions, his neighbors, Saturday nights in town, his shirt collar unbuttoned, and above all, a good soaking rain in August.

He is not much for droughts, ditches, throughways, experts, weeds, the eight–hour day, helping with the housework, or grasshoppers.

Nobody else is so far from the telephone or so close to God. Nobody else gets so much satisfaction out of modern plumbing, favorable weather, and good ice cream.

Nobody else can remove all these things from his pockets and on wash day still have overlooked: five staples, one cotter key, a rusty spike, three grains of corn, the end of a old lead pencil, a square tape, a $4.98 pocket watch, and a cupful of chaff in each trouser cuff.

A farmer is both Faith and Fatalist—he must have faith to continually meet the challenges of his capacities amid an ever-present possibility that an act of God (a late spring, an early frost, a tornado, a flood, a drought) can bring his business to a standstill. You can reduce his acreage but you can't restrain his ambition.

Might as well put up with him—he is your friend, your competitor, your customer, your source of fiber, and a self–reliant young citizen to help replenish your cities.

He is your countryman—a denim dressed, business–wise, fast growing statesman of stature.

And when he comes in at noon having spent the energy of his hopes and dreams, he can be recharged anew with the magic words: "The Market's Up."

Author Unknown

INDEX